The Executive Unbound

THE EXECUTIVE UNBOUND

After the Madisonian Republic

Eric A. Posner

Adrian Vermeule

OXFORD
UNIVERSITY PRESS

Oxford University Press, Inc., publishes works that further
Oxford University's objective of excellence
in research, scholarship, and education.

Oxford   New York
Auckland   Cape Town   Dar es Salaam   Hong Kong   Karachi
Kuala Lumpur   Madrid   Melbourne   Mexico City   Nairobi
New Delhi   Shanghai   Taipei   Toronto

With offices in
Argentina   Austria   Brazil   Chile   Czech Republic   France   Greece
Guatemala   Hungary   Italy   Japan   Poland   Portugal   Singapore
South Korea   Switzerland   Thailand   Turkey   Ukraine   Vietnam

Published by Oxford University Press, Inc.
198 Madison Avenue, New York, NY 10016

www.oup.com

Oxford is a registered trademark of Oxford University Press

Library of Congress Cataloging-in-Publication Data
Posner, Eric A.
The executive unbound : after the Madisonian republic / Eric A. Posner, Adrian Vermeule.
    p.   cm.
Includes bibliographical references and index.
ISBN 978-0-19-976533-1 (hardcover : alk. paper) 1. Executive power—United States. I. Vermeule, Adrian. II. Title.
KF5050.P67   2011
342.73'06—dc22   2010023201

Printed in the United States of America
on acid-free paper

CONTENTS

The Executive Unbound

Introduction

In the administrative state, what if anything constrains the enormous power of the executive—including both the presidency and the administrative agencies? In mainstream Anglo-American legal theory, the answer to this question emerges from a tradition that we will call liberal legalism. Liberal legalism cannot be defined in a sentence; it is a complex of theoretical views and institutional commitments related by a family resemblance, including elements of philosophical and political liberalism, constitutionalism, and deliberative democracy. But the simplest version of liberal legal theory holds that representative legislatures govern and should govern, subject to constitutional constraints, while executive and judicial officials carry out the law. The basic answer that liberal legalism supplies, then, is that law does and should constrain the executive.

More complex and realistic versions of liberal legal theory attempt to modify this picture to account for the facts of the modern administrative state, in which massive delegation to the executive and frequent crises threaten to relegate legislatures and courts to the sidelines. The twin problems of delegation and emergencies drive a great deal of liberal legal theory, which struggles to find conceptual devices and institutional mechanisms that can square liberalism's commitments, largely worked out by the end of the nineteenth century, with the accelerating development of administrative institutions in the twentieth and twenty-first. Liberal legalism is intensely anxious about executive power, and sometimes goes so far as to define tightly constrained executive power as an essential element of the rule of law.

Our thesis is that these modifications to liberal legalism fail. Either they do not go far enough to square with the facts, or they go so far as to effectively abandon the position they seek to defend. We live in a regime of executive-centered government, in an age after the separation of powers, and the legally constrained executive is now a historical curiosity. As against liberal constitutional theorists like James Madison, Bruce Ackerman,[1] and Richard Epstein,[2] and liberal theorists of the rule of law like Albert Venn Dicey[3] and David Dyzenhaus,[4] we argue that in the modern administrative state the executive governs, subject to legal constraints that are shaky in normal times and weak or nonexistent in times of crisis.

Whereas Madison is an exemplar of liberal legalism, particularly in the domain of constitutional theory, we draw upon the thought of the Weimar legal theorist Carl Schmitt. We do not agree with all of Schmitt's views, by any means. To the extent Schmitt thought that democratic politics do not constrain the executive, or thought that in the administrative state the executive is not only largely unconstrained by law but also unconstrained *tout court*, we disagree. Indeed, to the extent that Schmitt thought this, he fell into a characteristic error of liberal legalism, which equates lack of legal constraint with unbounded power. But Schmitt's critical arguments against liberal legalism seem to us basically correct, at least when demystified and rendered into suitably pragmatic and institutional terms.

A central theme in Schmitt's work, growing out of Weimar's running economic and security crises in the 1920s and early 1930s, involves the relationship between the classical rule-of-law state, featuring legislative enactment of general rules enforced by courts, and the administrative state, featuring discretionary authority and ad hoc programs, administered by the executive, affecting particular individuals and firms. The nub of Schmitt's view is the idea that liberal lawmaking institutions frame general norms that are essentially "oriented to the past," whereas "the dictates of modern interventionist politics cry out for a legal system conducive to a present- and future-oriented 'steering' of complex, ever-changing economic scenarios."[5] Legislatures and courts, then, are continually behind the pace of events in the administrative state; they play an essentially reactive and marginal role, modifying and occasionally blocking executive policy initiatives, but rarely taking the lead. And in crises, the executive governs nearly alone, at least so far as law is concerned.

In our view, the major constraints on the executive, especially in crises, do not arise from law or from the separation-of-powers framework defended by liberal legalists, but from politics and public opinion. Law and politics are hard to separate and lie on a continuum—elections, for example, are a complicated mix of legal rules and political norms—but the poles are clear enough for our purposes, and the main constraints on the executive arise from the political end of the continuum. A central fallacy of liberal legalism, we argue, is the equation of a constrained executive with an executive constrained by law. The pressures of the administrative state loosen legal constraints, causing liberal legalists to develop tyrannophobia, or unjustified fear of dictatorship. They overlook the de facto political constraints that have grown up and, to some degree, substituted for legal constraints on the executive.[6] As the bonds of law have loosened, the bonds of politics have tightened their grip. The executive, "unbound" from the standpoint of liberal legalism, is in some ways more constrained than ever before.

We do not claim that these political constraints necessarily cause the executive to pursue the public interest, however defined, or that they produce optimal executive decision-making. We do claim that politics and public opinion at least block the most lurid forms of executive abuse, that courts and Congress can do no better, that liberal legalism goes wrong by assuming that a legally unconstrained executive is unconstrained overall, and that in any event there is no pragmatically feasible alternative to executive government under current conditions. The last point has normative implications, because of the maxim "Ought implies can." Executive government is best in the thin sense that there is no feasible way to improve upon it, under the conditions of the administrative state.

In what follows, we support these claims by discussing the major elements of the legal and political framework for executive government. Although we pay special attention to times of crisis, our thesis is not limited to those times. Crises are just the limiting case of extremely rapid change in the policy environment, and thus exacerbate the inability of law to constrain the executive, but the underlying dynamics operate in normal times as well. In Schmittian terms, legality and legitimacy diverge in times of crisis, and legitimacy prevails. This divergence merely exposes that legitimacy rather than legality is the main determinant of authority—and of power—in the administrative state, so the fact that legality and legitimacy coincide in normal times does not mean that legality is ever important in its own right.

WHAT IS THE "EXECUTIVE"?

By the "executive," we mean the gigantic complex of national political institutions that are not part of either the legislative or the judicial branch. The scale of these institutions dwarfs all competitors. The federal government has nearly 2 million civilian employees.[7] Some 98 percent of these employees do not work for Congress or the judiciary, relatively tiny institutions that perch precariously atop the Leviathan of the administrative state. So defined, the executive includes both the president and the presidential apparatus (known as the Executive Office of the President, which includes dozens of institutions), and also the administrative agencies. The latter category includes both "executive agencies" whose heads can be dismissed at will by the president, and the "independent" agencies, whose heads can only be dismissed for cause; independent agencies are also somewhat insulated from presidential control by inchoate norms that operate within the Washington political culture.

Executive agencies have been brought under increasingly firm control by the White House, through the appointment of political loyalists and through institutional mechanisms such as oversight by the Office of Information and Regulatory Affairs (OIRA).[8] As we will discuss later, moreover, there is growing evidence suggesting that presidents often manage to assert effective control over the independent agencies, especially through appointments and requirements of consultation between independent and executive agencies. There is evidence that by the end of a typical president's first term the independent agencies are staffed by appointees who will reliably follow the president's program.[9] So the distinction between executive and independent agencies looms large for lawyers, who adore arguments about whether independent agencies are constitutional[10] and about the president's legal authority (or lack thereof) to control them,[11] but the real-world effects of the distinction may not be large, and seem to be diminishing over time; presidents have a great deal of influence over both types of agencies.

Another necessary qualification is that whether they are executive or independent, some agencies manage to obtain and retain some degree of autonomy, some of the time. Entrepreneurial leaders of agencies can play congressional committees and the White House off against one another, form coalitions with interest groups, and develop public reputations for expertise or competence that make it politically costly to interfere with their choices.[12] As we discuss in chapter 4, presidents who seek credibility sometimes use such reputations for their own benefit, appointing technocrats from the other party to important posts in order to signal their impartiality, as when President Clinton (re)appointed Alan Greenspan to chair the Federal Reserve, or when President Obama did the same with Ben Bernanke. Yet the world has changed since Truman joked that Eisenhower would, as president, be unable to get anyone to follow his orders. The Executive Office of the President is far larger in 2010 than in 1952, and—as liberal legalists emphasize[13]—presidents have far more control over agency policymaking today than yesterday. Even where bureaucracies enjoy some autonomy, presidents can often reroute decision making through subordinate bodies or otherwise circumvent the bureaucracy at lower cost than Congress can, increasing presidents' relative advantages.

Most generally, it is important to take account of relevant differences within the "executive," and we do so where appropriate. In chapter 3, for example, we separately consider the extent to which framework statutes constrain the president, on the one hand, and the administrative agencies, on the other. As the example of independent agencies suggests, however, our view is that the operative institutional differences are less important than the legal forms and organizational charts might suggest. Thus chapter 3 concludes that statutory constraints on both the president and the agencies are loose. Likewise, in chapter 1, we consider the interaction between independent agencies and cabinet departments during the financial crisis of 2008. Part of our story is that independent agencies like the Federal Reserve and the Securities and Exchange Commission reliably cooperated with Treasury to carry out the White House program. Although the executive branch is not "unitary" in theory or even in practice, it is hardly as indecisive and fragmented as Congress showed itself to be before, during, and after the financial crisis.

THE TWIN PROBLEMS OF LIBERAL LEGALISM

Having defined our terms as far as possible, our main critical thesis is that liberal legalism has proven unable to generate meaningful constraints on the executive. Two problems bedevil liberal legalism: delegation and emergencies. The first arises when legislatures enact statutes that grant the executive authority to regulate or otherwise determine policy, the second when external shocks require new policies to be adopted and executed with great speed. Both situations undermine the simplest version of liberal legalism, in which legislatures themselves create rules that the executive enforces, subject to review by the courts. Delegation suggests that the legislature has ceded lawmaking authority to the executive, de facto if not de jure,[14] while in emergencies, only the executive can supply new policies and real-world action with sufficient speed to manage events.

The two problems are related in practice. When emergencies occur, legislatures acting under real constraints of time, expertise, and institutional energy typically face the choice between doing nothing at all or delegating new powers to the executive to manage the crisis. As we will see, legislatures often manage to do both things; they stand aside passively while the executive handles the first wave of the crisis, and then come on the scene only later, to expand the executive's de jure powers, sometimes matching or even expanding the de facto powers the executive has already assumed.

A great deal of liberal legal theory is devoted to squaring delegation and emergencies with liberal commitments to legislative governance. Well before World War I, the Madisonian framework of separated powers began to creak under the strain of the growing administrative state, typically thought to have been inaugurated by the creation of the Interstate Commerce Commission in 1887. For Madisonian theorists, delegation threatened the separation of powers by effectively combining lawmaking and law-execution in the same hands, and emergencies threatened legislative primacy by requiring the executive to take necessary measures without clear legal authorization, and in some cases in defiance of existing law. (We refer to the Madisonian tradition as it has developed over time and as it exists today, not to Madison himself, whose views before the founding were less legalistic than they would become during the Washington and Adams administrations.)

As to both delegation and emergencies, Madisonian liberals have repeatedly attempted to compromise with the administrative state, retreating from one position to another and attempting at every step to limit the damage. In one prominent strand of liberal legal theory and doctrine, which has nominally governed since the early twentieth century, delegation is acceptable as long as the legislature supplies an "intelligible principle"[15] to guide executive policymaking ex ante; this is the so-called "nondelegation doctrine." This verbal formulation, however, proved too spongy to contain the administrative state. During and after the New Deal, under strong pressure to allow executive policymaking in an increasingly complex economy, courts read the intelligible principle test so capaciously as to allow statutes delegating to the president and agencies the power to act in the "public interest," nowhere defined.[16] Before 1935, the U.S. Supreme Court mentioned nondelegation in dictum but never actually applied it to invalidate any statutes; in 1935, the Court invalidated two parts of the National Industrial Recovery Act on nondelegation grounds;[17] since then, the Court has upheld every challenged delegation.

Subsequently, liberal legal theorists turned to the hope that legislatures could create administrative procedures and mechanisms of legislative and judicial oversight that would enforce legal constraints on the executive ex post, as a second-best substitute for the Madisonian ideal. In American administrative law, a standard account of the Administrative Procedure Act (APA), the framework statute for the administrative state, sees it as an attempt to translate liberal legalism into a world of large-scale delegation to the executive, substituting procedural controls and judicial review for legislative specification of policies. The APA applies to administrative action in a broad range of substantive areas, but does not apply to presidential action, so Congress has also enacted a group of framework statutes that attempt to constrain executive action in particular areas. Examples are the War Powers Resolution, which regulates the presidential commitment of armed forces abroad, the National Intelligence Act, which structures the intelligence agencies and attempts to require executive disclosure of certain intelligence matters to key congressional committees, and the Inspector General Act, which installs powerful inspectors general throughout the executive branch.

As to emergencies, starting at least with John Locke's discussion of executive "prerogative," liberal political and constitutional theorists have struggled to reconcile executive primacy in crises with the separation of powers or the rule of law or both. Such questions have become all the more pressing in the twentieth and twenty-first centuries, when a series of wars, economic emergencies, and other crises have multiplied examples in which the executive proceeded with dubious legal authority or simply ignored the laws. Here too, the response has been a series of legal constraints, such as the APA's restrictions on emergency administrative action, and framework statutes such as the National Emergencies Act, which regulates the president's ability to invoke grants of emergency powers granted under other laws.

One of our main claims is that these approaches are palliatives that have proven largely ineffective, and that fail to cure the underlying ills of liberal legalism. The same institutional and economic forces that produce the problems of delegation and emergencies also work to undermine legalistic constraints on the executive. The complexity of policy problems, especially in economic domains, the need for secrecy in many matters of security and foreign affairs, and the sheer speed of policy response necessary in crises combine to make meaningful legislative and judicial oversight of delegated authority difficult in the best of circumstances. In emergencies, the difficulties become insuperable—even under the most favorable constellation of political forces, in which the independently elected executive is from a different party than the majority of the Congress. Liberal legalism, in short, has proven unable to reconcile the administrative state with the Madisonian origins of American government. The constitutional framework and the separation-of-powers system generate only weak and defeasible constraints on executive action.

Madisonian oversight has largely failed, and it has failed for institutional reasons. Both Congress and the judiciary labor under an informational deficit that oversight cannot remedy, especially in matters of national security and foreign policy, and both institutions experience problems of collective action and internal coordination that the relatively more hierarchical executive can better avoid. Moreover, political parties, uniting officeholders within different institutions, often hobble the institutional competition on which Madisonian theorizing relies.[18] Congressional oversight does sometimes serve purely political functions—legislators, particularly legislators from opposing parties, can thwart presidential initiatives that are unpopular—but as a legal mechanism for ensuring that the executive remains within the bounds of law, oversight is largely a failure.

The same holds for statutory constraints on the executive—unsurprisingly, as these constraints are the product of the very Madisonian system whose failure is apparent at the constitutional level. In the terms of the legal theorist David Dyzenhaus, the APA creates a series of legal "black holes" and "grey holes" that either de jure or de facto exempt presidential and administrative action from ordinary legal requirements, and hence from (one conception of) the rule of law.[19] The scope of these exemptions waxes and wanes with circumstances, expanding during emergencies and contracting during normal times, but it is never trivial, and the administrative state has never been brought wholly under the rule of law; periodically the shackles slip off altogether.

As we will also try to show, the subject-specific framework statutes intended to control delegations and to constrain presidential emergency powers have fallen into abeyance, de facto; the War Powers Resolution, for example, is said to have died when President Clinton, in clear defiance of its terms, conducted a 68-day bombing campaign in Kosovo—a conflict that was itself impossible to square with prevailing rules of international law. When the hour of crisis tolls, Congress has little incentive or capacity to enforce such attempted precommitments, which typically arise from an ephemeral political consensus and lose their base of political support over time.

EXECUTIVE GOVERNMENT

Liberal legalism's struggles with delegation and emergencies are symptomatic of a core underlying problem, which is that it gets the center of institutional gravity wrong. In the administrative state, it is not the case that legislatures govern, even subject to constraints and the need for cooperation with other branches. Rather the executive governs, in the sense that it drives the policy agenda even where the cooperation of other branches is needed for political reasons. The fraction of time that Congress spends occupied with the president's agenda has steadily increased over the years.[20] Moreover, in many domains, the executive—most dramatically the president, but the agencies as well—can proceed through unilateral action. Although the Constitution, read literally, gives the president few express unilateral powers, he enjoys (and agencies enjoy) a mass of delegated powers, whose breadth and ambiguity mean that there is usually some statute or other in the picture to which the president or an agency can plausibly appeal.

Even more important, legal analysts often go wrong by overlooking that the "presidential power of unilateral action"[21] is a de facto power as well as a de jure one. The executive—alone of national institutions—has the capacity to take action in the real world, outside the law books, and that action changes the status quo facing other institutions. Where it is more difficult for those institutions to undo the new status quo the executive has set than it would have been to block the change initially, the power of unilateral de facto action becomes highly consequential. In the American quadricameral lawmaking system (president, House, Senate, and Supreme Court) de jure change can often be blocked, and the executive's power to change the status quo unilaterally and de facto is accordingly critical. Sometimes the executive will have strictly political incentives to obtain congressional support,[22] but this is not a legal constraint, and if anything it underscores the failure of the separation-of-powers framework central to liberal legal theory.

A corollary is that the executive's power can sometimes be exercised in defiance or violation of statutes, even where they arguably or indeed clearly prohibit what the executive has done, so long as the executive can block retaliation by other branches after the fact. When President Clinton violated the War Powers Resolution in Kosovo, the military action created new facts in the world to which Congress and other actors had to adjust, regardless of the legal niceties. This is an old theme in American politics— when Lincoln exceeded his legal powers at the beginning of the Civil War,

Congress had little choice but to ratify the *fait accompli*—but in the administrative state, the president's power to affect the world in this way, whatever the law books might say, has grown enormously.

CONSTRAINTS ON EXECUTIVE GOVERNMENT

In this depiction, do the president or the agencies enjoy imperial powers? The agencies clearly do not; executive agencies are legally and practically controlled by the White House, while the independent agencies are not legally subject to presidential control but are controlled to a large degree by the president's exercise of the power to appoint their members and by legal and customary obligations to consult and collaborate with executive agencies and cabinet secretaries.

Does the president himself, then, possess imperial power? Not in the overheated sense in which liberal historians and political scientists refer to the "imperial presidency."[23] Liberal legalists equate the absence of effective *legal* constraints on the executive with the absence of *any* constraints, yet even an imperial president is constrained by politics and public opinion.[24] Most fundamental is the reelection constraint, which shapes the horizon of presidential decision-making in a first term, and thus indirectly shapes the behavior of the executive agencies that the president oversees, and to some degree the behavior of the independent agencies that the president influences, and whose members he nominates. Although elections are, to a degree, regulated by courts and law, reelection is primarily a political constraint rather than a legal one, which is why a norm of regular elections first evolved in democratic polities without written constitutions, such as the United Kingdom. Politically, in a polity dominated by a mass public accustomed to exercising a large degree of democratic control, presidents need elections to legitimate their power. Even Lincoln, who has been called a "constitutional dictator," shied away from postponing elections in the depths of the Civil War.

Most important, perhaps, is the initial election of the president. Candidates for high office are stripped bare of the physical and social veils that protect the privacy of the rest of us. Every word they have uttered is scrutinized, as is their political and personal histories, and even the lives of their parents, relatives, friends, and associates. The extraordinary scrutiny that they undergo both reflects the magnitude of the stakes and helps ensure that the public selects someone whose ideological positions, character, habits, and abilities are acceptable.

Even between elections, the president needs both popularity, in order to obtain political support for his policies, and credibility, in order to persuade others that his factual and causal assertions are true and his intentions are benevolent. In the longer run, presidents—especially second-term presidents—worry about their policy legacy and their place in history. So the president cannot simply attempt to maximize the satisfaction of his own policy preferences in every situation. Rather he must trade off those satisfactions against the need to maintain popularity and credibility, which means that he must sometimes satisfy others' preferences rather than his own, and must invest in a favorable reputation among officials, elites, and people. Indeed, the greater the president's power becomes, both through delegation and other de jure mechanisms and through the debilities of oversight institutions, the more essential popularity and credibility become, as the public focus on the presidency grows. In the administrative state, the executive is in some ways a victim of its own swelling power, and must take steps to bind itself through institutional mechanisms that generate credibility.

Political constraints, unlike most legal constraints, operate even in times of crisis. Indeed, counterintuitively, some political constraints actually increase during perceived emergencies. Crises tend to produce broad delegations to the executive and cause the public and officials to rally 'round the flag. Yet crises create pressure for bipartisanship and an appearance of public solidarity across ideological lines, which in turn pressure presidents to offer concessions necessary to bring legislators from other political parties on board. Crises also create a sense of urgency, and while urgency helps to produce broad delegations, which in effect speed up the pace of policy change by handing the reins to the president, urgency can also help legislators in bargaining with the president, who usually needs to demonstrate to the public that he will take swift and resolute action. Overall, crises enhance presidential power, including delegated power, but by no means eliminate all political constraints. We will support these claims with case studies of several statutes involving both security emergencies and economic emergencies: the Authorization to Use Military Force, enacted days after 9/11, the Patriot Act, enacted in the succeeding months, and the Emergency Economic Stabilization Act of 2008.

Crises arise not only from exogenous shocks, such as 9/11 or the financial meltdown of 2008, but also when lawmaking institutions engage in high-stakes brinksmanship over the allocation of lawmaking powers or the choice of policies. We call these moments "constitutional showdowns," and show that popularity and credibility are decisive in such moments. The executive, legislature, and judiciary bargain and bluff their way to a resolution; the outcome is determined by popular support and by the credibility of the players' threats. Public opinion, not Madisonian deliberation, rules the day. However expansive his legal powers, the president must anticipate such moments and work, even in normal times, to build public support for his policies and to generate credibility for his threats.

Overall, we suggest that political constraints on executive government are real, even as legal constraints have atrophied.[25] Our most ambitious claim relates these two points in a causal framework. The economic and political conditions of the administrative state have a dual effect: they both cause the relaxation of legal constraints on the executive, and also create new political constraints, in part substituting the rule of politics for the rule of law. Demographic and economic conditions that both help to produce, and are produced by, the administrative state—among them a highly interdependent and complex economy and continually falling information costs—require more rapid adjustments in policy, and so induce an increase in delegation and executive power generally. Yet those same conditions also help to produce a wealthy and highly educated population, whose elites continually scrutinize executive action and tighten the constraints of popularity and credibility. The administrative state generates the cure for its own ills.

An implication is that the demise of liberal legalism, of the separation of powers, even of the rule of law itself, need not imply autocracy; across nations, a wealthy and educated population is a strong safeguard of democracy, according to empirical evidence we will review. The critics of the imperial presidency focus to excess on the role of law in constraining the executive, assuming that the only alternative is tyranny, but this is an unjustified belief, given the evidence—akin to a fear of genetically modified foods. In what follows, we trace the persistence of this tyrannophobia through American history and suggest that whatever its social utility in the past, it has none today.

However, the critics of the imperial presidency are not wholly wrong. Although they downplay the purely political constraints on the executive in the administrative state, they correctly describe an administrative state whose centerpiece is executive government, rather than the government of a representative legislature. From the standpoint of liberal legalism, the administrative state does indeed feature an imperial executive; the critics are wrong only in thinking that anything can be done about this fact. Our contrary thesis is that executive-centered government in the administrative state is inevitable, and that law cannot hope to constrain the modern executive. If our claim that the administrative state also tends to produce political constraints on the executive is correct, however, liberal legalism's fears of executive tyranny are overblown. Liberal legalism's essential failing is that it overestimates the need for the separation of powers and even the rule of law. The administrative state itself generates political substitutes for legal constraints on executive power.

PLAN OF THE BOOK

The book is structured around our two main claims: law does little to constrain the modern executive, contrary to liberal legalism's hopes, whereas politics and public opinion do constrain the modern executive, contrary to liberal legalism's fears.

The first claim—the debility of liberal legalism in the administrative state—is laid out in chapters 1, 2, and 3. Chapter 1 focuses on the constitutional framework for the administrative state, deriving from Madison and his colleagues. The Madisonian framework is broken and cannot be translated or otherwise adapted to the administrative state, or so we argue. Chapter 2 focuses on the problem of constitutional change and argues that liberal legalism has no adequate theory of how change in fundamental law can be accomplished, at least under the American constitution. Rather the main mechanism of constitutional change is a political one—the "constitutional showdown," in which institutions and officeholders use political weapons in a struggle for authority. Showdowns are resolved not by law, but by appeals to the court of mass public opinion. In this sense, constitutional change in the American system is plebiscitary. Chapter 3 focuses on the statutory framework for the administrative state, examining both framework statutes intended to check presidential power, and the APA, intended to channel and constrain the power of the bureaucracy. Here too, the circumstances of modern government ensure that the rule of law will always remain critically incomplete, and that its gaps will expand during crises. As throughout, we study cases from the post-9/11 period and from times of economic emergency, in order to triangulate on the common features of two major types of crises.

Our second claim—the substitution of political for legal constraints on the executive—is the subject of chapters 4, 5, and 6. Chapter 4 examines domestic political constraints on the executive. Chief among these are the credibility constraint, which gives the executive incentives to use various self-binding mechanisms to generate credibility across lines of party, ideology, and interest, and the popularity constraint, which gives the executive incentives to satisfy the preferences of some sufficient fraction of the public. Here we recur to our running comparison between the security crisis of 2001 and the economic crisis of 2008, showing that the Bush administration's behavior in the two crises can most simply be explained by reference to its public standing, rather than law or other secondary factors. Chapter 5 examines international political constraints on the executive and contrasts them with international legal constraints, or "global liberal legalism." While the former are real, the latter are evanescent, despite the hopes of legal liberals. Chapter 6 focuses on tyrannophobia—the false and unjustified belief that the alternative to liberal legalism, with its executive tightly constrained by law, must be executive tyranny. This is a bogeyman of liberal legal and political theory that rests on little or no evidence. The real alternative to liberal legalism is not tyranny but a plebiscitary presidency,[26] constrained by the shifting tides of mass opinion.

AFTER MADISON

What comes after the Madisonian regime of liberal legalism and the separation of powers? Our answer is a new political order in which government is centered on the executive. By virtue of "Ought implies can," it is useless for liberal legalists to bemoan the decline of legal constraints on the executive. Long-term economic and institutional forces—most generally, as Schmitt observed, the rapidity of change in the policymaking environment and the institutional incapacity of legislatures and courts to supply the necessary policy adjustments—make executive governance inevitable. The only useful response is to think about how executive government can be improved, and we offer prescriptions for making executive government more credible and more responsive to public opinion. After liberal legalism and the decline of the separation of powers, executive government is not despotic, but it is or can be popular and broadly credible among the citizenry. The aim of legal theorists, in this new world, should be to help make it more so—to act as midwives to the postliberal order of executive government.

The new political order holds sway in the United States, whose law and institutional arrangements are central to our discussion. We do not claim that the new order can be discerned everywhere, in every liberal democratic polity that has an administrative state. Although the institutional mechanisms we discuss will have implications for other polities, insofar as conditions are similar, differences in local conditions will affect the observable results. One of our main claims, for example, is that the Madisonian separation of powers is obsolete. This claim will not apply in any straightforward way to parliamentary systems, as opposed to systems with an independently elected president; mixed presidential-parliamentary systems, like France, present further complications. However, the crucial Schmittian insight that the increasing pace of economic and social change produces increasingly executive-centered government does affect parliamentary systems as well, and was of course initially formulated to characterize the parliamentary system of Weimar Germany.

CHAPTER 1

The Constitutional Framework

We begin with the constitutional framework, and with the official constitutional theory of liberal legalism. In this theory, lawmaking powers are separated among three different branches—legislature, executive, and judiciary—in order to promote an institutional division of labor and to protect liberty. The liberty-protecting function of the separation of powers, Madison suggested, is that the combination of powers in one institution would be "the very definition of tyranny."[1] Mutual checking and monitoring by the branches of government would prevent concentration of power, suppress the evils of factionalism, and conduce to better policymaking overall.

This theory has collapsed. Its fit with reality is no longer merely imperfect, in the way that all regulative ideals are imperfect; rather it does not even approximate the political terrain it purports to cover. We will proceed to explain this conclusion in three steps. First, we examine the checking function of the separation of powers. Here Madison made two crucial mistakes: first in assuming that the individual ambitions of government officials would cause them to support the power of the institutions they occupy, and second in assuming that some invisible-hand mechanism would cause the mutual contest among institutions to produce a socially beneficial system of mutual checks. Nothing in the actual separation-of-powers system, however, guarantees or even generally tends to produce socially beneficial results. In particular, we show that the system will predictably lead to suboptimal checking—to a political regime in which some institutions (such as legislature and judiciary) do too little to check the swelling power of others (such as the executive).

Second, we examine the monitoring function of the separation of powers, focusing particularly on legislative and judicial monitoring of the executive. The vastly increased complexity and scale of the executive, since Madison's day, ensures that the monitoring function is largely obsolete. In the administrative state, the scope of the executive's responsibility is vast, and legislative and judicial institutions lack the capacity to monitor any important fraction of what the executive does, even where opposing polit- ical parties occupy the executive and other branches, and even with the help of "fire alarms"—alerts from interest groups with stakes in particular issues.[2] In many of the most important domains, and those most difficult to monitor—those involving intelligence, foreign affairs and national security, or highly complex questions of economic policy—legislators and the courts are overmatched, for enduring structural reasons that prevail no matter what the contingent political constellation. We thus reject any strong version of the "congressional dominance" thesis—the idea that Congress, sometimes enlisting the aid of interest groups and the courts, exerts im- plicit but effective control over executive and administrative behavior.[3]

Third, we examine the relationships among the separation of powers, dele- gation to the executive, and the pace of policymaking in the administrative state. Schmitt famously claimed that legislatures and courts "come too late" to crises in the administrative state, meaning that in crises the rate of policy change becomes so great that legislators and judges have little choice but to hand the reins to the executive. Crises, however, are merely the endpoint on a con- tinuum, and Schmitt's more general point is that the administrative state requires rapid ongoing adjustments in complex policy matters, adjustments that cumbersome legislative and judicial processes are unable to supply. The main engine of adjustment is delegation to the executive. The two solvents of liberal legalism are delegation and emergencies; taken separately, each dissolves the premises of liberal legalism, and their interaction is all the more corrosive.

We make these claims concrete by examining two episodes of crisis gov- ernment in the modern administrative state: the post-9/11 security crisis and the economic meltdown of 2008. These episodes reveal, in extreme form, the basic debility of the separation-of-powers framework in the ad- ministrative state.

MADISONIAN CHECKING?

In the Madisonian account of the separation of powers, mutual checking by institutions arises because the individual interests and ambitions of officials give them incentives to promote the power of the institutions they occupy (as Madison put it, the "interests of the man must be tied to the rights of the place"); when this occurs, institutions will engage in a process of political competition such that "ambition [will] counteract ambition." So there are two levels to the Madisonian argument: the aggregation of individual interests into institutional behavior, and the aggregation of institutional behavior into a system of mutual checks—a system that is thought to produce socially desirable effects, such as liberty and the prevention of tyranny.

Madison's argument, however, is flawed at both levels. We will proceed backward, first supposing that individuals indeed have incentives to promote the power of the institutions they occupy, and then questioning that assumption. First, there is no mechanism that predictably produces optimal checking through the interaction of the branches, in part because future generations are not represented in lawmaking institutions and in part because of problems of collective action among (as opposed to within) branches. Second, as the legal theorist Daryl Levinson has shown,[4] there is no reason to accept Madison's assumption that "the interests of the man" would be aligned with "the rights of the place." Because of collective action problems within Congress (as opposed to among the branches), the interests of individual legislators do not necessarily align with the interests of Congress qua institution.

CHECKING AND FUTURE GENERATIONS

Suppose we have a theory stating that a separation of powers of strength S is optimal, where S specifies the ratio of the power of each branch of the national government to the total power of the national government. This theory might be legal, based on an account of the constitutional distribution of power, or might instead be rooted in democratic theory or political morality. For our purposes the source of the theory is irrelevant.

If one branch has taken over the whole government, $S = 1$ for the victorious branch and $S = 0$ for the others; if each of the three branches is of equal strength, $S = 1/3$ for each. An S-function might, for example, specify that the distribution of power should be president $= .5$, Congress $.25$, and Supreme Court $.25$. Obviously these numbers are simplistic, but they suffice to illustrate our point. Suppose also that one institution— say, the presidency—is increasing its strength, such that its strength exceeds what is specified in the social S-function. Then current citizens and future generations will benefit from checking the expanding power of that branch.

However, current institutions will be too passive—will challenge the expanding institutions too rarely, and with too little intensity—because they will not fully capture the benefits to future generations of exercising the checking function. The largest harms from an unbalanced government will be likely to materialize in the medium-run and long-run future, beyond the time horizon of current institutions. Suppose that one thinks the current power of the presidency is excessive—that the president's S-factor is too high. Then one might regret the many occasions in the past two generations on which Congress and the Supreme Court have foregone opportunities to challenge the president's power—including the many cases in which the Court employed the "passive virtues," including creative or disingenuous statutory interpretation, in order to duck a confrontation.[5]

Particular political mechanisms may cause some of these externalities to be internalized. Thus the interests of current citizens and litigants will be partly taken into account by the more-or-less representative national institutions, the presidency and Congress. Yet large literatures in public choice and political economy detail the agency slack and other failures of representation that affect these institutions. The courts are less directly representative; although they tend to follow the national election returns eventually, they do so only with a time lag, and are used by outgoing political parties to entrench their preferences against the incoming political tide.[6]

CHECKING AND COLLECTIVE ACTION: DIVIDE AND CONQUER

The point that current checking will fail to internalize the interests of future generations would hold even if there were only two branches in the picture. With three branches, however, externalities among *current* actors are also possible. One possibility is that the strongest branch—the one with the highest S-value—can play a divide-and-conquer game, alternating alliances with the weaker branches until it effectively dominates both. Here, the externality is that each of the weaker branches fails to take into account the full costs of its short-run opportunism to the other weak branch and to the balance of the whole system. Conversely, the weaker branches will be tempted to free ride on each other's investment in checking the strongest branch, so long as there is a positive cost to a showdown that checks aggrandizement.

Counterintuitively, a configuration of president = .5, Congress = .5, Supreme Court = 0 might yield far more aggressive checking of presidential expansion than would a configuration like president = .5, Congress = .25,

Supreme Court = .25. In the latter scenario Congress and the Court will face temptations to mutual free-riding, while in the former scenario the concentration of nonpresidential power in a single place reduces the scope for presidential aggrandizement. Potentially offsetting the free-rider problem is the very multiplicity of checking agents, which may raise the likelihood that at least one of them will step forward to challenge an expansion of power. However, as we discuss shortly, there is no general mechanism ensuring that one effect precisely compensates for the other. Note, in this regard, that interbranch conflicts—"constitutional show-downs"—need not help to check aggrandizement. Showdowns might instead provide the very opportunity the stronger branch has been seeking to crush its adversaries or to clarify their impotence, creating a highly visible precedent that will underscore its power.

AN INVISIBLE HAND?

So far, we have suggested that there is no general reason to think that the decentralized decisions of lawmaking branches and institutions will result in socially optimal checking. It might be suggested that decentralized decisions might result in socially optimal checking by some sort of invisi-ble-hand mechanism. Even if each institution considers only its private costs and benefits, rather than social costs and benefits, perhaps a kind of analogy to markets operates, such that the social optimum arises as "the result of human action, but not the execution of any human design."[7] For similar or related suggestions, consider the claims that the "fog" of legal uncertainty in constitutional law has the systemically beneficial effect of deterring aggrandizement,[8] or the suggestion that "[t]he governmental order that arises in our system of separation of powers paradoxically has much in common with the more spontaneous order that may arise where individuals work out mutually advantageous arrangements without the aid of a central coordinator."[9] The basic form of the argument is that emergent constitutional norms, customs, conventions, and precedents are or may be systemically optimal, even if no actor aims to promote an optimal system.

Of course this is possible, but there is no reason to think that it actually is so. In general, these are methodologically suspect functional explanations;[10] they speculate that private decisions produce social benefits without speci-fying how exactly this outcome occurs. For a genuine invisible-hand process to operate, there must be some mechanism that explains the connection between individual-level behavior and the systemic optimum.[11] Absent intentional optimizing by a social planner, the social optimum will be produced only by some sort of evolutionary or feedback mechanism.

In ideal markets, there is just such a mechanism: the price system, enforced by competition. Economic actors who are not aiming to produce public benefits will do so by rationally pursuing their self-interested ends; doing so embeds information about supply and demand in prices and propagates that information through the economic system.[12] Under the idealized conditions of textbook welfare economics, the price system ensures that all Pareto-improving trades are consummated. However, nothing in the separation-of-powers system corresponds in any robust way to the role of the price system (in ideal markets).[13] There is no general mechanism ensuring that the decentralized decisions of branches will produce the optimal level of checking, except possibly in an accidental and temporary fashion. The separation-of-powers system has it in common with the ideal market, and some real markets, that there is no central director, but the conclusion does not follow that the separation-of-powers system displays "spontaneous order" or that it will produce mutually advantageous arrangements. Furthermore, even if all such arrangements are made, there is no guarantee that the resulting distribution of political power will be socially optimal, because there are enduring divergences between private and social costs and benefits.

BRANCHES, INDIVIDUALS, AND PARTIES

So far we have assumed, with Madison, that branches of the national government can be personified as rational actors. Madison thought that the design of the relevant institutions would align the "interests of the man" with the "right of the place." As we mentioned, however, Madison's picture is vulnerable at this level as well.[14] The interests of individuals who fill the branches will often, perhaps systematically, diverge from the institutional interests of those branches. Moreover, individual officials are members of parties whose interests cut across those of institutions. Relaxing the assumption of personification should generally strengthen our conclusions, because introducing a divergence between individual and institutional interests, or party interests and institutional interests, makes it even more unlikely that institutions will act so as to produce the socially optimal level and distribution of mutual checking among branches.

Consider, as an example, the problem of underinvestment in checking aggrandizement—here again defining aggrandizement as any change that gives one institution more power than specified in an ideal S-function. We saw two mechanisms that might cause a current Congress to underinvest in showdowns that would check the expanding powers of the presidency. The first is that the current Congress would not fully internalize the interest of future generations in enjoying an optimal separation-of-powers system; the second is that Congress might attempt to free ride on the checking function of the Supreme Court, which might in turn be trying to free ride on the checking function of Congress.

The divergence between the interests of individual legislators and the institutional interests of Congress provides a third mechanism, quite possibly cumulative with the first two. David Hume argued, in effect, that lack of coordination among members of Parliament enabled the Crown to buy a decisive bloc of legislative support on the cheap.[15] Modern commentators have extended the point, showing that because Congress is a they, not an it,[16] and is a they with many members, legislators face severe problems of collective action in organizing to oppose the executive, even where it would be socially optimal to do so. The internal multiplicity of Congress increases the probability that Congress as a whole will underinvest in checking the executive. The executive too is a they, not an it, but as we discuss subsequently, in relative terms the executive is more unified and hierarchical than Congress. By the same token, although there is a divergence between the interests of individual Presidents and the institutional power of the presidency, the two are more closely aligned than are the interests of individual legislators and the institutional power of Congress.

Of course, the same collective action problems that hamper Congress in opposing the executive might also prevent Congress from aggrandizing power at the expense of the executive or the courts, and that result might itself be socially desirable. Consider that internal legislative disagreement, preventing formation of a sufficiently large coalition, was all that saved Andrew Johnson from being convicted after he was impeached. It has been claimed, plausibly enough, that a successful impeachment of Johnson would have decisively tilted the American separation-of-powers system in the direction of a quasi-parliamentary form of government.[17] But there is no reason to think that this second possibility somehow balances out the first; there is no big ledger where the beneficial effects of internal legislative conflict balances out the detrimental effects, and no pricelike mechanism that makes the former equal to the latter in any event. The effects of Congress's collective action problems are, at best, a random variable with respect to the socially optimal level and distribution of constitutional checking. Once the divergence between individual and institutional interests is taken into account, there is even less reason to think that decentralized institutional interaction will have any systematic or predictable tendency to supply checking in a socially desirable manner.

MADISONIAN MONITORING?

We turn from checking to the related, but distinctly different idea of monitoring—especially the monitoring by Congress (particularly through congressional committees), or by judges, of executive authority, including delegated authority. The connection between checking and monitoring is that in the liberal legalist separation-of-powers theory stemming from Madison, institutional competition produces monitoring or oversight of executive discretion. Congressional and judicial oversight of executive action, on this account, will ensure that the executive exercises discretion only as directed by voter-principals, acting through legislators who are simultaneously agents (of the voters) and principals (of the executive).

This statement of the Madisonian position is intended to distinguish between the legal and political functions of oversight. It is clear that oversight—by legislators, judges, or other actors—can affect public opinion, which can in turn constrain the president. Congress and other institutions are participants in the game of public opinion, and that game is, in the administrative state, the major constraint on the executive. The political effects of oversight on the executive, however, are indirect. In this chapter, we focus on whether oversight directly accomplishes its legal function in the theory of liberal legalism. The legal function of oversight is to ensure that the executive exercises power within the boundaries set by law. In the Madisonian vision, legislators have an interest in monitoring the president to ensure that he faithfully executes the statutes they enact.

This account is no longer adequate, if it ever was. Legislators and judges are, for the most part, unable to effectively oversee or monitor the executive's exercise of delegated legal authority, especially in the domains of foreign policy and national security. We will examine some of the principal institutional problems, beginning with legislative oversight and then turning to the courts.

CONGRESS

Many institutional factors hamper effective legislative monitoring of executive discretion for legal compliance. Consider the following problems.

Information Asymmetries

Monitoring the executive requires expertise in the area being monitored. In many cases, Congress lacks the information necessary to monitor discretionary policy choices by the executive. Although the committee system has the effect, among others, of generating legislative information and expertise,[18] and although Congress has a large internal staff, there are domains in which no amount of legislative expertise suffices for effective oversight. Prime among these are areas of foreign policy and national security. Here the relative lack of legislative expertise is only part of the problem; what makes it worse is that the legislature lacks the raw information that experts need to make assessments.

The problem would disappear if legislators could cheaply acquire information from the president, but they cannot. One obstacle is a suite of legal doctrines protecting executive secrecy and creating deliberative privileges—doctrines that may or may not be justified from some higher-order systemic point of view as means for producing optimal deliberation within the executive branch. Although such privileges are waivable, the executive often fears to set a bad institutional precedent.

Another obstacle is the standard executive claim that Congress leaks like a sieve, so that sharing secret information with legislators will result in public disclosure. The problem becomes most acute when, as in the recent controversy over surveillance by the National Security Agency, the executive claims that the very scope or rationale of a program cannot be discussed with Congress, because to do so would vitiate the very secrecy that makes the program possible and beneficial. In any particular case the claim might be right or wrong; legislators have no real way to judge, and they know that the claim might be made either by a well-motivated executive or by an ill-motivated executive, albeit for very different reasons.

Collective Action Problems

Part of what drives executive reluctance to share information is that, even on select intelligence committees, some legislator or staffer is bound to leak and it will be difficult to pinpoint the source. Aware of the relative safety that the numbers give them, legislative leakers are all the more bold. This is an example of a larger problem, arising from the fact that there are many more legislators than top-level executive officials.

Compared to the executive branch, Congress finds it more costly to coordinate and to undertake collective action (such as the detection and punishment of leakers). To be sure, the executive too is a "they," not an "it." Much of what presidents do is arbitrate internal conflicts among executive departments and try to aggregate competing views into coherent policy over time. As a strictly comparative matter, however, the contrast is striking: the executive can act with much greater unity, force, and dispatch than can Congress, which is chronically hampered by the need for debate and consensus among large numbers. This comparative advantage is a principal reason why Congress enacts broad delegating statutes in the first place, especially in domains touching on foreign policy and national security. In these domains, and elsewhere, the very conditions that make delegation attractive also hamper congressional monitoring of executive discretion under the delegation.

There may or may not be offsetting advantages to Congress's large numbers. Perhaps the very size and heterogeneity of Congress make it a superior deliberator, whereas the executive branch is prone to suffer from various forms of groupthink. But there are clear disadvantages to large numbers, insofar as monitoring executive discretion is at issue. From the standpoint of individual legislators, monitoring is a collective good. If rational and self-interested, each legislator will attempt to free ride on the production of this good, and monitoring will be inefficiently underproduced. More broadly, the institutional prerogatives of Congress are also a collective good. Individual legislators may or may not be interested in protecting the institution of Congress or the separation of legislative from executive power; much depends on legislators' time horizons or discount rate, the expected longevity of a legislative career, and so forth. But it is clear that protection of legislative prerogatives will be much less emphasized in an institution composed of hundreds of legislators coming and going than if Congress were a single person.

"Separation of Parties, not Powers"

Congress is, among other things, a partisan institution.[19] Political scientists debate whether it is principally a partisan institution, or even exclusively so. But Madison arguably did not envision partisanship in anything like its modern sense. Partisanship undermines the separation of powers during periods of unified government. When the same party controls both the executive branch and Congress, real monitoring of executive discretion rarely occurs, at any rate far less than in an ideal Madisonian system. This appears to have a marked effect in the domain of war powers and foreign affairs, where a recent study by political scientists William Howell and Jon Pevehouse shows that congressional oversight of presidential war powers differs markedly depending upon the partisan composition of Congress.[20] When Congress is a co-partisan of the president, oversight is minimal; when parties differ across branches, oversight is more vigorous.

Partisanship can enhance monitoring during periods of divided government,[21] but this is cold comfort for liberal legalists. From the standpoint of liberal legalism, monitoring is most necessary during periods of unified government, because Congress is most likely to enact broad delegations when the president holds similar views; and in such periods monitoring is least likely to occur. The Congress of one period may partially compensate by creating institutions to ensure bipartisan oversight in future periods—consider the statute that gives a minority of certain congressional committees power to subpoena documents from the executive[22]—but these are palliatives. Under unified government, congressional leaders of the same party as the president have tremendous power to frustrate effective oversight by the minority party.

The Limits of Congressional Organization

Congress as a collective body has attempted, in part, to overcome these problems through internal institutional arrangements. Committees and subcommittees specialize in a portion of the policy space, such as the armed forces or homeland security, thereby relieving members of the costs of acquiring and processing information (at least if the committee itself maintains a reputation for credibility). Intelligence committees hold closed sessions and police their members to deter leaks (although the sanctions that members of Congress can apply to one another are not as strong as the sanctions a president can apply to a leaker in the executive branch). Large staffs, both for committees and members, add expertise and monitoring capacity. And interest groups can sometimes be counted upon to sound an alarm when the executive harms their interests.

Overall, however, these arrangements are not fully adequate, especially in domains of foreign policy and national security, where the scale of executive operations is orders of magnitude larger than the scale of congressional operations. Congress's whole staff, which must (with the help of interest groups) monitor *all* issues, runs to some 30,000 persons.[23] The executive branch has some 2 million civilian employees, in addition to almost 1.4 million in the active armed forces.[24] The sheer mismatch between the scale of executive operations and the congressional capacity for oversight, even aided by interest groups or by leakers within the bureaucracy, is daunting. Probably Congress is already at or near the limits of its monitoring capacity at its current size and budget.

We neither make, nor need to make, any general empirical claim that Congress has *no* control over executive discretion. That is surely not the case; there is a large debate, or set of related debates, about the extent of congressional dominance. We have reviewed the institutional problems piecemeal; perhaps some of them are mutually offsetting, although we do not see any concrete examples. But we do think that in the administrative state there is a significant structural gap, and during emergencies and wars an even larger gap, between the extent of executive discretion and legislative capacity for monitoring.

COURTS

Problems for Judicial Oversight of the Executive

Information asymmetries

The gap between the executive and the judiciary, in information and expertise, is even wider than between the executive and Congress. Whereas many legislators have a narrowly defined field of policy expertise, particularly in the House of Representatives, federal judges are mostly generalists, barring a few specialized courts. Furthermore, the partial insulation from current politics that federal judges enjoy, by virtue of life tenure and salary protection, brings with it a kind of informational impoverishment.[25] Legislators, who must please other people at least some of the time, interact with the outside world far more systematically than generalist judges, whose main source of information is the briefs and arguments of litigants. When the executive says that resolving a plaintiff's claim would require disclosure of "state secrets," with dangerous consequences for national security, judges know that either an ill-motivated or a well-motivated executive might be making the claim and that they have no easy means to assess whether the claim is credible.

Collective action problems and decentralization

If congressional monitoring of executive discretion is hampered by collective action problems, judicial monitoring is hampered by a similar condition, the decentralized character of the federal judiciary. The judiciary too is a "they," not an "it," and is decentralized along mainly geographic lines. Different judges on different courts have different views of the costs and benefits of oversight and of the appropriate level of monitoring. The Supreme Court is incapable of fully resolving these structural conflicts. Because the Court presides over a large institutional system and lacks the capacity to review more than a fraction of cases submitted to it, its role is restricted by necessity to the declaration of general principles of law and episodic, ad hoc intervention in the system.

The legitimacy deficit

In the federal system, appointed judges are not overtly partisan, though they are sometimes covertly so. The very condition that enables this relative lack of overt politicization—that federal judges are, at least in one familiar conception, legal technocrats appointed for their expertise rather than elected on a partisan basis—also creates a serious legitimacy deficit for the judiciary, understanding legitimacy in a strictly sociological sense.[26] Aroused publics concerned about issues such as national security may have little tolerance for robust judicial oversight of executive discretion, which can always be condemned as "activism" by "unelected judges." This charge sometimes succeeds and sometimes fails, but for the judges it is always a concern that acts as a drag on attempts to monitor executive behavior.

Here too, we do not claim that judicial oversight is a total failure. Doctrinal lawyers focus, sometimes to excess, on a handful of great cases in which judges have checked or constrained discretionary executive action, even in domains involving foreign policy or national security. Cases such as *Youngstown*,[27] the Pentagon Papers case,[28] and recently *Boumediene v. Bush*[29] head this list. Undoubtedly, however, there is a large gap between executive discretion and judicial capacities, or even between executive discretion and the sum of congressional and judicial capacities working in tandem. In times of emergency, especially, both Congress and the judiciary almost always defer to the executive. *Boumediene*, which held that alleged enemy combatants detained at Guantánamo Bay could bring habeas corpus claims, was strictly procedural in character; it ordered no one to be released, something that the judges who issued it doubtless appreciated. Legislators and judges understand that the executive's comparative institutional advantages in secrecy, force, and unity are all the more useful during emergencies, so that it is worthwhile transferring more discretion to the executive even if it results in an increased risk of executive abuse. The result is that cases such as *Boumediene* are the exception, not the rule, especially during the heat of the emergency.

CRISIS AND DELEGATION

So far we have examined problems with checking and monitoring that occur in normal times. The administrative state, however, is beset by recurring crises, in part because the scope of its responsibilities is so vast. Crises exacerbate the problems of liberal legalism, or so we will suggest.

Delegation is a defining feature of the administrative state. Congress has shown that it has powerful incentives to delegate vast powers to the president, for both good reasons and bad (from the standpoint of liberal legalism). In the late nineteenth and early twentieth centuries, the demand for regulation outstripped the capacity of legislatures to supply regulation directly, requiring delegation to administrative agencies, some of which are controlled de jure by the president, some of which are influenced by the president de facto, especially through the power to appoint their members. The complexity of policymaking and the rapid pace of change in the policy environment make it prohibitively costly for relatively underspecialized legislators, burdened with cumbersome processes of collective action in large-number bodies, to attempt to specify all policy choices themselves, even if they would want to. And as we have seen, courts proved systematically unable to enforce a constitutional doctrine of "nondelegation" and have basically abandoned any attempt to do so.[30]

Emergencies are also a defining feature of the administrative state. As the scope of government's power and responsibility expand continually, events that in earlier centuries would have been seen as the punishment of the gods or as bad luck, and thus merely to be suffered, became a problem for government to solve. The climate itself, proverbially beyond human control, is now seen as a regulatory problem, and many talk of the problem of climate change as a "crisis." The expanding administrative state witnesses a continual series of "small emergencies"[31] and an episodic succession of large emergencies whose timing and nature is unpredictable, but whose existence is not.

When emergencies occur, the standard legislative response is delegation, for all the same reasons that delegation is a standard legislative tool in normal times—only more so. The factors that induce delegation in normal times are not different in nature than the factors that induce delegation in perceived emergencies, but they take a more extreme form. Emergencies and crises, in our definition, are just one end of a continuum, in which the economic and political environment changes with maximum speed; problems or threatened problems require immediate response and large-scale, extremely rapid shifts in government policy. Delegation is the legislature's tool of first resort for coping with such problems, because legislatures are incapable of supplying the necessary policy adjustments at the necessary pace.

What makes crises significant is that fundamental institutional reform takes place in a brief period of time even as existing institutions struggle to fulfill their mandate. Sometimes, existing institutions simply claim more power than it was understood that they had. At other times, Congress rouses itself to act, but only for the purpose of confirming a seizure of power or discretion by the executive, or in order to delegate large new powers. Our goal is to understand these dynamics.

A SCHMITTIAN VIEW

We first turn to the best general analysis of institutional capacities and crisis management in the administrative state, stemming from Carl Schmitt. Schmitt was a Weimar and Nazi jurist, and a searching critic of the constitutional and legal commitments of liberal democracies.[32] Schmitt's general constitutional theory[33] has long been a major influence on continental legal theorists, and his scathing critique of parliamentary democracy is also famous.[34]

Schmitt's work, at least as interpreted by recent commentators like William Scheuerman, addresses the relationship between the classical rule-of-law state, featuring legislative enactment of general rules enforced by courts, and the administrative state, featuring discretionary authority and ad hoc programs, administered by the executive.[35] We do not need, and will dispense with, some of Schmitt's more jurisprudential and abstract claims and concerns, such as his critique of legal positivism. (We also reject his political extremism, which is not justified by his critique of liberal democracy but requires additional assumptions about political psychology that are implausible.)[36] Rendered in suitably institutional and pragmatic terms, Schmitt's work contains essential insights for understanding how Congress, the courts, and the executive can and cannot manage crises, economic or otherwise.

Here the main inspiration is not solely Schmitt's famous work on emergencies, on "the exception" as opposed to normal law, or his famous pronouncement that "sovereign is he who decides on the exception."[37] Although we will draw on those themes in chapter 3, we focus here on Schmitt's analysis of the general debility of legislatures and judges in the modern administrative state, not only in times of war but also or especially in economic crises.[38] Such crises underscore legislative debility, making it plain for all to observe, but the causes of the debility are structural and ever-present.

As we have seen, Schmitt holds that liberal lawmaking institutions, such as legislatures and courts, frame and apply general norms that are essentially "oriented to the past," whereas "the dictates of modern interventionist politics cry out for a legal system conducive to a present- and future-oriented steering of complex, ever-changing economic scenarios."[39] Only the executive is institutionally capable of reacting with sufficient speed and force as the rate of change in the policy environment increases; legislatures and courts increasingly fall behind the pace of events in the administrative state, and are forced to play an essentially reactive and marginal role. As Scheuerman puts it,

> Given the demands of a capitalist economy that to an ever greater extent requires fast, constantly changing forms of state intervention in accordance with the rapid-fire dictates of economic life, it is no surprise that even liberal democratic polities tend to hand over vast open-ended authority to executive and administrative bodies widely seen as best suited to the tasks of quick and immediate action.[40]

Crises, economic or otherwise, represent the extreme manifestation of this phenomenon. In crises, legality and legitimacy diverge, and legitimacy prevails; but this suggests that even in normal times, where they happen to coincide, legitimacy may be the only force that matters. States of exception merely reveal the underlying dynamics that operate de facto in all periods.

Legislatures may be asked to delegate new authority to administrators after a crisis is already under way, but the frontline response is inevitably administrative, and the posture in which legislators are asked typically to grant new delegations of authority, with the crisis looming or in full blast, all but ensures that legislators will give the executive much of what it asks for. Courts, for their part, get involved only much later, if at all, and essentially do mop-up work after the main administrative programs and responses have solved the crisis, or not. The result is that in the administrative state, broad delegations to executive organs will combine lawmaking powers with administrative powers; "only then can the temporal distance between legislation and legal application be reduced."[41]

These points are abstract. We will illustrate them by examining the role of Congress and the courts in the aftermath of 9/11 and the 2008 financial crisis. Our main claim will be that the Schmittian view supplies a better account of institutional capacities and behavior in these crisis episodes than does the liberal legalist view stemming from Madison.

TWO CRISES

Terrorism

On September 11, 2001, a terrorist attack on the World Trade Center in New York killed over three thousand people. The markets plunged, and airlines reeled toward bankruptcy. Executive action and legislation followed, both to stabilize the markets and to counter terrorism. The Bush administration and Congress bailed out the airlines, and the economic issues temporarily receded from center stage. Legally and politically, the main focus turned toward counterterror policies and, in 2003, the war in Iraq, which the administration sometimes linked to the counterterror issue.

In the immediate aftermath of 9/11 the legal framework for counterterrorism policy came, for the most part, from the Constitution and from two major statutes: the Authorization for Use of Military Force (AUMF) enacted on September 18, 2001, and the USA Patriot Act, enacted on October 26, 2001. In subsequent years new statutes were added, notably the Detainee Treatment Act of 2005, the Military Commissions Act of 2006, and the FISA Amendments Act of 2008. In some cases, the Bush administration initiated or pursued post-9/11 counterterror policies based on claims of inherent executive power stemming from Article II of the Constitution, particularly the commander-in-chief clause. In other cases, however, the administration sought legislative authorization for its actions.

The AUMF gave the administration broad authority to use "necessary and appropriate force" against Al Qaeda and related entities. How broad this authority actually was became controversial in later years; a plurality of the Supreme Court eventually ruled that it authorized executive detention of enemy combatants, yet in controversies over surveillance the administration's attempts to invoke the statute were widely rejected. Civil-libertarian critics derided the "hasty" and "panicked" process by which the AUMF and the Patriot Act were passed, and portrayed them as massive delegations of unchecked power to the executive.

The reality, however, was more complex, as we discuss shortly. The administration partially lost control of the legislative process in both cases, and although it got most of what it wanted, it did not get everything it asked for. Measured from the baseline of the executive's initial proposals, legislative pushback was substantial. However, there is a great deal of truth in the critics' complaints: measured from the baseline of the legal status quo ante 9/11, the administration did receive large delegations of new powers in response to the crisis.

What about the judges' reaction? Here the picture fits a standard cyclical pattern in American history: courts remain quiet during the first flush of an emergency, and then reassert themselves, at least symbolically, as uncertainty fades and emotions cool. Between 2001 and 2004, the courts were conspicuously silent about counterterror policy. Indeed, in 2003 the Supreme Court denied certiorari in a case questioning the constitutionality of closed hearings in deportation proceedings, despite the existence of a circuit split on the issue[42]—in tension with the Court's usual certiorari practice, and a clear example of Alexander Bickel's "passive virtues."

In 2004, the Court for the first time reached the merits of a case about presidential authority over counterterror policy, in *Hamdi v. Rumsfeld*.[43] Despite initial impressions that the Court had asserted itself against executive power, the administration won most of what it had wanted. Especially useful to the administration was the plurality's holding that the AUMF authorized detention of alleged enemy combatants. Newspaper accounts and civil libertarians focused on a different holding, that constitutional due process might demand some minimum procedures to determine which detainees are actually enemy combatants. However, the main opinion conspicuously declined to require that *judicial* process be used, and the government constructed a system of administrative tribunals to make enemy-combatant determinations.

By 2006, the Bush administration had lost a great deal of credibility both at home and (especially) abroad, in part because of setbacks in Iraq, in part because of scandals, such as Abu Ghraib, and in part because of spectacular incompetence in the management of Hurricane Katrina. Moreover, with the passage of time and the absence of new terrorist attacks in the homeland, the sense of threat waned. Predictably, the judges reasserted themselves. In *Hamdan v. Rumsfeld*[44] in 2006, the Court held that the administration's military commissions set up to try alleged enemy combatants for war crimes violated relevant statutes and treaties. When Congress reacted by passing the Military Commissions Act in 2006, the Court went on to hold in 2008, in *Boumediene v. Bush*, that the statute violated the Suspension Clause of the Constitution by denying habeas corpus to detainees at Guantánamo Bay. Even in these cases, however, the Court did not actually order anyone released; in both cases, the result was simply more legal process. There remain sharp pragmatic limits on what courts are willing to do when faced with executive claims of security needs.

Those limits are underscored by recent systematic studies of the post-*Boumediene* litigation, in which Guantanamo detainees have brought *habeas corpus* petitions in federal court in the hopes of obtaining release.[45] Although there are various ways to interpret the data, we will recount some undisputed points:

(1) Overall, "less than four percent of releases from [Guantanamo] have followed a judicial order of release".[46] These numbers may understate the *in terrorem* effect of judicial oversight, which might cause the government to release detainees in anticipation of litigation; but that hypothesis is belied by the low variation in the rate of releases over time, whose apparent insensitivity to the course of litigation in the courts suggests that the prime motor is internal bureaucratic imperatives rather than legal considerations or fear of judicial oversight.[47] Moreover, the 4% figure may actually overstate the effect of judicial oversight, because in some fraction of that subset of cases the government would have released the detainee anyway, when the bureaucratic wheels stopped spinning. It seems safe to conclude that the overwhelming supermajority of releases occur because the government has no interest in holding individuals who are unlikely to be a threat, or because the government incurs political costs from holding detainees, or because the government happens to strike a deal with a foreign nation who will accept the detainee. Judicial oversight is a sideshow.

(2) Even in the cases in which the judges "order release," the actual orders – with only two exceptions as of December 31, 2009—have turned out to be merely hortatory. The judges urge the government to negotiate with foreign nations to find a country willing to accept the detainee at issue,[48] but stop short of ordering that the detainee be immediately allowed

to walk through the gates of Guantanamo. The judges, leery of the political and policy consequences of ordering possible terrorists to be released, almost always pull their punches at the last second, despite what the headlines report.

(3) Releases from Guantanamo slowed dramatically after 2008, when *Boumediene* was decided and President Obama was elected.[49] This may be because the government has already released most of the harmless detainees, and is now down to the hard core of the dangerous. At the same time, however, the number of detainees at the government's facility in Bagram, Afghanistan has swelled. An alternative (and not necessarily inconsistent) hypothesis, then, is that Obama is not seriously constrained by what the judges are doing, but does face political imperatives to be tough on terrorism, resulting in fewer releases at Guantanamo and new detentions elsewhere. As we discuss in later chapters, presidents have more political freedom to act on their off-side. A conservative president like Nixon can strike a deal with Red China, while a liberal president like Obama can expand detention at Bagram while brushing aside complaints from civil-libertarian elites, whose carping gets no traction with the general public so long as detention is ordered by a president perceived in some general way to be sensitive to claims of liberty. On this hypothesis, the pattern of executive detention, over time, is fundamentally driven by political imperatives, not judicial orders or legal norms.

Finance

On September 18, 2008, after months of economic anxiety and several massive bailouts of distressed firms by the government, the stock market had its largest single-day drop since September 11, 2001. The stock market crash was caused by, and helped exacerbate, the worst financial crisis since the Great Depression. Investment banks and other financial institutions had loaded up on mortgage-backed securities and other derivatives tied to the value of the housing market. When housing prices across the country peaked and began their decline, bankers realized that the assumptions they had used to value the derivatives were false. Lenders who took these securities as collateral for their loans stopped extending credit, and those who held those assets discovered that they could not raise cash by selling them because no one would buy securities they could not value except at a steep discount. The reduction of liquidity threatened the highly leveraged investment banks, and indeed many commercial banks as well. If these institutions were to fail, then businesses and consumers would not be able to borrow. Businesses would have to fire workers they could not pay, and consumers, many of them newly unemployed workers, would not be able to borrow to pay for goods, further reducing the receipts of businesses, and sending the economy into a recession or depression.

As happened after 9/11, executive officials declared an economic emergency and moved on two fronts: unilateral executive action and the acquisition of new authority through delegation. The Federal Reserve dusted off a 1932 statute that granted it massive powers to pump liquidity into the economy during financial emergencies, and in the course of the crisis would effectively take over a number of credit markets—including the market in commercial paper, which funds many corporations. The Fed also provided additional liquidity to banks and investment banks, and gave support to money market mutual funds. The Treasury dipped into its Exchange Stabilization Fund, so that it could guarantee money market mutual funds, which were threatened with a run. The Exchange Stabilization Fund was created by a statute designed to enable Treasury to manage foreign currency instability, but was written so broadly that the money could be used for virtually anything. Even these massive authorities were not enough. To rescue AIG, the Fed effectively purchased its shares—one of the few things *not* allowed by the 1932 statute—but structured the deal as a loan so as to meet that statute's formal requirements. And throughout, the Fed and Treasury used their informal authority. Reminding bankers that the regulatory agencies had enormous discretionary authority, Fed and Treasury officials wheedled and cajoled and, most importantly, made vague but ominous threats.[50]

The Fed and Treasury did *not* simply apply general norms established by a policymaking Congress. The nature of the crisis, including the overwhelming uncertainty, forced these two agencies to take an ad hoc approach. As is always the case in financial crises, the government faced a dilemma. If it let firms fail, they would be appropriately punished for their excessively risky investments. But they would also bring down other firms, with the result that credit would dry up, and economic activity would be stifled. The initial response was a series of transactions and measures designed to prop up failing firms—"regulation by deal."[51] After some hesitation—Lehman Brothers was allowed to fail, with disastrous short-term consequences because so many other firms had accounts with Lehman— the Fed and other government institutions began pumping liquidity into the system at unprecedented levels. They were apparently persuaded by the scale of the failures, the quite obvious contagion effect, and independent evidence of a credit crunch, such as the extremely high rate of interest that banks began to charge each other for interbank loans.

It soon became clear that the financial crisis would require more resources than the Fed could supply—at least, without risking its democratic legitimacy, according to Fed chief Ben Bernanke.[52] On September 19, Henry Paulson, the Treasury secretary, submitted a bill to Congress that would authorize Treasury to borrow $700 billion and use it to purchase mortgage-related assets. The bill provided that the secretary's purchasing decisions would be final, not subject to judicial review. Paulson apparently believed that by purchasing mortgage-related assets, the government would help reduce uncertainty about banks' balance sheets, allowing them to borrow if they turned out to be solvent. Judicial review or other oversight would slow down this process when quick action was essential.

The boldness of the secretary's bill initially produced an enthusiastic reaction, and the financial markets rose, but quickly the reception turned sour. Critics argued that the bill was a "blank check" that gave the Treasury too much discretion and subjected it to too little oversight; that the bill favored the rich—the investment banks, their managers, their shareholders—at the expense of the taxpayer, while providing no relief to distressed homeowners; and that Secretary Paulson, with the support of Chairman Bernanke, sought to stampede Congress into action by predicting dire consequences if inaction occurred, rather than acknowledging that Congress should hold hearings, solicit the advice of independent experts, and deliberate.

Leaders of both parties in the House, with the support of Paulson, President Bush, and both candidates for the presidency greatly expanded the Paulson bill, partly in response to these criticisms, but on September 29, the House voted down the revised version by a vote of 228 to 205. The stock market crashed, with the Dow Jones Index falling by 778 points. Senate leaders promptly took up the bill and overwhelmingly passed a revised version on October 1. The Senate version largely retained the provisions of the House bill but added numerous, mostly unrelated provisions designed to appeal to the marginal dissenters. On October 3 this bill passed the House and was signed by the president.

The EESA differed from the Paulson bill in numerous ways. But most important, for our purposes, it did not reduce Treasury's power to purchase mortgage-related securities; in fact, it expanded Treasury's power, authorizing it to purchase virtually any security when doing so could help resolve the financial crisis. Democrats in Congress also sought to compel Treasury to regulate executive compensation and provide relief to homeowners subject to foreclosure in limited circumstances, but the authorities they gave Treasury were largely discretionary. EESA also provided for limited judicial review and set up various oversight mechanisms that, however, lacked coercive power.

Even before Treasury put into operation its plan to purchase mortgage-related assets, it became clear that this approach would not be adequate, and Treasury announced that it would inject equity directly into financial institutions by buying preferred stock, as the Fed did with AIG. Indeed, Treasury later announced that it would not use Troubled Asset Relief Program (TARP) funds to purchase troubled assets at all, and would rely *solely* on equity purchases. The White House, for its part, tried and failed to obtain a bill giving Treasury specific statutory authority to prop up faltering automakers, who offer credit as an adjunct to their main operations. Despite the failure, Treasury used TARP funds to bail out the automakers in December 2008 and January 2009, relying on the broad definition of "financial institution" in the EESA.

Meanwhile, the Fed was increasing the money supply, buying up commercial paper, and purchasing other assets that it traditionally left to the private markets. Treasury directed Fannie Mae and Sallie Mae to buy up mortgage-backed securities. The Federal Deposit Insurance Corporation (FDIC) was brokering purchases of failed banks such as Wachovia, and, citing its emergency statutory authority, it eliminated the $250,000 ceiling on deposit insurance and guaranteed virtually all newly issued senior unsecured debt, potentially exposing itself to more than $1 trillion in liability.

The Obama administration followed the lead of the Bush administration in broad outline, with small differences in emphasis, including greater attention to foreclosure relief. Its major accomplishment in its first months was the enactment of a stimulus bill that sought to address the underlying economic crisis. In a twist, on February 10, 2009, the new secretary of the Treasury, Timothy Geithner, announced a new plan for using the remaining $350 billion or so of TARP funds. In addition to measures for mortgage relief and further capital injections to banks, the secretary indicated that Treasury would, in part, revive the idea of purchasing toxic assets. This time around, however, the strategy would take the form of a joint public-private venture to buy the assets, rather than direct government transactions.

The Obama administration also tried to squeeze the maximum amount of authority out of new and old statutory provisions. To evade the EESA limitations on executive pay and other policies of TARP recipients, it proposed funneling funds though special-purpose vehicles set up solely as conduits for government funds. To finance the Home Affordable

Modification Program, a project to pay loan servicers to modify privately held mortgages, it drew on TARP funds that by statute should have been used only to purchase financial instruments (such as mortgage-backed securities) or to renegotiate mortgages owned by the government. And to authorize the FDIC to insure purchasers of toxic assets under its toxic asset purchase program while evading statutory limitations on FDIC exposure to liability, the administration rested on a strained interpretation of the FDIC statute—in essence, reading a statute that limits the FDIC's exposure to $30 billion as permitting the FDIC to insure up to $850 billion on the theory that the FDIC can always cover its losses by increasing the fees that it charges banks. All of these interpretations are, at best, questionable.

CONGRESS, CRISES, AND DELEGATION

We now turn to an assessment of legislative performance in these episodes; later we will examine the role of the courts. When crises strike the administrative state, how well does Congress carry out the functions of policy-making, checking, and monitoring that are the *raison d'être* of legislatures in liberal legal theory? In order to answer these questions, we must first specify the liberal legalist view of legislative power and behavior during crises.

Liberal legalists, following Madison, describe Congress as the deliberative institution par excellence. On this view, Congress is a summation of local majorities, bringing local information and diverse perspectives to national issues. The bicameral structure of Congress aids deliberation; the House shifts rapidly in response to changing conditions and national moods, while the Senate provides a long-term perspective, and cools off overheated or panicky legislation. The Madisonian emphasis on the cooling-off function of the Senate functions as a check on executive claims that an emergency is at hand.

The application of the Madisonian view to crises or emergencies is the default position among legal academics. On this view, even in crisis situations the executive may act only on the basis of clear congressional authorization that follows public deliberation, and the executive's actions must presumptively be subject to judicial review. A proviso to the Madisonian view is that if immediate action is literally necessary, the executive may act, but only until Congress can convene to deliberate; if the executive's interim actions were illegal, it must seek ratification from Congress and the public after the fact.[53]

In the Schmittian view, by contrast, the Madisonian vision of Congress seems hopelessly optimistic. Even in normal times, Schmitt believed, the deliberative aspirations of classical parliamentary democracy have become a transparent sham under modern conditions of party discipline, interest-group conflict, and a rapidly changing economic and technical environment. Rather than deliberate, legislators bargain, largely along partisan lines. Discussion on the legislative floor, if it even occurs, is carefully orchestrated posturing for public consumption, while the real work goes on behind closed doors, in party caucuses.

How does this picture relate to Schmitt's point that legislatures invariably "come too late" to a crisis? Crises expose legislative debility to view, but do not create it. Indeed, legislative failure during crises is in part a consequence of legislative failure during the normal times that precede crises. *The basic dilemma, for legislators, is that before a crisis, they lack the motivation and information to provide for it in advance, while after the crisis has begun, they lack the capacity to manage it themselves.* We will describe each horn of the dilemma in detail.

BEFORE THE CRISIS

In the precrisis state, legislatures mired in partisan conflict about ordinary politics lack the motivation to address long-term problems. Legislators at this point act from behind a veil of uncertainty about the future, and may thus prove relatively impartial; at least high uncertainty obscures the distributive effects of legislation for the future, and thus reduces partisan opposition. However, by virtue of these very facts, there is no strong partisan support for legislation, and no bloc of legislators has powerful incentives to push legislation onto the crowded agenda. The very impartiality that makes ex ante legislation relatively attractive, from a Madisonian perspective, also reduces the motivation to enact it.

This point is related to, but distinct from, Schmitt's more famous claim about the "norm" and the "exception." In a modern rendition, that claim holds that ex ante legal rules cannot regulate crises in advance, because unanticipated events will invariably arise. Legislatures therefore either decline to regulate in advance or enact emergency statutes with vague standards that defy judicial enforcement ex post. Here, however, a different point is at issue: even if ex ante legal rules could perfectly anticipate all future events, legislatures will often lack the incentive to adopt them in advance.

Occasionally, when a high-water mark of public outrage against the executive is reached, legislatures do adopt framework statutes that attempt to regulate executive behavior ex ante; several statutes of this kind were adopted after Watergate. The problem is that new presidents arrive, the political coalitions that produced the framework statute come apart as new issues emerge, and public outrage against executive abuses cools. Congress soon relapses into passivity and cannot sustain the will to enforce, ex post, the rules set out in the framework statutes. As we will discuss more fully in chapter 3, the post-Watergate framework statutes have thus, for the most part, proven to impose little constraint on executive action in crisis, in large part because Congress lacks the motivation to enforce them.

DURING THE CRISIS

The other horn of the dilemma arises after the crisis has begun to unfold. Because of their numerous memberships, elaborate procedures, and internal structures, such as bicameralism and the committee system, and internal problems of collective action, legislatures can rarely act swiftly and decisively as events unfold. The very complexity and diversity that make legislatures the best deliberators, from a Madisonian perspective, also raise the opportunity costs of deliberation during crises and disable legislatures from decisively managing rapidly changing conditions. After 9/11, everyone realized that another attack might be imminent; only an immediate, massive response could forestall it. In September 2008, the financial markets needed immediate reassurance: only credible announcements from government agencies that they would provide massive liquidity could supply such reassurance. Indeed, though commentators unanimously urged Congress to take its time, within weeks the Bush administration was being criticized for not acting quickly enough. In such circumstances, legislatures are constrained to a reactive role, at most modifying the executive's response at the margins, but not themselves making basic policy choices.

Liberal legalists sometimes urge that the executive, too, is large and unwieldy; we pointed out in the introduction that the scale of executive institutions dwarfs that of legislative and judicial institutions. On this view, the executive has no systematic advantages in speed and decisiveness. Yet this is fatally noncomparative. The executive is internally complex, but it is structured in a far more hierarchical fashion than is Congress, especially the Senate, where standard procedure requires the unanimous consent of a hundred barons, each of whom must be cosseted and appeased. In all the main cases we consider here, the executive proved capable of acting with dispatch and power, while Congress fretted, fumed, and delayed.

The main implication of this contrast is that crises in the administrative state tend to follow a similar pattern. In the first stage, there is an unanticipated event requiring immediate action. Executive and administrative officials will necessarily take responsibility for the front-line response; typically, when asked to cite their legal authority for doing so, they will either resort to vague claims of inherent power or will offer creative readings of old statutes. Because legislatures come too late to the scene, old statutes enacted in different circumstances, and for different reasons, are typically all that administrators have to work with in the initial stages of a crisis. "Over time, the size and complexity of the economy will outgrow the sophistication of static financial safety buffers"[54]—a comment that can also be made about static *security* safety buffers, which the advance of weapons technology renders obsolete. In this sense, administrators also "come too late"—they are forced to "base decisions about the complex, ever-changing dynamics of contemporary economic [and, we add, security] conditions on legal relics from an oftentimes distant past."[55]

Thus Franklin Roosevelt regulated banks, in 1933, by offering a creative reading of the Trading with the Enemy Act of 1917, a statute that needless to say was enacted with different problems in mind. Likewise, when in 2008 it became apparent on short notice that the insurance giant AIG had to be bailed out, lest a systemwide meltdown occur, the Treasury and Federal Reserve had to proceed through a strained reading of a hoary 1932 statute. While the statute authorized "loans," it did not authorize government to purchase private firms; administrators structured a transaction that in effect accomplished a purchase in the form of a loan. Ad hoc "regulation by deal,"[56] especially in the first phase of the financial crisis, was accomplished under the vague authority of old statutes. The pattern holds for security matters as well as economic issues, and for issues at the intersection of the two domains. Thus after 9/11, the Bush administration's attempts to choke off Al Qaeda's funding initially proceeded in part under provisions of the International Emergency Economic Powers Act, a 1977 statute whose purpose, when enacted, was actually to restrict the president's power to seize property in times of crisis.[57]

At a second stage typical of administrative crises, Congress writes new statutes delegating broad powers to the executive to handle the crisis. It is simplistic to say, and we do not claim, that legislatures write the executive a blank check. On the other hand, it is equally false to say that during crises, Congress acts as a Madisonian deliberator, with institutions like bicameralism cooling of the heated passions of the public and of executive officials. The basic pattern is that the executive asks to take three steps forward; Congress, pushing back somewhat, has no choice but to allow it to take two.

We will examine this pattern in the post-9/11 context and in the context of the 2008 economic emergency. In the first setting we focus on the Authorization to Use Military Force (AUMF) and the USA Patriot Act; in the second setting we focus on the EESA.

September 14 AUMF

Passed by Congress three days after 9/11, in the white heat of the emergency, the AUMF is where one might expect to find a hasty blank-check delegation to the executive. Surprisingly, however, the AUMF resulted from a process of tough bargaining among the White House, Democratic leaders in the Senate, and Republican leaders in the House.[58]

The White House's initial proposal provided

> That the President is authorized to use all necessary and appropriate force against those nations, organizations or persons he determines planned, authorized, harbored [sic], committed or aided in the planning or commission of the attacks against the United States that occurred on September 11, 2001, *and to deter and preempt any future acts of terrorism or aggression against the United States.*[59]

Other authorities proposed by the White House included a request that Congress give the president standing authority to appropriate whatever sums he deemed necessary to fight terrorism, that Congress waive any restrictions on foreign assistance, and that relevant congressional committees acquiesce in restrictions on the provision of classified or "sensitive" information.

These proposals, however, were quickly and decisively rejected by legislative leaders, apparently on a bipartisan basis. The decisive worry involved, not principally civil liberties, but the institutional power of Congress vis-à-vis the executive branch: "Given the breadth of activities potentially encompassed by the term 'aggression,' the President might never again have had to seek congressional authorization for the use of force to combat terrorism."[60] Accordingly, "[A] consensus quickly developed that the authority should be limited to those responsible for the September 11 attacks, and to any country harboring those responsible." The final clause in the White House proposal, underlined above, was transformed into a purpose clause that limited the president's authority by requiring a nexus to the perpetrators of 9/11, and that deleted sweeping powers to fight "terrorism" and "aggression." In the final version, the operative section of the AUMF stated that "the President is authorized to use all necessary and appropriate force against those nations, organizations, or persons he determines planned, authorized, committed, or aided the terrorist attacks that occurred on September 11, 2001, or harbored such organizations or persons, in order to prevent any future acts of international terrorism against the United States by such nations, organizations or persons."[61]

Besides insisting on this partially constrained authorization, legislators charted a middle course on many dimensions. Procedurally, they rejected amendments that would have imposed explicit periodic reporting requirements, but similar requirements were imposed by implication, through a cross-reference bringing the AUMF under the War Powers Resolution. Substantively, legislators declined to make it textually explicit that the authorization was only for the use of military force abroad, although many legislators so claimed during the debates. By the same token, however, legislators successfully resisted last-minute pressure from the White House— despite the extreme urgency of the situation—to insert the words "in the United States" so as to give the president express authority to use military force against terrorism domestically.[62]

Patriot Act

This 342-page statute defies easy summary, and in any event some excellent overviews are available.[63] The statute contains a variety of measures expanding law enforcement powers to conduct searches and surveillance; enacts prophylactic measures against illegal money laundering and financial transactions by terrorist groups; creates some new substantive crimes; and adjusts some rules of immigration and federal criminal procedure. As enacted, the measure contained a sunset provision for many of the more controversial provisions.

The final version differed in major respects from the administration's first draft, which was called the Anti-Terrorism Act (ATA). That draft contained several provisions that provoked opposition from civil-libertarian legislators in both parties, such as a grant of power to the attorney general indefinitely to detain any alien on national security grounds, without judicial review. The opposition was sufficiently intense that the House Judiciary Committee, with a Republican majority, rebelled and refused to mark up the bill.[64] The ATA as such died; the final enactment combined a draft bill by Senator Leahy (the USA Act), a consensus bill developed by House Republicans and Democrats (the PATRIOT Act), and administration provisions.

Overall, "[t]he administration did not get everything it asked for in the draft Anti-Terrorism Act. The administration also got a lot it did not ask for."[65] The final enactment, for example, sharply cut back on the administration's request for the power to detain aliens indefinitely without review; the statute only allowed detention for seven days, and added an express right of judicial review. Moreover, the statute contained several civil-libertarian provisions inserted by House Republicans, including a federal cause of action for executive release of wiretap information, a provision establishing an Inspector General for Civil Liberties and Civil Rights in the Department of Justice, and the sunset provisions, which House Republicans insisted upon retaining despite vehement objections from the president's negotiators.

In the first case, the White House initially proposed a blank-check delegation to the president of power to respond as appropriate to "deter and preempt terrorism."[66] The bargaining, although accomplished in a matter of days, ended up introducing a more restrictive nexus test, which limited the president's authority to the use of force against entities that had aided the 9/11 attacks.[67] In the case of the Patriot Act, a rebellion by civil-libertarian Republican legislators in the House caused the administration to temporarily lose control of the bargaining process, resulting in a reduced grant of powers combined with a sunset provision.[68]

Emergency Economic Stabilization Act

In the case of the EESA, the administration's initial plan was sketchy in the extreme, and would have granted legally unreviewable power to the secretary of the Treasury to spend some $700 billion dollars on the acquisition of mortgage-related assets, essentially without legislative standards. Rebellious House Republicans rejected one version of the bill, but the final legislation retained the core of the administration's proposal, while modifying it on several margins. The statute actually gave the secretary additional new powers that the administration had not requested or perhaps even desired, such as the powers to buy an equity stake in distressed firms and to regulate executive pay. The former power would allow the Treasury to "nationalize" banks—that is, take them over and operate them. On the other hand, several oversight mechanisms were introduced, although as we will discuss shortly, their effectiveness is questionable. Finally, the legislation introduced some new substantive restrictions on the secretary's new authority, and provided for staggered disbursement of the funds in a fashion reminiscent of the Patriot Act's sunset provisions.

IN THE WAKE OF THE CRISIS

Crises give Congress an opportunity to exercise post hoc oversight and enact legislation that ensures that executive overreaching does not recur. This exercise, a recurrent feature of the American system, with famous precedents during the Great Depression and after the Pearl Harbor attack, is in the spirit of the Madisonian view. But the Madisonian view requires that this process lead to results. In fact, the process today is largely empty.

The last great example of post hoc oversight took place during and after the Watergate scandal, and led to a series of statutes in the 1970s that placed formal constraints on executive power. The effectiveness of these statutes remains a matter of debate, and we consider them in chapter 3. But they at least give us a baseline sense of what the Madisonian view might require from Congress after crises end.

The executive's crisis response to the 9/11 attack did lead to congressional hearings and other forms of post hoc review, such as the 9/11 Commission's investigation and report. But controversial executive actions, including torture and wiretapping, which arguably broke existing law, led to only sporadic and uninformative congressional hearings, not to the prosecutions and truth commissions demanded by the administration's critics. This is all the more remarkable, given that in 2008 the executive and Congress fell into the hands of the Democratic Party, the opposition party during the bulk of the 9/11 crisis. Rarely does the opportunity for political revenge coincide so perfectly with the demands of public virtue and liberal legalism. Why didn't the Democrats in the executive and Congress seize this opportunity?

The answer brings together all the problems with the Madisonian view that we have discussed so far. Hearings, truth commissions, and trials would require revealing secrets about interrogation, detention, and other counterterror tactics that would compromise national security. These procedures would also bring to light unsavory practices that would harm America's standing in the world. Even years after the harshest tactics were abandoned, these costs are high because Al Qaeda and other terrorists groups remain a threat, and testimony and photographic evidence revealing new abuses would be a propaganda boon for America's enemies. In addition, the American public is divided over counterterror tactics, with large minorities and even majorities passionately believing that the U.S. government should use any and all means to counter terrorist threats. The Obama administration cannot afford the political backlash that would take place if it tried to punish officials of the Bush administration.

Yet another factor, we suspect, is that the Obama administration does not want to deter its own soldiers and CIA agents from acting aggressively against terrorist threats. We do not mean that President Obama himself or any of his lieutenants condone torture. But in other respects, the Obama administration has followed Bush administration policies on national security, including the reliance on broad surveillance powers, detention, military commissions, rendition, and targeted assassination—many aspects of which remain questionable under both domestic and international law. Prosecution and other forms of public humiliation of Bush administration officials can only send a signal to the people who carry out Obama's counterterror policies that they are in legal jeopardy as well, which would sap them of confidence and morale. The Obama administration cannot afford to take this risk.

The financial crisis also led to congressional hearings. In addition, with EESA Congress established a number of oversight commissions with the tasks of investigating the government's response to the crisis and monitoring its expenditure of TARP funds. So far, these committees and commissions have done little to shed light on the government's handling of the crisis, again in part because they must contend with the executive branch's secrecy claims, and in part because these committees and commissions have multiple masters with different interests. More important, Congress has not produced a legislative structure for controlling the government during the next financial crisis. This is not to say that Congress was happy with the performance of Treasury and the Fed. Members of Congress battered Treasury secretary Henry Paulson with complaints, and a large minority of the Senate voted against Fed chief Ben Bernanke's reappointment by President Obama in 2010. In 2009 Representative Ron Paul proposed a bill to bring some of the Fed's activities within the purview of Congress's accounting body, the Government Accountability Office, but although the bill received a great deal of symbolic support from other members of the House, it was never enacted.

For all of the complaints about executive power, the conventional wisdom today is that the Fed and the Treasury acted forcefully to solve the worst financial crisis since the Great Depression. Therefore, there is no political support for curtailing their powers for the next financial crisis. The Fed emerged from the crisis more powerful than ever, having established by precedent (almost certainly unchallengeable in court) emergency powers enabling it to spend hundreds of billions of dollars to tame a financial emergency, using virtually any means, subject to no oversight by the other branches of government. Current legislative proposals would delegate yet more regulatory powers to the Fed and other oversight bodies.

We are left with a picture of congressional (and judicial) passivity in the wake of the two major crises of the first decade of the twenty-first century. Institutionally unable to make policy before and during crises, Congress can hardly complain about the policy choices made by the executive after the crisis is over. Within the strict limits created by national security, and the need to protect and encourage deliberation among government officials during both security and economic emergencies, Congress has helped bring some government activities to light. But because it cannot punish people who acted improperly, it cannot set precedents for the next crisis. And as its silence demonstrates, it has no interest in doing so.

CONGRESS AND CRISES: A SUMMARY

In all the cases we have examined, the overall result was the same. Measured either from the baseline of (1) what the executive initially requested or (2) what the executive actually desired (as best we can tell from indirect evidence), Congress pushed back somewhat, despite the speed of legislative enactment; it narrowed proposed delegations or added delegations that the administration did not desire, added sunset provisions or similar mechanisms, and created oversight mechanisms. These points should not obscure, however, that measured from the baseline of (3) the legal status quo ante the emergency, executives obtained broad new delegations of power, and that oversight mechanisms were of only dubious efficacy. After the AUMF, the president possessed a great deal of statutory authority to combat terrorism, especially abroad; after the Patriot Act, that authority was extended to domestic criminal law and immigration matters. After the EESA, the president enjoyed broad statutory authority to rescue the economy from crisis.

The overall picture of Congress's role in emergency lawmaking, then, is as follows. Congress lacks motivation to act before the crisis, even if the crisis is in some sense predictable. Thus the initial administrative response will inevitably take place under old statutes of dubious relevance, or under vague emergency statutes that imposes guidelines that the executive ignores and that Congress lacks the political will to enforce, or under claims of inherent executive authority. After the crisis is under way, the executive seeks a massive new delegation of authority and almost always obtains some or most of what it seeks, although with modifications of form and of degree. When Congress enacts such delegations, it is reacting to the crisis rather than anticipating it, and the consequence of delegation is just that the executive once again chooses the bulk of new policies for managing the crisis, but with clear statutory authority for doing so.

In this pattern, Congress's structural incapacities ensure that, while Congress can shape and constrain the executive's response at the margins, it is fundamentally driven by events and by executive proposals for coping with those events, rather than seizing control of them. Schmitt's broad claim that the fast-moving conditions of the administrative state produce a marginal, reactive, and essentially debilitated Congress is closer to the mark than the Madisonian vision of a deliberative legislature that might rise to the occasion in times of crises, rather than handing power to the executive and hoping for the best.

The role of the Senate during the passage of the EESA is particularly hard to square with the Madisonian view. Far from dampening hasty legislation with a calmly deliberative perspective, the Senate played two main roles. The first, a pluralist role, was to lubricate the bill's passage with pork-fat, such as a tax break for producers of wooden arrows (but not plastic ones) intended to gain the support of the senators from Oregon, where the wooden-arrow makers were located.[69] The Senate's second role was to put pressure on the House to act even more quickly and to approve the new delegation of executive authority. The Senate vote was accelerated by Senate leaders in order to approve the bill before the House's final vote, a move intended to underscore the obstructionism of House Republicans and to raise the political costs of their resistance. Rather than cooling off the sense of urgency behind the legislation, the Senate helped bring it to a boil.

To be sure, it is difficult to extract from the Madisonian view specific and clear implications or predictions about how Congress will or should act during emergencies, in order to compare with the facts. Both the Schmittian view and the Madisonian view offer broad accounts of political processes and probabilistic tendencies, rather than point predictions. The Schmittian view, however, could clearly be falsified by imaginable outcomes. If Congress had rejected the bailout bill altogether, or decided to handle mortgage-related purchases itself, through its committees—and a great many detailed policy choices and appropriations matters were handled in exactly that way during the nineteenth century—then the Schmittian view would have been falsified. After 9/11, if Congress had adopted a statute that restricted the president's power in future security emergencies, the Schmittian view would have been falsified in the security context. By the same token, however, if we are right that Congress played a marginal and reactive role during both crises, bucking against executive proposals but eventually giving in on the major points, griping from the stands, and reaching decisions mostly through bargaining rather than deliberation, it is fair to think that the Madisonian view does not capture the dynamics of crisis governance.

THE COURTS

We now turn from Congress to the courts, the other main hope of liberal legalism. In both economic and security crises, courts are marginal participants. Here two Schmittian themes are relevant: that courts come too late to the crisis to make a real difference in many cases, and that courts have pragmatic and political incentives to defer to the executive, whatever the nominal standard of review. The largest problem, underlying these mechanisms, is that courts possess legal authority but not robust political legitimacy. Legality and legitimacy diverge in crisis conditions, and the divergence causes courts to assume a restrained role. We take up these points in turn.

The Timing of Review

A basic feature of judicial review in most Anglo-American legal systems is that courts rely upon the initiative of private parties to bring suits, which the courts then adjudicate as "cases and controversies" rather than as abstract legal questions. This means that there is always a time lag, of greater or lesser duration, between the adoption of controversial government measures and the issuance of judicial opinions on their legal validity.

Common lawyers sometimes praise this delayed review precisely because the delay ensures that courts are less likely to set precedents while crises are hot, precedents that will be warped by the emotions of the day or by the political power of aroused majorities.[70]

Delayed review has severe costs, however. For one thing, courts often face a *fait accompli*. Although it is sometimes possible to strangle new programs in the crib, once those measures are up and running, it is all the more difficult for courts to order that they be abolished. This may be because new measures create new constituencies or otherwise entrench themselves, creating a ratchet effect, but the simpler hypothesis is just that officials and the public believe that the measures have worked well enough. Most simply, returning to the pre-emergency status quo by judicial order seems unthinkable; doing so would just re-create the conditions that led the legislature and executive to take emergency measures in the first place.

For another thing, even if courts could overturn or restrict emergency measures, by the time their review occurs, those measures will by their nature already have worked, or not. If they have worked, or at least if there is a widespread sense that the crisis has passed, then the legislators and public may not much care whether the courts invalidate the emergency measures after the fact. By the time the courts issue a final pronouncement on any constitutional challenges to the EESA, the program will either have increased liquidity and stabilized financial markets, or not. In either case, the legal challenges will interest constitutional lawyers, but will lack practical significance.

Intensity of Review

Another dimension of review is intensity rather than timing. At the level of constitutional law, the overall record is that courts tend to defer heavily to the executive in times of crisis, only reasserting themselves once the public sense of imminent threat has passed. As we will discuss in chapter 3, federal courts deciding administrative cases after 9/11 have tended to defer to the government's assertion of security interests, although more large-number work is necessary to understand the precise contours of the phenomenon. Schmitt occasionally argued that the administrative state would actually increase the power of judges, insofar as liberal legislatures would attempt to compensate for broad delegations to the executive by creating broad rights of judicial review; consider the Administrative Procedure

Act (APA), which postdates Schmitt's claim. It is entirely consistent with the broader tenor of Schmitt's thought, however, to observe that the very political forces that constrain legislatures to enact broad delegations in times of crisis also hamper judges, including judges applying APA-style review. While their nominal power of review may be vast, the judges cannot exercise it to the full in times of crisis.

Legality and Legitimacy

At a higher level of abstraction, the basic problem underlying judicial review of emergency measures is the divergence between the courts' legal powers and their political legitimacy in times of perceived crisis. As Schmitt pointed out, emergency measures can be "exceptional" in the sense that although illegal, or of dubious legality, they may nonetheless be politically legitimate, if they respond to the public's sense of the necessities of the situation.[71] Domesticating this point and applying it to the practical operation of the administrative state, courts reviewing emergency measures may be on strong legal ground, but will tend to lack the political legitimacy needed to invalidate emergency legislation or the executive's emergency regulations. Anticipating this, courts pull in their horns.

When the public sense of crisis passes, legality and legitimacy will once again pull in tandem; courts then have more freedom to invalidate emergency measures, but it is less important whether or not they do so, as the emergency measure will in large part have already worked, or not. The precedents set after the sense of crisis has passed may be calmer and more deliberative, and thus of higher epistemic quality—this is the claim of the common lawyers, which resembles an application of the Madisonian vision to the courts—but the public will not take much notice of those precedents, and they will have little sticking power when the next crisis rolls around.

OTHER INSTITUTIONS AND ACTORS

So far we have discussed only ordinary congressional and judicial processes, but sometimes other actors come into play. The EESA, for example, creates a variety of institutions to monitor the authority it delegates. However, their force is at best unclear. We will focus on two of the EESA's oversight mechanisms that are of theoretical interest. The first involves review by Congress itself, assisted by a congressional oversight panel; the second involves oversight by an independent board.

Congressional Review

The EESA provides that the secretary's second $350 billion in purchasing authority is subject to a joint resolution of disapproval.[72] On January 16, 2009, however, the Senate blocked a disapproval bill,[73] making the release automatic, and that vote was entirely predictable. The theory of such provisions is to secure a kind of congressional review, akin to a sunset clause (which the EESA also contains). Yet this type of mechanism requires affirmative action by the future Congress, or at least a credible threat of such action; thus, it is even less likely than a sunset clause to result in a real check on the executive. A joint resolution is just a statute by another name, so a disapproval would have had to obtain a congressional supermajority in order to override a veto. Similar statutes that require affirmative congressional action to check the executive, such as the National Emergencies Act, have tended to become dead letters, as we will detail in chapter 3.

Separately, the EESA creates a "Congressional Oversight Panel" whose members are chosen by congressional leaders. By early 2009, the panel had issued several reports outlining questions that "the American people" should ask of Treasury, and had expressed the view that there is a "foreclosure" crisis at the root of the financial crisis. The major problem with the Congressional Oversight Panel is that it possesses only the standard powers of a congressional committee, the powers to obtain information and produce reports. While those powers are not negligible in ordinary times, they become inadequate as the pace of events quickens in economic emergencies. Congress's own committees have usually proven unable to do more than follow the action, rather than shape it, while occasionally criticizing the players in the arena; it is unlikely that an ad hoc committee will do better.

Independent Boards

The EESA also creates oversight by a putatively independent board, the Financial Stability Oversight Board, which consists of the secretary himself, the chairman of the Federal Reserve, the chairman of the Securities and Exchange Commission (SEC), the director of the Federal Housing Finance Agency (an independent commission recently created in other legislation), and the secretary of Housing and Urban Development.[74] Of these five, three are chairs or heads of "independent agencies," whose principals cannot be fired without cause, and this suffices to create a patina of independent oversight. In the case of the SEC, there is some degree of legal uncertainty about the independence of the commission, in part because the D.C. Circuit recently issued an expansive interpretation of the grounds for firing permitted by the statute.[75] So one might describe the EESA as creating a board consisting of two-and-a-half independent agencies and two-and-a-half executive agencies—another display of Congress's Solomonic wisdom.

However this may be, the aura of independence fades quickly when one considers the board's powers and the actual conduct of its members. The board is authorized to "review[] the exercise of [the secretary's powers]," to ensure that the secretary is carrying out the purposes and policies of the statute, to recommend action to the secretary, and to send reports to appropriate congressional committees.[76] These provisions are another exercise in "studied ambiguity."[77] Their scope and force is vague, the crux of the ambiguity being whether the board has power to actually countermand the secretary's purchasing decisions and other orders, or whether its power to "review" simply amounts to a power to find out what the secretary is up to and transmit information to Congress. The high-minded interpretation is that Congress declined to give the board clearly controlling authority because of lurking constitutional questions about whether the powers of a "core" executive agency like the Treasury could be subjected to independent control, even under the Court's latitudinarian precedents. The low-minded interpretation is that legislators benefited politically by creating an oversight mechanism whose atmospherics suggest independent supervision of the secretary's massive new powers, but whose operational reality is far less impressive. "'[The board is] sort of a joke in terms of oversight,' a congressional aide said."[78]

Even if the board had crystal-clear legal power to actually countermand the secretary's decisions, a separate problem is whether the board would in practice function as an autonomous check on the secretary's extraordinary economic authority. The answer is likely to be no. Even before the EESA was enacted, the chair of the Fed, Ben Bernanke, acted hand in glove with the Treasury secretary, Henry Paulson, with the latter in the role of lead partner. Part of the explanation here is that independent agencies face the same problems of legality and legitimacy that plague independent judiciaries in times of crisis. Lacking a direct channel of accountability to the president, they are partially insulated from politics, but are also vulnerable to criticism as "unelected bureaucrats."

Moreover, recent empirical work suggests that the heads of independent agencies and executive agencies tend to have common preferences and beliefs, both aligned with those of the reigning president; at least this is especially likely to be so late in the second term of an eight-year presidency.[79] Two mechanisms, one political and one legal, bring about this result. The political mechanism is that because the two main political parties are increasingly polarized, presidents can reliably select and appoint independent agency heads whose preferences and views track their own. While the opposition party in the Senate can slow down the rate of such appointments, and thus delay the time when presidents take control of the independent agencies, polarization means that when presidents do gain a majority on the agency, their appointees reliably work to promote the president's agenda.[80] Eventually presidents can do a great deal to coordinate all agency heads on common preferences and a common program, whatever their nominal legal status.

The legal mechanism is in fact a diverse collection of statutes, proposed statutes and internal executive-branch procedures, norms and practices that require independent agencies to consult or collaborate with cabinet departments and executive agencies in the formulation of policy.[81] In actual practice, even before the financial crisis, Treasury was coming to play a larger role in securities regulation, despite the nominal independence of the Securities and Exchange Commission. During the crisis, as we have mentioned, Treasury and the Fed worked hand in glove. Norms or legal requirements of consultation and collaboration give the president, through his agents, increasing influence over the independent agencies. "Even if an independent agency is not under the thumb of the President, it might still feel the hand of the President."[82]

The Whole and the Parts

It is tempting to think that, even if these oversight mechanisms are feeble taken individually, their cumulative force is more impressive. The reverse is more likely to be true, however: because the very multiplicity of overseers dilutes the responsibility of each, the whole will be less than the sum of the parts. In the savings-and-loan crisis, Congress also set up a variety of oversight bodies, including an independent board structured very similarly to the one created by the EESA. The consequence was unclear lines of authority and fractured responsibility: "[O]verlapping oversight ensured that . . . no one agency would bear the blame for the problems that inevitably would emerge. The alphabet soup of overseers distanced both the president and the Congress from the oversight as well, so it helped minimize the electoral fallout from the bailout."[83] It would be no surprise to see the same dynamic at work under the EESA.

A NOTE ON THE FED

The Federal Reserve Board is an independent agency. Although the president appoints its seven members with Senate consent, he does not have the power to remove them. Indeed, the president does not even appoint the chiefs of the twelve independent Federal Reserve Banks, even though their heads participate in the decision-making process. We have so far treated the Fed, acting in concert with Treasury (an executive Cabinet Department), as a part of the executive. A brief refinement is warranted.

The Fed does not fit comfortably in either the Madisonian scheme or a scheme of executive primacy. It has immense policymaking authority, which it exercises by (in effect) setting the price of money, in this way influencing the business cycle and the entire operation of the economy, and by regulating the safety and soundness of major banks. The Fed is at least partly responsible for both the financial crisis of 2008–2009 and for its resolution. The easy-money policy of the early 2000s fueled the housing bubble; the credit facilities it opened during the financial crisis helped keep the economy running. The Fed also has executive authority: it directly manipulates the money supply by purchasing and selling securities, making loans, setting reserve requirements, and so forth. As we have seen, during the financial crisis it took over a great deal of the credit market by establishing credit facilities that issued loans to and bought securities from market actors. Finally, the Fed's activities are subject to only the most deferential judicial review, if any.[84]

Yet the Fed is not a plenary dictator in the Schmittian sense. It has authority only over its regulatory domain. Congress retains the power to withdraw powers from the Fed, dismantle it, and subject it to controls, and it seems clear that Fed chiefs believe that they need the support of Congress and the executive in order to maintain their authority. As noted above, Bernanke worried that the Fed could not go too far during the financial crisis without sacrificing its democratic legitimacy, and this is what led him and Paulson to seek legislation from Congress.

The central role of the Fed in the financial crisis raises the question of whether the executive is checked, in some sense, by its own internal divisions. These divisions result from the existence of both bureaucracies such as the EPA that are formally subject to presidential control but in practice enjoy some autonomy because of the limits of presidential oversight, and bureaucracies such as the Fed that enjoy both formal and substantive independence (or quasi independence) from presidential control.

The upshot of the massive size of the executive is that the president can exert control only in certain areas—for example, counterterrorism policy during the Bush administration, and then subject to numerous constraints, and not over many other areas, where he can at best set the tone (which may well be ignored by subordinates), or through appointments of people who may not act in the president's interest or may not be able to control those below them. So the sheer complexity of the government response to regulatory problems limits the impact of a single person, and renders inappropriate the use of words like "dictator" to describe the president.[85] What this means is that a large area of public policy is determined by a self-replicating career bureaucracy that probably roughly shares the political preferences of the center (albeit no doubt with occasional significant deviations) and in general acts with typical bureaucratic caution with an eye to avoiding scandal. The traditional separation-of-powers model does not, of course, capture this phenomenon. The bureaucracy is not a representative institution like the legislature, nor a judicial institution—although efforts have been made to introduce representative and judicial elements to it, as though to take up the slack left by the collapse of liberal institutions outside the executive.[86]

THE SELF-FULFILLING CRISIS OF AUTHORITY

Finally, we mention a dynamic that further tightens the political constraints on legislatures and courts in times of crisis. Precisely because markets expected the House to pass the EESA, its initial failure to do so created a perceived "crisis of authority,"[87] suggesting a risk that dysfunctional political institutions would not be able to coordinate on any economic policy at all. That second-order crisis supervened on the underlying economic crisis, but acquired force independent of it. The Senate had to scramble to undo the damage and did so in world-record time. The House quickly fell into line.

In this way, measures urged by the executive to cope with a crisis of unclear magnitude acquired a kind of self-created momentum. Rejection of those measures would themselves create a political crisis that might, in turn, reduce confidence and thus trigger or exacerbate the underlying financial crisis. A similar process occurred in the debates over the AUMF and the Patriot Act, where proponents of the bills urged that their rejection would send terrorist groups a devastating signal about American political willpower and unity, thereby encouraging more attacks. These political dynamics, in short, create a *self-fulfilling crisis of authority* that puts legislative institutions under tremendous pressure to accede to executive demands, at least where a crisis is even plausibly alleged.

Critics of executive power contend that the executive exploits its focal role during crises in order to bully and manipulate Congress, defeating Madisonian deliberation when it is most needed. On an alternative account, the legislature rationally submits to executive leadership because a crisis can be addressed only by a leader. Enemies are emboldened by institutional conflict or a divided government; financial markets are spooked by it. A government riven by internal conflict will produce policy that varies as political coalitions rise and fall. Inconsistent policies can be exploited by enemies, and they generate uncertainty at a time that financial markets are especially sensitive to agents' predictions of future government action. It is a peculiar feature of the 2008 financial crises that a damaged president could not fulfill the necessary leadership role, but that role quickly devolved to the Treasury secretary and Fed chair who, acting in tandem, did not once express disagreement publicly.

CONCLUSION

American government in the period 2001 to 2008 bears little resemblance to the constitutional framework erected, or wished for, by liberal legalism. In the liberal-legalist view, legislatures are said or at least hoped to be the primary actors, with executive and judicial power following suit—through law-execution and law-interpretation respectively. Both legislatures and courts are supposed to check and monitor the executive, keeping its power tightly cabined. In these episodes, however, executive officials take center stage, setting the agenda and determining the main lines of the government's response, with legislatures and courts offering second-decimal modifications. Legislative and judicial monitoring and checking is largely hopeless, in part because of the necessarily ad hoc character of the government's initial reaction ("regulation by deal"),[88] in part because legislatures and courts come too late to the scene. The overall impression is that the constitutional framework of liberal legalism has collapsed under the pressure of fact, especially the brute fact that the rate of change in the policy environment is too great for traditional modes of lawmaking and policymaking to keep pace. Although crises demonstrate the problem with particular clarity, it is embedded in the structure of the administrative state.

None of this means that the president is all-powerful; that is not our claim. As political science assessments of executive power show,[89] the president does face some checks even from a generally supine Congress and even in the domains of war and foreign affairs where presidential power reaches its zenith.[90] However, these checks are not primarily legal. Even Congress's main weapon for affecting presidential behavior is not the cumbersome and costly legal mechanism of legislation. Rather legislators appeal to the court of public opinion, which in turn constrains the president. Oversight and various forms of "soft law"[91]—congressional statements and resolutions short of legally binding legislation—affect public support for presidential action in the realm of foreign policy, and in many other domains as well. There are real constraints on executive government, but formal constitutional procedures are not their source.

CHAPTER 2
Constitutional Change

Under liberal legalism, how does constitutional law change over time? The question is theoretically crucial. If constitutional law is frozen at its inception, then any positive rate of change in the policy environment will eventually render it obsolete. In the administrative state, moreover, the rate of change in the policy environment is high and plausibly accelerating over time,[1] making constitutional rules set down in past generations particularly suspect. Liberal legalism needs a theory of constitutional change through legal mechanisms.

But there is no such theory, or so we will argue. We will begin by reviewing some legal mechanisms by which liberal legal theorists have attempted to reconcile constitutional change with the constitutional rule of law, such as the formal amendment process, judicial interpretation, and "constitutional moments" of higher lawmaking. None of these is both descriptively accurate and normatively appealing; whether taken separately or together, none can account for more than a small fraction of the constitutional change that a dynamic polity demands.

We then lay out an affirmative theory of constitutional change, which attempts to show that constitutional norms change through political processes—especially shifts in public opinion—rather than through any legal mechanism. The main process, we suggest, is the "constitutional showdown"—episodes of conflict between and among institutions over the distribution of policymaking authority. Such conflicts are settled by bargaining, brinksmanship, bluffing, and ultimately by the force of public opinion, rather than by any distinctively legal form of decision making.

Although showdowns are often accompanied by legal arguments, such arguments are just another move in the bargaining game, and showdowns are best understood as a special kind of politics accompanied by legalized rhetoric. Madisonian liberal legalism has little to say about this phenomenon.

LIBERAL LEGALISM AND CONSTITUTIONAL CHANGE

In the original Constitution, the official mechanism of constitutional change is the formal amendment process set out in Article V. The rules actually lay out several different mechanisms for amendment, but we will focus on the standard case in which amendments are initiated in Congress, enacted by a two-thirds vote, and then approved by three-fourths of state ratifying conventions. In American history this procedure has been used some twenty-odd times, depending on how one counts the Bill of Rights amendments, which were enacted in a clump, and on whether one counts the disputed Twenty-seventh Amendment. Whatever the precise number, it is clear that at the federal level the amendment process is invoked rarely, as compared to many states and foreign constitutions that have hundreds of amendments. The comparison is somewhat blurred, however, by the fact that states and foreign nations replace their constitutions wholesale with surprising frequency,[2] which makes the U.S. Constitution an extreme outlier on the score of longevity.

The well-known problem is that the Article V procedures for formal constitutional amendment are cumbersome. Putting aside the wholesale replacement of constitutions, and simply comparing formal amendment mechanisms across jurisdictions, it has been shown that the Article V process is an extreme outlier; very few polities have equally onerous supermajority requirements.[3] While the amendment process can be used for major constitutional surgery after a significant trauma, such as the Reconstruction Amendments after the Civil War, it cannot be routinely used for the incessant midlevel changes that are needed to keep pace with economic, social, and political changes. Although amendments could be used more frequently than they are, it is unlikely that the formal amendment process could supply all needed change.

Given the cumbersome quality of Article V, liberal legal theory has thus added epicycles to attempt to square constitutional change with its basic commitment to the constitutional rule of law. We will examine two such epicycles: judicial interpretation and higher lawmaking.

JUDICIAL INTERPRETATION

One source of constitutional change is judicial updating of constitutional law over time through various modalities of "dynamic" interpretation.[4] There is no doubt that judicial interpretation is a real mode of constitutional change in American constitutional law. Because of the rigidity of the Article V amendment process, constitutional obsolescence will inevitably result unless there is some other process for producing change, and judicial updating might be this process. Comparison across polities shows that there is a substitution relationship between judicial updating and the rigidity of the formal amendment process: the more difficult it is to obtain formal amendments, the more de facto amendment through judicial interpretation must be permitted, or the shorter the constitution's life span will be.

From the standpoint of liberal legalism, however, the problems with this mechanism of change are familiar and important. First is the dubious political legitimacy of judge-made constitutional change, a central problematic of constitutional theory. The official theory of liberal legalism squares liberal constitutionalism with democracy by claiming that constitutional rules are adopted with the direct or indirect consent of the people, through their representatives in legislatures, constituent assemblies, or ratifying conventions. It requires further theoretical epicycles to square judge-made constitutional change with this picture. In the American federal system judges are selected and approved by elected representatives, but this is a further step removed from the popular will that it supposed to determine the legitimacy of constitutional rules. And it is not obvious, at all, that judges selected by representatives a generation or so ago should have superior authority to interpret (and de facto amend) the constitutional rules than current legislatures or executives, whose connection to the people—at least in the sense of current majorities—is far more immediate. Taken to an extreme, judge-made constitutional change threatens to produce a regime of liberal legalism without democracy.

A second problem, less discussed but perhaps even more serious, is that judicial interpretation takes place on far too small a scale to provide a comprehensive mechanism of constitutional change. As the legal theorist Frederick Schauer emphasizes,[5] the Supreme Court's agenda is a small subset of the nation's agenda, and this remains true even if the denominator is confined to the nation's constitutional agenda. The Supreme Court restricts itself to a small fraction of the constitutional questions that arise daily in the operation of government, most of which are either never settled or settled only through bargaining between and among nonjudicial institutions.

Within the pages of the U.S. Reports, constitutional law is centrally concerned with hot-button questions of affirmative action, abortion, and the rights of detainees, although the justices throw in a few cases of commercial importance, such as litigation under the "dormant commerce clause." Outside the law books, however, there is an enormous world of constitutional problems that the judges rarely touch, involving the structure and function of government and the operation of the branches. Manifold issues about executive privilege, the crucial power to make appointment to agencies and other official bodies, the power to direct or supervise agency officials in the execution of their statutory powers, and other structural questions almost never become the subject of formal judicial precedents. These questions go unsettled for generations as far as doctrinal law is concerned; we will provide examples of this phenomenon later in the chapter. The upshot is that because of its sharply restricted scope, and dubious legitimacy even within its scope, judge-made constitutional change cannot supply more than a small fraction of the necessary constitutional adjustments.

HIGHER LAWMAKING

Finally, there is the theory of higher lawmaking during "constitutional moments," offered by constitutional scholar Bruce Ackerman.[6] This theory rejects the "monist" liberal legal conception, in which the sole modality of constitutional change is formal amendment, in favor of a "dualist" conception in which de facto amendments can occur in moments of higher lawmaking. Lower lawmaking is the quotidian process of legislative horse-trading and grubby interest-group politics; moments of higher lawmaking occur when the polity is aroused to mass participation in constitutional reconstruction, and adopts principles that endure until the next higher moment. Ackerman's scheme recognizes constitutional moments in the founding era, after the Civil War, and during the New Deal, but rejects other proposals, such as the so-called Reagan Revolution. In between these times, the judges' task is to synthesize the commitments of the various periods.

Ackerman's theory is arresting, but has grave weaknesses. The theory is another attempt to square the circle by combining liberal legalism and popular democracy, but it can do so only at the price of theoretical vagueness. Having abandoned the formalities of constitutional amendment, the obvious question is what criteria sort out moments of higher lawmaking from moments of quotidian politics, and Ackerman has nothing convincing to say on this score. The New Deal, he thinks, is a moment of higher lawmaking despite the absence of any formal constitutional amendment to embody New Deal principles. The Reagan Revolution, by contrast, does not count as higher lawmaking for Ackerman, even though the latter, like the former, produced a sea change in government policymaking and yielded a cadre of judges dedicated to implementing the movement's principles. It is by no means obvious what distinguishes the two episodes.

For our purposes, a related deficiency in the theory is that, like the others, it cannot supply a comprehensive mechanism of constitutional change. Even assuming the validity of Ackerman's periodization of constitutional moments, they are too sporadic to supply routine medium-size adjustments to the constitutional framework. Ackerman suffers from the common tendency to equate "constitutional" with "higher" or "really important," whereas one of our points is that constitutional conflict over the distribution of policymaking authority is continual and ubiquitous. Higher lawmaking through mass deliberation by a temporarily aroused populace is too large-scale and too rare to do the job.

CUMULATIVE MECHANISMS?

The main mechanisms of constitutional change in liberal legal theory— formal amendments, judicial interpretation, and higher lawmaking—are independently inadequate, in the dual sense that they are all normatively dubious and that each fails to supply more than a small portion of constitutional change. Is it possible that they are fully adequate when taken cumulatively? Is there a substantial domain of necessary constitutional change that cannot be produced by either formal amendment, judicial interpretation, or higher lawmaking?

There is, and it is the very domain in which constitutional change is most often necessary. It involves the shifting distribution, over time, of routine policymaking authority in the administrative state, between and among Congress, the courts, and various components of the enormous and heterogeneous executive establishment, here taken to include the independent agencies. Many of these questions have large consequences for first-order policy and for the operation of government, but any one of these questions may be too small-scale or too obscure to rouse supermajoritarian sentiment, which is necessary to activate the costly processes of formal amendment or higher lawmaking. Moreover, many of these questions never reach the courts, in part because they are settled through bargaining and political processes before the slow processes of litigation can catch up, in part because the judges themselves are nervous about intervening in struggles between other branches and nervous about disrupting the internal mechanics of other branches. This world of midrange institutional struggle with constitutional dimensions is crucial terrain for the administrative state, yet it is a world in which liberal legalism has little purchase.

CONSTITUTIONAL SHOWDOWNS

The upshot is that Madisonian liberal legalism has no adequate legal mechanism or combination of mechanisms to supply needed constitutional change. Yet "the constitution," in the sense of the operative rules and norms that allocate authority across institutions, does change continuously. How does this occur? We suggest that the central mechanism of constitutional change is not amendments, higher lawmaking, or even judicial doctrine, but episodes of conflict between institutions over the distribution of policymaking authority. Constitutional change is a special kind of politics, one that emerges from institutional struggle in a twilight world without clear or settled rules. This process is far removed from the clear rule of law that is central to liberal legalism.

Constitutional law is pervasively shaped by (what the headlines call) "showdowns" between and among branches of government.[7] When the Democratic Congress began investigating the dismissal of U.S. attorneys in 2007, congressional committees issued subpoenas, and the White House asserted executive privilege to block advisers to the president from being forced to testify.[8] This is a familiar Washington pattern, which usually ends in a compromise between the legislative and executive branches, but occasionally ends up in a large-scale showdown. In the latter case, the result may be litigation that creates a judicial precedent, a political settlement that creates a nonjudicial precedent, or both.

Showdowns occur between the president and the courts and between Congress and the courts as well as between the president and Congress. Indeed, some showdowns involve all three branches simultaneously, or threaten to do so. When congressional committees issue subpoenas and the executive asserts privilege, the courts may eventually be asked to enforce the subpoenas. When Franklin Roosevelt attempted to pack the Supreme Court, the attempt implicated congressional as well as judicial prerogatives, because a bill was necessary to expand the number of seats on the Court. Some legislators opposed the bill even though (they claimed) they would have favored a constitutional amendment.[9]

The idea of a constitutional showdown seems, at first, hopelessly vague. But informal talk of showdowns is extremely widespread and persistent in both scholarship and in the popular press, and there is undoubted pretheoretical appeal to the category, which seems to capture a major mechanism of constitutional development. Our project here is to put some theoretical backbone into the idea of a constitutional showdown[10] and to demonstrate that showdowns are a special kind of legalized politics.

PRELIMINARIES

We will define constitutional showdowns both extensionally, by examples and paradigm cases, and intensionally, by necessary and sufficient criteria. The former procedure is appropriate for family-resemblance complexes, where there are many related ideas that may share no single common property or defining feature; the idea of a constitutional showdown doubtless has a family-resemblance structure of this sort. Nonetheless we think it will be useful to the reader to attempt a conceptual definition as well, if only to indicate more clearly where our theoretical concerns lie.

EXAMPLES

To indicate the sorts of cases we have in mind, consider the following examples of the three major categories of showdowns we will discuss.

Presidential-Congressional Showdowns

Impeachments are the most dramatic constitutional showdowns, and inevitably create precedents. Andrew Johnson, having been impeached for violating the Tenure of Office Act, which forbade presidential removal of certain cabinet officers without congressional approval, escaped conviction in the Senate by a single vote; the Supreme Court later cited this episode to support a conclusive constitutional rule in favor of presidential power to remove executive officers,[11] or at least "purely" executive officers.[12]

The Nixon impeachment had a double precedential effect, both creating legal forms that were used in the Clinton impeachment, and provoking a constitutional showdown between Nixon and the Court that itself created a judicial precedent on executive privilege.[13]

Struggles over appointments and executive privilege can, of course, result in constitutional showdowns even where no impeachment eventuates. A pure example of a constitutional showdown occurred when

[o]ne year into President [George H. W.] Bush's term, Congress passed . . . a provision prohibiting the United States from spending any money authorized for international conferences on the U.S. delegation to the Conference on Security and Cooperation in Europe unless that delegation included representatives of the Commission on Security and Cooperation in Europe. This Commission was composed almost entirely of members appointed by the legislative branch. . . . Given the far-reaching challenge to powers of the presidency, President Bush's response was extremely forceful. He announced that the provision was unconstitutional, and that he would refuse to enforce it. . . . [W]hile the House of Representatives' lawyer bitterly complained about the President's refusal to enforce the law, Members of Congress took no further action.[14]

Presidential-Judicial Showdowns

Here too some cases result in a judicial precedent and some do not. In the latter case, consider Lincoln's decision to defy a habeas corpus order issued by Chief Justice Taney (in *Ex parte Merryman*) during the opening days of the war.[15] This counts as a showdown because Lincoln's action was based on a particular view of presidential power to defy the courts in situations of extreme crisis, where doing so is necessary to save "all the laws but one"; because the judges acquiesced through inaction, and through extreme deference to Lincoln until the end of the Civil War; and because Lincoln's action created a (nonjudicial) constitutional precedent that clarified the constitutional lines and is cited to this day by constitutional theorists with various views of presidential power, judicial power, and the role of emergencies in constitutional law.[16]

The former case is exemplified by some of the most famous cases in constitutional law, such as the Steel Seizure Case (*Youngstown v. Sawyer*) and the Watergate tapes case, *United States v. Nixon*. In the former the Court rejected a claim by President Truman that he had constitutional power to seize steel plants to prevent a work stoppage that would have cut off war material for America forces in Korea;[17] in the latter the Court rejected a "generalized" claim of executive privilege and forced Nixon to turn over Oval Office recordings that had been lawfully subpoenaed in a grand jury investigation.[18] In both cases the president promptly acquiesced by obeying the Court's orders, unlike Lincoln, and the cases have set the terms of various separation-of-powers controversies to the present day.

Congressional-Judicial Showdowns

A central storyline of American constitutional history involves showdowns between Congress and the judiciary.[19] As usual, such showdowns have created precedents even when no judicial decision ensued. During Reconstruction, the Republican Congress manipulated the number of justices in order to deny Democrat Andrew Johnson appointments to the Court, first lowering the number of seats and then raising the number when Ulysses S. Grant came into office.[20] Congress's actions during this period were a prominent precedent for Franklin Roosevelt's Court-packing plan; the failure of that plan itself set a precedent that weighs against future manipulation of the Court's membership.

Other actions of the Reconstruction Congress did result in judicial precedents. One was to enact legislation that deprived the Court of jurisdiction to hear a pending case, thus preventing the Court—were the legislation upheld—from limiting congressional power to deploy military commissions in the former Confederacy. Bowing to the political winds, the Court upheld the jurisdiction-stripping statute in *Ex Parte McCardle*.[21] The decision has served as an important precedent in many later episodes and cases; although its authority has been questioned by commentators,[22] and the Court has in later episodes typically used aggressive statutory construction to find jurisdiction while avoiding the constitutional questions, this sort of controversial posthistory is the fate of many prominent precedents, both judicial and nonjudicial.

DEFINITIONS

We will also attempt to define showdowns intensionally, with special attention to the precedential effect of showdowns. The legal scholar Peter Spiro offers an illuminating treatment of the way in which war-powers controversies acquire precedential force. In his words,

> [T]he legal significance of any such episode will hinge on three elements. First, it is actions that count, not words; mere assertions of executive or legislative authority are largely irrelevant in the long run, the chaff of institutional bravado. Second, in order to take on lawmaking significance, the conduct must be known to the other branch; secret operations will have no constitutional significance until they are made known to Congress and it has had an opportunity to respond. Third, the other branch must have accepted or acquiesced in the action. Any conduct that satisfies (or even arguably satisfies) these requirements will become part of the precedential mix; a single historical episode can create incremental elements of custom in the same way that a single judicial decision will incrementally change court-made doctrine.[23]

Our definition draws on Spiro's but generalizes it to a broader range of constitutional settings. We will say that a constitutional showdown is (1) a disagreement between branches of government over their constitutional powers that (2) ends in the total or partial acquiescence by one branch in the views of the other and that (3) creates a political precedent couched in constitutional terms. Constitutional showdowns are a subset of showdowns generally; the latter would include, for example, a disagreement between the president and the courts over whether the president has been granted particular powers by statute, rather than by constitutional law.

This definition embodies several assumptions. First, we will often speak of "institutional interests" or the interests of branches of government; these formulations are just shorthand for the point that individuals are in some cases motivated to promote the interests of institutions to which they belong, although in other cases they are not.[24] We relax this simplifying assumption in later discussion, but for now will use personified branches—the president, Congress, and the courts. The justification for this assumption is twofold: it simplifies the presentation of our claims without serious loss of accuracy, and each branch contains internal rules for aggregating individual votes into institutional decisions, such as statutes, judicial precedents, and executive orders.[25] Likewise, we also bracket the role of political parties in a separation-of-powers system, and take up that issue in later discussion as well.

Second, we assume that constitutional showdowns create precedents, almost always nonjudicial, and that these precedents have some positive force in decision making during later periods. The force of such precedents may be large or small, depending upon circumstances and context. Despite skepticism about the force of both judicial and nonjudicial precedents, our assumption is minimal. Nonjudicial precedents, like judicial ones, are rarely the only consideration that later decision-makers take into account, and are often overridden or ignored because preferences or political circumstances have changed; but this does not mean the precedents never existed in the first place. "Individual episodes will, of course, have more or less weight in the same way that decisions from some courts are more meaningful than from others, and in this respect such factors as frequency, consistency and regularity will be important to determining the constitutional probity of a particular practice."[26]

Several mechanisms can cause the settlements that do occur in earlier episodes to have positive force in later times. The "civilizing force of hypocrisy"[27] makes it positively costly for decision makers to disavow a principle they relied on to their benefit at an earlier time, although in some cases the benefits of opportunistic disavowals of precedent are worth the cost. Political precedents may create focal points that coordinate behavior;[28] indeed, focal points can affect behavior even in interactions that mix cooperative and distributive motives[29]—circumstances where all branches involved want to coordinate, yet the branches have different preferences about which rule or practice to coordinate upon. Political precedents reduce the costs of decision making, so that in later periods decision makers may follow them even if they would have preferred a different rule if deciding on a blank slate. More nebulously, precedents set in an earlier showdown tend to ossify into institutional routines and individual habits, and may even become internalized by actors who develop a sense of legal obligation to follow the precedent.

The precedent that is created by a showdown may, but need not, be a judicial precedent. Instead it will usually be an unwritten constitutional norm or convention[30]—a practice that is widely understood as a settlement of a constitutional question and that is regular or stable over time, although it need not be eternal. Constitutional conventions in this sense include the refusal of any president after Washington and before Franklin Roosevelt to stand for a third term, a convention that eventually collapsed, and the norm that the president need not submit treaties to the Senate during the negotiating phase, but need only obtain ex post Senate ratification; the latter practice was also established by Washington but has persisted to the present day.[31]

We have called showdowns a species of legalized politics, and it is important to be clear that the precedents created in showdowns are as much political as conventionally legal. They are rarely judicial precedents, and even if as a jurisprudential matter there are nonjudicial precedents that might count as "legal" on some theory of law, such an account would be excessively spongy, even meaningless, if extended to cover all the consequences of showdowns. Showdowns usually produce settlements of political conflicts in which the participants cite more or less legal arguments, but which do not become conventionally legal for that reason. Note also that showdowns may produce no settlement at all. What starts off as a showdown might end as a compromise, with the disagreement papered over and neither side acquiescing in the other side's claim to authority. Or the underlying source of dispute might resolve itself before a true impasse is reached.

A further twist is that it is common for branches to give in, or strike a bargain that effectively acquiesces in the views of another branch, all the while disclaiming any surrender of official powers and disclaiming any intention to set a precedent. Presidents, for example, routinely waive claims of executive privilege in practice, allowing even their closest advisers to testify, while denying that they have compromised their constitutional prerogatives.[32] Such events count as showdowns that have set nonjudicial precedents in favor of the constitutional power of Congress to require testimony from executive officials. Yet another complication is that acquiescence can be total or partial; one branch might clearly cede to another some, but not all, of what the other branch claims. This does not affect the analysis, but complicates the exposition, so we will usually address only the limiting case.

Finally, we will focus on showdowns between or among the three major branches of the national government. However, other actors engage in showdowns as well. There can be showdowns between political parties, as when the majority and minority parties in the Senate disagree about the extent to which the minority party can block votes, put members on committees, and influence procedural rules. A dramatic example of a showdown occurred when members of the Texas legislature tried to leave the state in order to prevent a quorum from forming, and the majority party tried to have them arrested.[33] There can be showdowns between sections of the country: the showdown over slavery between the North and the South led to the Civil War. There can be showdowns between the national government and the state governments, as occurred when Orval Faubus, the governor of Arkansas, refused to comply with an order of the Supreme Court, and President Eisenhower deputized the Arkansas national guard. And showdowns often involve overlapping political divisions, as when a branch controlled by one party reaches an impasse with a branch controlled by another party. In all cases, agents granted political authority by the Constitution disagree about the contours of their authority, and refuse to back down in the face of competing claims by other agents.

CUSTOM AND *OPINIO JURIS*

Our assumption that showdowns can create nonjudicial precedents is related, but not identical, to the idea that customary practices are a source of law. In the theory of international law, customary law consists of practices—behavioral regularities—followed from an internalized sense of legal obligation, or *opinio juris*. Theorists of domestic constitutional law[34] and foreign relations law[35] have adapted *opinio juris* to identify law that arises from interbranch interactions, such as the president's power to withdraw public land from private acquisition[36] or to deploy forces abroad in small-scale operations, like the invasion of Grenada, without congressional approval.[37] All these theorists deploy the idea as a criterion for winnowing law out of the larger set of behavioral regularities or governmental practices; the idea is that some behavioral regularities, such as the practice that nations send diplomats to the funerals of past heads of state, or the practice of Supreme Court justices attending the State of the Union address, are not felt by the actors themselves to have any legally obligatory character and thus cannot count as law.

For our purposes, however, *opinio juris* is a sufficient but not a necessary condition for showdowns to have precedential force. All that matters is that showdowns create some sort of precedential constraint that enters into the decisions of subsequent actors, whether or not it is decisive (just as judicial precedents might or might not be decisive, but are always relevant). One way that positive precedential force might arise is that actors internalize, and take to be legally obligatory, the practices of the past; but there are

	Agreement about authority	Disagreement about authority
Agreement about policy	(1) No showdown	(2) Possible showdown
Disagreement about policy	(3) Acquiescence	(4) Showdown

Table 2.1

purely political mechanisms that also give rise to precedential force, as we have mentioned. Precedents may just be patterns of behavior that parties recognize as providing focal points that permit cooperation or coordination.[38] Under the civilizing force of hypocrisy, actors will incur a cost if they act too opportunistically in disavowing earlier positions whenever it suits their interests, and this cost will affect their later decisions. But that does not require, indeed it implicitly denies, that the actors have internalized the earlier practices as legally obligatory.

AUTHORITY, POLICY, AND PUBLIC OPINION

Here we clarify some crucial elements of our definition, particularly the condition that actors must disagree about the allocation of constitutional authority. Such disagreements, we will suggest, are usually settled in the short term by the force of public opinion rather than by distinctively legal sources. In these cases—which account for the mine-run of constitutional change—our constitution is plebiscitary, a phenomenon antithetical to the aspirations of liberal legalism.

Showdowns occur when the location of constitutional authority for making an important policy decision is ambiguous, and multiple political agents (branches, parties, sections, governments) have a strong interest in establishing that the authority lies with them. Although agents often have an interest in negotiating a settlement, asymmetric information about the interests and bargaining power of opposing parties will sometimes prevent such a settlement from being achieved. That is when a showdown occurs. Ultimately, however, someone must yield; this yielding to or acquiescence in the claimed authority of another agent helps clarify constitutional lines of authority, so that next time the issue arises, a constitutional impasse can be avoided. From a normative standpoint, constitutional showdowns thus have an important benefit, but they are certainly not costless. As long as the showdown lasts, the government may be paralyzed, unable to make important policy decisions, at least with respect to the issue under dispute.

We begin by examining a simplified version of our problem, one involving just two agents—Congress and the executive. We assume for now that each agent is a unitary actor with a specific set of interests and capacities. We also assume that each agent has a slightly different utility function, reflecting their distinct constituencies. If we take the median voter as a baseline, we might assume that Congress is a bit to the left (or right) of the median voter, while the president is a bit to the right (or left). We will assume that the two agents are at an equal distance from the median, and that the preferences of the population are symmetrically distributed, so that the median voter will be indifferent between whether the president or Congress makes a particular decision, assuming that they have equal information.[39] But we also will assume that the president has better information about some types of problems, and Congress has better information about other types of problems, so that, from the median voter's standpoint, it is best for the president to make decisions about the first type of problem and for Congress to make decisions about the second type of problem.[40]

Suppose, for example, that the nation is at war and the government must decide whether to terminate it soon or allow it to continue. Congress and the president may agree about what to do, of course. But if they disagree, their disagreement may arise from one or both of two sources. First, Congress and the president have different information. For example, the executive may have better information about the foreign policy ramifications of a premature withdrawal, while Congress has better information about home-front morale. These different sources of information lead the executive to believe that the war should continue, while Congress believes the war should be ended soon. Second, Congress and the president have different preferences because of electoral pressures of their different constituents. Suppose, for example, that the president depends heavily on the continued support of arms suppliers, while crucial members of Congress come from districts dominated by war protestors. Thus, although the median voter might want the war to continue for a moderate time, the president prefers an indefinite extension, while Congress prefers an immediate termination.

So far, we have explained why the president and Congress might disagree about when to terminate the war, but mere policy disagreement does not result in a showdown. Showdowns arise only when there is a disagreement about authority. If Congress believes that the president has the sole authority to terminate the war, then his view will prevail. Congress may try to pressure him or influence him by offering support for other programs desired by the president, or by trying to rile up the public, but these activities are part of normal politics, and do not provoke a constitutional showdown. Similarly, if the president believes that Congress has the sole authority to terminate the war, then Congress's view will prevail. This outcome is shown in cell 3 in table 2.1. Similarly, no showdown occurs when the two branches agree both about authority and policy—for example, that the president decides, and Congress agrees with his decision (cell 1). The first column represents the domain of normal politics.

Showdowns can arise only when Congress and the president disagree about who decides. Here, there are two further possibilities. First, Congress and the president disagree about who decides but agree about the correct policy outcome (cell 2). In these situations, which arise with some frequency, the two branches are often tempted to paper over their differences because an immediate policy choice is not at stake. But sometimes a showdown will occur. We will discuss this special case later. Second, Congress and the president disagree about the policy outcome *and* about authority (cell 4). In this case, showdowns are likely, because a policy decision must be made, and if the parties cannot agree about what it should be, then they cannot avoid resolving the question of authority. We focus on this case for now.

WHY SHOWDOWNS OCCUR

In our war example, Congress and the president disagree about when the war should end, and who should make the decision. Let us suppose that they can both make reasonable constitutional arguments, and that the judiciary will not step in to resolve the dispute. What happens next? If each branch asserts its power, we have a full-blown constitutional crisis. No ordinary legal means exists for resolving the dispute. Consider how this crisis might play out. One possibility is that Congress enacts a law declaring the war at an end, and the president directs the military to disobey the law. The military would need to decide whether to obey the president or Congress. The military might make this decision on the basis of a good-faith legal analysis, or it might not. Whether or not it does, there is a further question whether soldiers would obey the decisions of the generals, and the public would support the decisions of the soldiers. The soldiers might fear that if the generals take an unlawful stance, the soldiers might subsequently be found guilty of committing crimes. And even if they do not, they might fear that the public might fault them for obeying (or disobeying) the generals. A great deal of delay and paralysis could result as people decide for themselves what they ought to do. But eventually only two outcomes are possible. One is that the nation divides into factions and a civil war erupts—a real possibility in many countries, but one sufficiently remote in the United States today that we can safely ignore it. The other is that through the mysterious process by which public opinion forms, the public will throw its weight behind one branch or the other, and the branch that receives public support will prevail.

We will call the public's final decision about the location of constitutional authority "public constitutional sentiment." The "public" here does not necessarily mean a fair aggregation of the views of all citizens; it is a stand-in for the complex process by which the views of elites, interest groups, ordinary citizens, and others ultimately determine the de facto lines of political authority, views that might be mediated, or not, by good-faith interpretation of relevant texts and traditions. Nor does it refer to an episodic or superficial political fancy, such as what can be read off a public opinion poll. If a showdown occurs, and the government is paralyzed, then the public or at least important groups will rouse themselves to attention, and so the view that prevails will reflect more fundamental, quasi-constitutional instincts than the views that prevail in ordinary politics. We will generally assume that public constitutional sentiment is exogenous—determined by social and economic trends and thus not directly controlled by political agents—but it is quite possible that public constitutional sentiment is itself influenced by earlier constitutional showdowns and settlements, given the powerful role of tradition and precedent in public thinking. At any given moment, public opinion appears as a fixed constraint from the standpoint of institutional actors, but over time it is itself formed endogenously by earlier showdowns.

Public constitutional sentiment is the bedrock, but that does not mean that it will be profound or even intelligent. There is no reason to believe that public constitutional sentiment actually reflects the optimal allocation of authority: it may be that public constitutional sentiment is simply uninformed, or is heavily influenced by the private interests of advocacy groups or elites. It might be that social welfare is maximized if Congress has the authority to terminate the war, but public constitutional sentiment nonetheless places that authority with the president. Our focus is not on whether public constitutional sentiment is optimal but what, given that sentiment, is the optimal way for Congress and the president to act. We will bracket the possibility that Congress and the president may care sufficiently about the public interest, while knowing that public constitutional sentiment is uninformed and bad for the country, that they would cooperate in allocating powers and avoid impasses which would be resolved by public constitutional sentiment. This possibility is not absurd: it is reflected in the views of people who oppose proposals for constitutional conventions because of the risk that the constitution that emerges will be worse than the constitution that we have. However, if Congress and the president can maintain such an allocation of powers voluntarily, then showdowns do not occur. Thus, we can ignore this possibility for purposes of our discussion.

If public constitutional sentiment will ultimately settle the question of whether Congress or the president has the power to terminate the war, why do showdowns occur? One might think that Congress and the president will simply resolve their dispute by consulting public constitutional settlement. The alternative would only be a showdown that would last long enough to rouse the public, and the paralysis of government during this interval could damage both institutions and ruin the electoral chances of their occupants.

The question is a familiar one in the game theoretic literature on bargaining, and we adopt that literature's findings.[41] Game theorists would treat the problem in the context of a standard bargaining game between two agents over a pool of resources or a "pie" whose value declines over time as the agents haggle. When two agents bargain over an asset, the eventual outcome is determined by the parties' valuations of the asset, their relative bargaining power, and the degree of information asymmetry.

Generally speaking, the asset will end up in the hands of the party who values it more. If a seller owns an asset and a buyer values the asset more than the seller does, then a sale will occur and, all else equal, they will split the surplus—the price will be midway between the seller's valuation and the buyer's valuation. If another buyer offers the seller a price higher than the seller's valuation but lower than the first buyer's valuation, then the seller now has an outside option that improves her bargaining position vis-à-vis the first buyer, and hence the agreed-upon price will rise. The price will also reflect inside options, such as the value that the seller receives from using the asset while bargaining proceeds.

Bargaining power refers to the relative time preferences of the agents. If bargaining is likely to take a great deal of time and the seller values future payoffs more than the original buyer does, the seller will be able to hold out for a still higher price. The reason is that the seller loses less than the buyer as a result of delay caused by a bargaining impasse, and so the buyer will pay a higher price to avoid the delay.

Information asymmetry exists when one or both agents lack information about the valuation of the other. Information asymmetry is always a matter of degree. At one extreme, in a purely theoretical world where information asymmetry does not exist, the agents would come to an agreement in the first round of bargaining, because they can only become worse off from delay. As the degree of information asymmetry increases, however, agents might gain an advantage from delay. For example, suppose that the seller does not know whether the buyer values the asset a great deal or very little. If a great deal, the seller would charge a high price; if very little, the seller would charge a low price. Not knowing which buyer she faces, the seller might offer a high price. The high-value buyer would accept the price in order to avoid the cost of delay, while the low-value buyer would hold out an extra round. In the second round, the seller knows that only the low-value buyer would have turned down the initial offer, and accordingly lowers the price. Thus, in equilibrium delay, and the resulting loss of value of the asset, occurs with some probability.

The "asset" in our example is the right to determine when the war will be terminated. Congress and the president may value this asset to a different degree, simply because the relevant officials' electoral prospects depend to a different degree on the outcome of the war. One source of asymmetric information, then, arises from uncertainty that each agent may have about the other agent's valuation of the right.[42] Another source of asymmetric information arises from uncertainty about public constitutional sentiment, and each agent might have different views about the probability that public constitutional sentiment will favor its claim. If the president announces that he will refuse to obey a statute that terminates the war, even if the government will collapse, he is making a strong statement that he values the right to terminate the war a great deal. This statement may or may not be credible; all of this depends on how much Congress knows about the president's incentives. But if the president really does value the right a great deal, and Congress does not believe him, then a long time will pass before a resolution is achieved.

It should be immediately clear that a showdown is a matter of degree. After Congress passes the law declaring the end of the war, the executive branch might engage in some tentative actions designed to gauge public constitutional sentiment. It might begin by expressing some reservations about Congress's authority, or leaking unofficial statements of disagreement. If the public responds favorably, the executive might take a strong stance, and, correlatively, Congress might back off. If the public's views are ambiguous, both sides might dig in their heels. In the meantime, the military might temporize, hoping for a political resolution. As time passes, the fact of an impasse will become clear, the cost from delay will increase, and an atmosphere of crisis may develop. At some point, one side or the other will back down, a compromise will be achieved, or there will be a breakdown in authority such as civil war.

The agent that prevails gains two benefits. First, its policy view will prevail. The war will be terminated or not. Second, its authority over the policy domain will be established, in the following sense. When the issue arises again in the future—in some future war, where the president and Congress have different views as to the timing of withdrawal—the agent that made the decision earlier will have presumptive authority to make the decision the second time. The reason is that the first decision will establish that public constitutional sentiment confers authority on that agent. If the president prevails the first time around, then Congress will fear that if it resists the president the second time, it will be defeated yet again. To be sure, public constitutional sentiment could change in the intervening period, but this is only a possibility, and if general political conditions have not changed in the meantime, then it is unlikely that public constitutional sentiment has as well. Adding to this, the precedent itself might feed into and strengthen public constitutional sentiment, as people generally give weight to tradition and precedent, and the agent who resists a precedent might be faulted for carelessly provoking a crisis.[43]

Our picture, then, depicts political agents being tempted to advance their authority at the expense of other agents, while also fearing that if the other side does not back down, a politically damaging impasse or crisis could occur. Such a crisis would hurt both sides that participate in it, weakening them relative to other agents that stay on the sidelines, but one side will emerge with public constitutional sentiment on its side, and thus do better than the other side. To avoid showdowns, the sides attempt to predict public constitutional sentiment and reach a bargain, but they will sometimes fail.

CONCLUSION

Few people dispute that the meaning of the Constitution has changed a great deal since the founding, either de jure or de facto. On the de jure side, the simplest version of Madisonian liberal legalism holds that the Constitution many only change through formal amendments, but the formal amendment process is too cumbersome, and this view has buckled under the pressure of circumstances. How does the Constitution change, as a positive matter, if the formal amendment procedure is rarely used?

The two main alternatives offered in liberal legal theory are judicial interpretation and higher lawmaking. The first view draws on the analogy to common-law development. Judges interpret constitutional provisions in light of new conditions not anticipated by the founders, in doing so subtly (and sometimes not so subtly) changing its meaning. Over time, these interpretations accrete and yield new allocations of power.[44] This is undoubtedly a means of constitutional change, but it is of only secondary importance. The judges are chronically worried about their legitimacy and so confine themselves to a small portion of the constitutional terrain.

A second view finds constitutional change in moments of upheaval when the public is supposedly attuned to politics and constitutional issues to a greater extent than in normal times. The Civil War and the New Deal are cited as examples. The public approves of changes in higher law, and these changes are duly respected by political actors.[45] Yet this process is vaguely defined, and in any event has all the mobilization costs of formal amendment, so it occurs too infrequently to provide a full theory of constitutional change.

The picture we offer is neither as judge-centered as the first alternative nor as episodic as the second: constitutional showdowns occur regularly, but the most frequent and important cases occur outside the courts. Institutional struggle among the executive, legislative, and judicial branches, and between the national and state governments, is the main way in which disagreements over the allocation of policymaking authority are worked out. We think of constitutional change as a routine phenomenon that political actors have a special role in provoking. Public constitutional sentiment evolves in subterranean fashion, generally unperceived by those who exercise power. However, when political agents disagree about the allocation of authority, they must make predictions about how the public will react if a showdown occurs. The agents subtly shift their allocation claims in response both to their predictions about public reaction and to the clarifying effects of showdowns when they actually occur.

Our positive picture of constitutional development is inconsistent with Madisonian liberal legalism. However, it is plausibly consistent with (a suitably specified version of) popular constitutionalism, although the sponginess of the latter approach makes it hard to be sure. Some "popular" constitutionalists seem to envision widespread and genuinely inclusive debate over constitutional meaning,[46] while others tend to focus on political movements among the educated and other elites.[47] In our approach, the elites who control the institutions of government effectively decide whether or not to engage in precedent-setting showdowns, but public constitutional sentiment—which may or may not be very popular, depending on circumstances—is both a major political constraint and a major variable in the elites' political calculations. The populace at large exercises an indirect influence over constitutional development, but as a filter that rules out certain elite positions and as an ultimate court of appeal, rather than as a frontline participant. The process of constitutional change is roughly plebiscitary: the people do not propose, but they do dispose.

CHAPTER 3

The Statutory Framework

If the constitutional framework of liberal legalism is too rickety to contain executive power, perhaps statutes can substitute new legal constraints. A principal hope of liberal legal theory is that the deficiencies of the constitutional framework can be patched up by framework statutes that will channel and constrain executive power. The executive comprises the president and (various types of) agencies, and liberal legalism tries to constrain both, through different statutes. As to the agencies, liberal legalists hope that general procedural statutes such as the Administrative Procedure Act (APA) can "translate" the principles and values underlying the separation of powers into a world in which agencies routinely hold consolidated powers of lawmaking, law-execution, and law-interpretation.[1] As to the president, Congress has enacted many subject-specific framework statutes that attempt to constrain executive power, especially with regard to warmaking, foreign policy, and emergencies. And liberal legal theorists often propose new statutes of this sort—for example, a statute that would confine presidential emergency powers in the aftermath of a terrorist attack.[2]

These efforts all fall short of the aspirations of liberal legalism, in greater or lesser degree. The subject-specific framework statutes that attempt to constrain presidential power are the most conspicuous failure; most are dead letters. Seemingly more successful is the APA, which remains the central framework for the administrative state. We will suggest that this is something of an illusion; the greater specificity of the subject-specific statutes, and the greater plasticity and ambiguity of the APA, make the failure of the former group more conspicuous, while giving the latter a misleading appearance of constraining force.

The secret of the APA's "success"—its ability to endure in a nominal sense—is that it contains a series of adjustable parameters that the courts use to dial up and down the intensity of their scrutiny over time. The APA's basic flexibility allows courts to allow government to do what government needs to do when it needs to do it. The result is a series of legal "black holes" and "grey holes"—the latter being standards of reasonableness that have the appearance of legality, but not the substance, at least not when pressing interests suggest otherwise. This regime is a triumph for the nominal supremacy of the APA, but not for any genuine version of the rule of law. Liberal legalism's basic aspiration, that statutes (if not the Constitution) will subject the administrative state to the rule of law, is far less successful than it appears.

SUBJECT-SPECIFIC FRAMEWORK STATUTES

With a few exceptions, most of the subject-specific framework statutes that attempt to constrain executive power, particularly presidential power, are a product of the era after Watergate. As revelations of executive abuses by both federal and state governments multiplied and a backlash against executive power set in, all three branches of government acted to reduce the scope of executive discretion in matters touching on security and antiterrorism. In the middle to late 1970s, Congress imposed a range of statutory constraints on the powers and activities of the executive branch generally and the presidency in particular, especially in matters relating to foreign affairs and national security.

The most prominent examples are the War Powers Resolution,[3] which constrained executive use of force abroad; the National Emergencies Act,[4] which limited executive declarations of emergency; the International Economic Emergency Powers Act,[5] which limited the executive's power to impose various economic sanctions and controls; the Ethics in Government Act,[6] which created independent counsels to investigate government wrongdoing; and the Inspector General Act of 1978, described below. Other constraints were imposed by litigation and judicial decree. Finally, some constraints were self-imposed, by executive guidelines that curtailed FBI authority to investigate groups with the potential to engage in terrorism. The restrictive Levi Guidelines of 1976[7] exemplified this executive self-constraint.

This framework for national security law has not endured. Indeed, a large part of the story of national security law in ensuing decades, and especially after 9/11, has involved efforts by various institutions and groups to loosen the constraints of the post-Watergate framework. By and large, those efforts have succeeded.[8] The following are four major examples.

1. *The War Powers Resolution (1973)*. At its core, the resolution attempts to limit executive use of armed forces in conflicts abroad, without congressional approval, to a period of 60 or 90 days (omitting many complicated details). But the resolution has by many accounts become a dead letter, especially after President Clinton's rather clear breach of its terms during the Kosovo conflict.[9] Congress has proven unable to enforce the resolution by ex post punishment of executive violations or arguable violations; the courts have invoked various doctrines of justiciability to avoid claims for enforcement of the resolution by soldiers and others. As one Madisonian scholar puts it, "In the area of military policy making, the War Powers Resolution, in its current form, has simply proven inadequate to discipline executive branch unilateralism."[10]

2. *The National Emergencies Act (1976)*. This statute abolished all preexisting states of emergency declared by executive order, and substituted a process for congressional review of new declarations. The process has proven largely ineffective, in large part because later Congresses have usually proven unable to use the statutory mechanism for overriding executive declarations. The Act's default rule is set so that affirmative congressional action is necessary to block an executive proclamation of emergency, and congressional inertia has generally prevailed. In practice, "anything the President says is a national emergency is a national emergency."[11]

3. *The International Emergency Economic Powers Act (1977)*. Enacted to regulate and constrain executive action during international economic crises, the statute has been construed by the courts to grant broad executive power. The Supreme Court held that it implicitly authorized the president to suspend claims pending in American courts against Iranian assets, as part of a deal to free hostages.[12] And a lower court said that the president had unreviewable discretion to determine that the government of Nicaragua satisfied the statutory requirement of "an unusual and extraordinary threat," thus triggering enhanced executive powers.[13]

4. *Inspector General Act of 1978*. A final accountability mechanism is the cadre of inspectors general, who now hold offices within most federal agencies, including the Department of Justice. Inspectors general have the power to investigate legal violations, sometimes including crimes,

within the executive branch. Some can be discharged by the agency head, but some can be discharged only by the president, and in either case Congress must be notified. It is clear that inspectors general have created a large apparatus of compliance monitoring and bureaucratic reporting, and have used a great deal of paper; what is harder to assess is whether they have been effective at promoting executive accountability, either to Congress or to the citizenry. The leading systematic study[14] concludes that "the Inspectors General have been more or less effective at what they do, but what they do has not been effective. That is, they do a relatively good job of compliance monitoring, but compliance monitoring alone has not been that effective at increasing governmental accountability. Audits and investigations focus too much on small problems at the expense of larger systemic issues."[15]

Why did these statutes prove less effective than their proponents hoped or, in the extreme, become dead letters? In all the cases, the basic pattern is similar. The statutes were enacted during a high-water mark of political backlash against strong executive power, which supermajorities in Congress attempted to translate into binding legal constraints. However, once the wave of backlash receded and the supermajorities evaporated, there was insufficient political backing for the laws to ensure their continued vigor over time. Later Congresses have not possessed sufficient political backing or willpower to employ the override mechanisms that the statutes create, such as the override of presidential declarations of emergency created by the National Emergencies Act.

Even where the statutes attempt to change the legal default rule, so that the president cannot act without legislative permission—as in the case of the War Powers Resolution, after the 60- or 90-day grace period has passed—the president may simply ignore the statutory command, and will succeed if he has correctly calculated that Congress will be unable to engage in ex post retaliation and the courts will be unwilling to engage in ex post review. President Clinton's implicit decision to brush aside the resolution during the Kosovo conflict (albeit with the fig leaf of a compliant legal opinion issued by the Justice Department's Office of Legal Counsel)[16] shows that what matters is what Congress can do after the fact, not what it says before the fact.

Here a major problem for framework statutes is the "presidential power of unilateral action"[17] to which we referred in the introduction. Statutory drafters may think they have cleverly closed off the executive's avenues of escape when they set the legal status quo to require legislative permission.

Because the president can act in the real world beyond the law books, however—the armed forces did not threaten to stand down from their Kosovo mission until Congress gave its clear approval, but instead simply obeyed the President's orders—the actual status quo may change regardless of whether the legal situation does. Once armed forces are in action, the political calculus shifts and legislators will usually be unable to find enough political support to retaliate—especially not on the basis of an arcane framework statute passed years or decades before.

To be sure, if the framework statutes are very specific, then violating them may itself create a political cost for the president, whose political opponents will denounce him for Caesarism. This cost is real, but in the type of high-stakes matters that are most likely to create showdowns between the president and Congress in the first place, the benefits are likely to be greater than the costs so long as the president's action is popular and credible—the crucial constraints we will discuss in chapter 4. Moreover, if the president can credibly claim to the public that the violation was necessary, then the public will be unlikely to care too much about the legal niceties. As legal theorist Frederick Schauer argues for constitutional violations[18] (and, we add, the argument holds a fortiori for statutory violations), there is an interesting asymmetry surrounding illegality: if the underlying action is unpopular, then citizens will treat its illegality as an aggravating circumstance, but if the underlying action is popular, its illegality usually has little independent weight. Finally, if the president credibly threatens to violate the statute, then Congress will have strong incentives to find some face-saving compromise that allows the president to do what he wishes without forcing a showdown that, legislators anticipate, may well end badly.

The upshot is that subject-specific framework statutes have a Potemkin quality: they stand about in the landscape, providing an impressive facade of legal constraint on the executive, but actually blocking very little action that presidents care about. In some cases presidents will have strictly political incentives to obtain congressional permission before acting, even in the domain of foreign affairs and national security. Yet this is not a consequence of the legal structures erected by Madisonian theory, either through constitutional rules or framework statutes. Rather, as an important recent model suggests, it actually implies a very different regime in which presidents may, but need not, obtain congressional consent.[19] The intuition behind this result is that a regime of optional separation of powers puts presidents to a revealing choice between proceeding unilaterally or instead through Congress, and thus gives imperfectly informed voters the maximum possible information and the greatest possible scope for rewarding or punishing presidents and legislators for their actions. Needless to say, however, this political mechanism gives cold comfort to Madisonian liberal legalists, who would blanch at the idea that an *optional* version of the separation of powers is superior to a mandatory version.

Political scientist Andrew Rudalevige is correct to describe the collapse of the constrained post-Watergate executive as the most significant contributor in the growth of a "New Imperial Executive."[20] Framework statutes are one of liberal legalism's principal instruments of executive constraint, in a world of little constitutional constraint. But having been tried, they have been found wanting.

THE ADMINISTRATIVE PROCEDURE ACT

We turn now to the APA, and the larger body of American administrative law. How much does this law constrain the executive, particularly the administrative agencies? How does the APA respond to real or perceived emergencies? Our picture is that the APA places some constraints on the agencies in normal times. However, as we will see, the statute as such does not ever constrain the president, who is exempt from the statute's coverage, and it also entirely exempts a range of matters touching on military and foreign affairs. Assuming there is no other avenue for obtaining judicial review of administrative action, and sometimes there is not, then the administrative state is exempt from judicial review in a given area. Although in principle one may have legality without judicial review, the risk is that it will be a nominal legality without any mechanism of enforcement. Moreover, even where judicial review is available, whatever constraint the APA does create in normal times devolves into a facade of legalism whenever government's interests become pressing— in which case courts will either call the situation one of "emergency," or (more likely) will simply uphold what the government wants to do under general, amorphous standards of "reasonableness" or "good cause."

In short, administrative law contains, built right into its structure, a series of legal black holes and grey holes.[21] Legal black holes arise when statutes or legal rules "either explicitly exempt[] the executive from the requirements of the rule of law or explicitly exclude[] judicial review of executive action."[22] Grey holes, which are "disguised black holes," arise when "there are some legal constraints on executive action—it is not a lawless void—but the constraints are so insubstantial that they pretty well permit government to do as it pleases."[23] Grey holes thus present "the façade or form of the rule of law rather than any substantive protections."[24]

David Dyzenhaus and other theorists of the rule of law show that black holes and grey holes are best understood by drawing upon the thought of Carl Schmitt, in particular his account of the relationship between legality and emergencies. In this sense, American administrative law just *is* Schmittian. During times of perceived emergency, black holes and grey holes become especially consequential. Moreover, their existence is inevitable. Extending legality to eliminate the black and grey holes is impracticable; the liberal legalist aspiration to eliminate the Schmittian elements of our administrative law is utopian.

Although we will examine both the black and the grey holes of administrative law, we focus especially on the latter. Administrative law is built around a series of open-ended standards or adjustable parameters—for example, what counts as "arbitrary" or "unreasonable," whether evidence is "substantial," whether a statute is or is not "clear"—that courts can and do adjust to increase deference to administrative agencies when it seems appropriate to do so. When the intensity of review is reduced sufficiently far, judicial review becomes effectively a sham and a grey hole arises. This process requires no change in any of the nominal legal rules, and is difficult even to specify in the abstract, let alone to monitor or check. Importantly, these grey holes are a product both of legislative action in the text of the APA, and of judicial action in subsequent cases. As we will see, liberal legal theorists committed to the rule of law find grey holes more objectionable than black holes, because the latter are at least openly lawless, whereas the former present a facade of law; but as we will also see, grey holes are unavoidable in administrative law, so decrying their existence is a futile posture.

CARL SCHMITT VERSUS THE RULE OF LAW

Our starting point is Schmitt's most famous contribution: his claim that emergencies—what Schmitt called "the exception"—pose an insuperable problem for the aspiration of liberal democracies to govern through the rule of law. In a 1921 work on Roman dictatorship, Schmitt distinguished between "commissarial" and "sovereign" dictatorship.[25] The former he saw as a legally regulated form of dictatorship that temporarily suspends the ordinary law in order to take emergency measures aimed at restoring the status quo ante the emergency; the latter he saw as a type of dictatorship, exemplified by the Bolshevik dictatorship of the proletariat, that aims to remake the legal and social order according to some master plan. Schmitt thought that the former type of dictatorship could be subjected to the rule of law, in the sense that law could specify, in advance, the powers of the commissarial dictator and the mode of his appointment.

A year later, however, Schmitt broke with his own earlier view and sharpened his critique of the rule of law.[26] In a work titled *Political Theology*, Schmitt offered a more radical account of emergencies, arguing that liberal democracies committed to the rule of law have no theory of exceptional states and that "sovereign is he who decides on the exception."[27] The many interpretive ambiguities surrounding this work should not obscure its main import. The legal systems of the liberal democracies cannot hope to specify the substantive conditions that will count as an emergency, because emergencies are by their nature unanticipated, or even the procedures that will be used to trigger and allocate emergency powers, because those procedures will themselves be vulnerable to being discarded when an emergency so requires.[28] In general, "One cannot use law to determine when legality should be suspended."[29] At most, Schmitt thought, liberal legalism can specify who has the power to determine whether there is an emergency,[30] but not the procedures or substantive conditions by which and under which emergency powers are triggered.

Schmitt's complex thought has given rise to an ever-growing body of commentary, especially after 9/11 restored the topic of emergency powers to prominence.[31] A great deal of this work is jargon-laden, excessively conceptual and obscure, as is indeed a great deal of Schmitt's own work. Once the layers of interpretive dross and continental conceptualisms are cleaned off of Schmitt's thinking, what remains are several important midsized and largely institutional or empirical insights: emergencies cannot realistically be governed by ex ante, highly specified rules, but at most by vague ex post standards; it is beyond the institutional capacity of lawmakers to specify and allocate emergency powers in all future contingencies; practically speaking, legislators in particular will feel enormous pressure to create vague standards and escape hatches—for emergencies and otherwise—in the code of legal procedure that governs the mine-run of ordinary cases in the administrative state, because legislators know they cannot subject the massively diverse body of administrative entities to tightly specified rules, and because they fear the consequences of lashing the executive too tightly to the mast in future emergencies. As we will see, all of these institutional features are central to American administrative law, and they create the preconditions for the emergence of the legal black holes and legal grey holes that are integral to its structure.

Schmittian ideas have come in for important criticism after 9/11. For concreteness, we will focus on a recent book by David Dyzenhaus, which offers a powerful critique of Schmitt and a powerful expression of the aspirations of liberal legalism. Dyzenhaus distinguishes between the "rule of law" and "rule by law,"[32] a distinction that is roughly equivalent to the jurisprudential distinction between the "thick" and "thin" versions of the rule of law. "Rule by law" (or the thin rule of law) is compliance with whatever duly-enacted positive laws there happen to be. By contrast, the "rule of law" (or the thick rule of law) requires more than compliance with whatever duly-enacted laws there happen to be; it also requires adherence to a broader set of principles of legality, most famously expressed by Lon Fuller.[33] Rule by law lacks content, whereas the rule of law adds a broad set of procedural and substantive norms associated with liberal legalism and, in the Anglo-American and Commonwealth countries, the common law. In this sort of schema, "rule by law" authorizes legislators or other lawmakers to create legal black holes—law-free zones that are themselves created by law. Lawmakers may also create grey holes, which appear to comport with the rule of law but really do not; imagine a statute or other legal rule specifying that notice will be given of new executive rules, except when the executive deems it a bad idea to do so.

Against this backdrop, liberal legalist critics such as Dyzenhaus urge the elimination of legal black holes and (especially) grey holes.[34] They say that a body of law containing black holes and grey holes is inconsistent with the rule of law, by which they mean the thick rule of law. They worry that rule by law is a bad approach to regulating executive action during actual or perceived emergencies; the exclusion of the rule of law will end up by giving away even rule by law, resulting in a law-free zone of unfettered executive discretion. Dyzenhaus suggests that the appropriate lens for understanding these issues is the thought of Schmitt.[35] On Dyzenhaus' rendition, "[i]f we are to answer Schmitt's challenge, we have to be able to show that contrary to his claims the exception can be banished from the legal order."[36]

The desired end-state for liberal legal theorists is a legal regime for regulating executive action during emergencies that does not contain either black or grey holes. We claim, by contrast, that black and grey holes will inevitably be integral to administrative law, and that because their presence is inevitable, there is no point condemning them; to do so is quixotic. The claim is not that our system of administrative law is maximally Schmittian. One could easily imagine a system whose black holes and grey holes are far larger than in our system. In this counterfactual system of administrative law, there would be a presumption against judicial review of executive action, unless Congress clearly indicated otherwise; stringent requirements for access to courts; and aggressively broad construction of the APA's various exceptions for administrative action relating to military affairs and foreign affairs and for emergency administrative action. Our system is not like that, not always anyway.

At the other end of the continuum, however, liberal legalists imagine a system of administrative law that is minimally Schmittian or even not Schmittian at all. In this sort of system, all administrative action would be subject to review under "ordinary" legal tests for statutory authority and procedural validity and reasoned decision-making. There would be no categorical exclusions of executive action, no exceptions for military or diplomatic functions or for emergencies, and perhaps not even any special "deference" to executive decision-making on the merits. Rather, judges would quite simply decide whether, in their view, executive action comported with relevant statutes and constitutional rules, and would take a hard look at the reasonableness of agency policy choices. Crucially, in answering those questions, judges would draw upon thick background principles of legality, of procedural regularity and fairness.

This too is a hopeless fantasy. Our administrative law is not like that either, and it never will be. Rather our system has substantial black holes and grey holes and will, for institutional rather than conceptual reasons, inevitably continue to do so. That the black holes and grey holes could be still larger is, for present purposes, neither here nor there.

BLACK HOLES OF ADMINISTRATIVE LAW

We will begin by reviewing the many situations in which, expressly or by implication, executive or administrative action relating to war and emergencies is excluded from the reach of the APA. Of course this exclusion, by itself, does not create a legal black hole, for other statutes may supply special avenues of review, and in some cases there may also be an avenue of so-called "nonstatutory review." We return to this point below. However, the existence of an APA exclusion is a necessary and important first step in creating a legal black hole. Because the APA is the only general waiver of federal sovereign immunity in cases seeking nonmonetary relief[37]—in other words, the only general charter for judicial review of administrative action—exclusion from the APA means that a black hole will arise unless some special avenue of review is present. In some cases it will be present, in others it will not.

The definition of "agency."

One of the main functions of administrative law is to regulate the powers and duties of administrative agencies and the processes by which they act. The APA covers "agencies" and "agency action." But what it an "agency" anyway? Can there be federal government bodies that do not fall within one of the listed exceptions yet are not "agencies," and are therefore excluded from the whole structure of legal regulation of the administrative state?

There can be and are. For one thing, various types of military tribunals may not be "agencies," either because they are expressly excluded, or because they do not fall within the definition in the first place. The APA expressly excludes from the definition of agency "courts martial and military commissions" and "military authority exercised in the field in time of war or in occupied territory."[38] Even more consequentially, the Supreme Court has twice stated that the president is not an agency.[39] In both cases, the Court invoked the opposite default rule: because of the president's special status and responsibilities, he is not covered by the APA absent a clear statement to that effect.[40] These holdings exclude from the scope of the APA highly consequential presidential action, such as the questions whether to accept a proposed census count or to accept or reject the recommendations of a base-closing commission. In these cases, no other statutes or common-law rules provided review either; the relevant presidential actions were left unreviewable. The actions themselves did not, of course, concern emergencies or war in any direct way, but the base-closing opinion involved military affairs, and was larded with references to the president's special responsibilities in military and foreign policy.

What is "agency action"?

Suppose that a given governmental body does count as an "agency," and no explicit or implicit exclusion applies. The next question is whether the agency has engaged in "action" reviewable under the APA. When the plaintiffs in *ACLU v. NSA*[41] challenged the National Security Agency's program(s) for warrantless electronic surveillance of suspected terrorists, a Sixth

Circuit panel dismissed the case on procedural grounds; but the lead opinion, presumably in dictum, discussed the APA as well, stating that the terrorist surveillance program was not "agency action" covered by the APA. On this reading, whole programs may fall outside the scope of the APA.

Exception(s) for "military or foreign affairs functions."

Even if there is an "agency" in the picture that has engaged in "agency action," the APA explicitly excludes "military or foreign affairs" functions from its procedural requirements for both rulemaking and adjudication.[42] This means that even where a military or foreign affairs function otherwise falls within the definition of rulemaking or adjudication, there are no applicable procedural requirements under the APA (although of course other constraints, such as due process, may apply). The question is what counts as a military or foreign affairs function.

The legislative history of the APA and the Attorney General's Manual both suggested that the exception should be narrowly construed.[43] What exactly this means is deeply unclear, as the exceptions are rarely litigated. Where cases do arise, they seem inconsistent, varying with some vague judicial impression of the strength of government interests and how central foreign policy was to the administrative action. In litigation over the Haitian refugee crisis of the early 1980s, one court held that a program of administrative detention for refugees did not fall within the exception.[44] On the other hand, courts in the same period invoked the exception to immunize from APA review administrative programs for the "voluntary" departure of Iranian nationals during the hostage crisis.[45] And a noteworthy recent case, *United States v. Ventura-Melendez*,[46] interprets the military functions exception in expansive terms, holding that a rule regulating civilians—even one that indirectly triggered criminal penalties—could fulfill a military function. In particular, the court said, "A rule designed to render safe and feasible the performance of a military function by preventing interference on the part of civilians necessarily serves a military function as well as a civilian one."[47]

"Committed to agency discretion by law."

Even if the relevant governmental body is an "agency," even if the agency has engaged in "action," and even if there is no exclusion for a military or foreign affairs function, courts may still decline to review the agency action for conformity with APA requirements. The main mechanism for doing so is the pair of exclusions in APA § 701(a)(1) and (2), which overcome the APA's background presumption of reviewability for final agency action where "statutes preclude judicial review" or where "agency action is committed to agency discretion by law."

After 9/11, lower courts applied the "committed to agency discretion" exception capaciously in national security contexts. In *Riverkeeper, Inc. v. Collins*,[48] the petitioner requested that the license for two nuclear plants be conditioned on the creation of a no-fly zone and defense measures to protect against terrorist attacks; the Second Circuit held that such issues are committed to the discretion of the Nuclear Regulatory Commission. A striking example in which agency action directly impinged on individual interests, yet was held unreviewable with regard to the important claims, was the Tenth Circuit's decision in *Merida Delgado v. Gonzales*.[49] A citizen of Panama received flight training at a federally regulated school in Oklahoma, where one of his fellow students was Zacarias Moussaoui, a coconspirator in the 9/11 attacks. Under a federal statute enacted after 9/11, the Aviation and Transportation Security Act, the attorney general could direct the school not to provide the requested training "because the Attorney General has determined that the individual presents a risk to aviation or to national security."[50] The attorney general so determined, and Delgado was excluded from flight training. The Tenth Circuit barred Delgado's claims by invoking the general principle that "it is rarely appropriate for courts to intervene in matters closely related to national security."[51]

This is a perfect example of a generality that contains an adjustable parameter. How rarely is rarely? How much weight is the national security context to be given, and when? Under tests like this it is easy for courts to adjust the parameter implicitly, as the security environment changes and circumstances vary, while adhering in every case to the nominal rules. As we will see, this is the hallmark of a grey hole, rather than a black one; the case law concerning agency action "committed to agency discretion by law" thus straddles the two major threats to the thick rule of law.

GREY HOLES

Let us now turn to the grey holes. For two reasons, the rules in this category are theoretically even more consequential than the black holes. First, some liberal legalist critics like Dyzenhaus find the grey holes even more objectionable than the black ones.[52] The problem with grey holes, they suggest, is that the apparent constraints on executive action mask the lack of actual constraints; better to expose the executive's lack of constraint for all to see. Second, and conversely, some critics overlook the pervasive character of the grey holes; these critics suggest that there is such a thing as "ordinary" administrative law that could be used to constrain executive action during emergencies.[53]

Our claim is that quite ordinary administrative-law doctrines, such as "arbitrary and capricious" review of agency policy choices and factual findings, function as grey holes during times of war and real or perceived emergency. By their nature, these doctrines are not, of course, explicitly tied to emergency circumstances (with the partial exception of the "good cause" exception to the main requirements of notice-and-comment rulemaking, discussed below). Rather, these doctrines represent adjustable parameters that courts can and do use to dial up or dial down the intensity of judicial review, as wars, security threats, and emergencies come and go. What makes these doctrines potential grey holes is that even when the parameter is adjusted down near zero—even when the intensity of review is very weak—the facade of lawfulness is preserved.

"Soft Look" Review

One of the main adjustable parameters of administrative law involves so-called "arbitrary and capricious review" under § 706(2)(a) of the APA. The arbitrary and capricious standard governs judicial review of agency policy choices and some types of agency fact-finding. The convention among administrative lawyers of a certain generation is to call this "hard look" review, because of language in the major Supreme Court cases, the high level of scrutiny evident in those decisions, and the searching scrutiny the D.C. Circuit and other appellate courts have often applied to agency policy choices.

In many cases, however, "hard look" is a misnomer; these cases employ a kind of "soft look" review, under which courts accept looser reasoning in support of agency policies and looser fact-finding than would usually be accepted. Nothing in these cases changes the nominal legal rules in any way. Rather courts simply adjust the intensity of scrutiny in ways that are entirely consistent with the linguistic formulas in the governing case law. Courts at different times can give more or less intense scrutiny to government action while reciting and applying these tests in all good faith. The more subterranean deference courts give to administrative action, the softer the look, and the more the arbitrary and capricious test starts to resemble a grey hole—a facade of lawfulness.

To illustrate these points, consider a series of cases from the D.C. Circuit in which the court has reviewed decisions by the Treasury Department's Office of Foreign Assets Control (OFAC). Originally an obscure government agency, OFAC has become an important counterterrorism agency by virtue of its powers to announce "Specially Designated Global Terrorist" organizations (SDGTs) and to block the assets of such organizations, on the theory that they are giving financial assistance to terrorist organizations. OFAC derives its powers from an executive order issued after 9/11, an order authorized in turn by the International Economic Emergency Powers Act.[54]

The D.C. Circuit has considered and rejected several challenges, brought by Islamic charities, to OFAC blocking orders. In *Holy Land Foundation for Relief and Development v. Ashcroft*,[55] the petition for review was brought by one of the largest Muslim charities in the United States. Finding that the charity was closely linked to Hamas, OFAC blocked all of the charity's assets. Describing the "arbitrary and capricious" standard as "highly deferential"—signaling soft- rather than hard-look review—the D.C. Circuit briskly found the designation decision and the blocking order nonarbitrary and also supported by "substantial evidence."[56] Moreover, the court also said that the core question was whether the agency's decision was supported by a "rational basis."[57] This formulation often signals a permissive application of the arbitrary-and-capricious standard.

The parameter was adjusted downward even farther in a later case, *Islamic American Relief Agency (IARA) v. Gonzalez*.[58] The D.C. Circuit upheld OFAC's blocking order under the arbitrary-and-capricious standard and the substantial evidence standard. Acknowledging that "the unclassified record evidence is not overwhelming," the court "reiterate[d] that our review—in an area at the intersection of national security, foreign policy, and administrative law—is extremely deferential."[59] Here the facade of law has become awfully flimsy. Nonetheless the court purports to be applying regular legal standards. It is just that those standards are applied with an additional large, but unquantifiable, measure of deference.

Holy Land Foundation and *IARA v. Gonzalez* exemplify arbitrary-and-capricious review whose intensity has been dialed down to a minimum. Where this occurs, bare rationality is all that is required, whereas it is conventional to observe that on more familiar regulatory issues in normal times, review often becomes a searching inquiry that threatens to cause "ossification" of the regulatory process. There is a continuum that runs from hard-look review to soft-look review to a legal grey hole—arbitrary-and-capricious review that lacks all substance, although it retains the form of law. Cases like the D.C. Circuit's decisions reviewing OFAC orders move a long way toward the latter pole.

The "Good Cause" Exception

Informal notice-and-comment rulemaking is a central administrative in-strument; the APA's procedural requirements for notice and comment rulemaking, and also the exceptions to those requirements, are a critical testing ground for the administrative law of emergencies. Here an impor-tant adjustable parameter involves the APA's exemption, from otherwise-applicable requirements, for informal rules "when the agency for good cause finds . . . that notice and public procedure thereon are impracticable, unnecessary, or contrary to the public interest."[60] What does this mean?

The legislative history of the APA expressly anticipated that this language—especially a finding that the usual procedure is "impracti-cable"—would cover administrative action in emergencies. As the Attorney General's Manual put it, impracticability would arise where "an agency finds that due and timely execution of its functions would be impeded" by compliance with notice-and-comment procedures.[61] The leg-islative history did caution that "[t]he exemption of situations of emer-gency or necessity is not an 'escape clause' in the sense that any agency has discretion to disregard its terms or the facts. A true and supported or sup-portable finding of necessity or emergency must be made and published."[62] But what exactly are the "terms" that the agency must obey? The APA's text is largely vacuous on this point; "good cause" is an open-ended standard that essentially delegates the issue to future agencies and judges.

By contrast to the exceptions for "military and foreign affairs functions," the exception for "good cause" has often been litigated. However, the cases are exceedingly fact-bound. In one illuminating sequence, in the wake of the Arab oil embargo and the gasoline crisis of 1973, agencies invoked the good-cause exception to make emergency price-control rules and rules designed to increase supply. The Temporary Emergency Court of Appeals, set up under the Economic Stabilization Act of 1970 and the Emergency Petroleum Allocation Act of 1973, initially upheld the emergency regula-tions. However, in 1975 the emergency court "distinguished between the initial start-up phase and later phases of both the price control and energy regulation programs, invalidating several later regulations for failure to provide notice and comment."[63] By 1975, of course, the oil embargo had ended and the crisis had eased. The episode suggests that courts adjust the good-cause parameter in accordance with their changing perceptions of emergency.

In recent years, the major case about emergencies and good cause is *Jifry v. FAA*,[64] a D.C. Circuit opinion from 2004. The Federal Aviation Administration (FAA) revoked the airmen certificates—licenses to operate commercial airliners—from a group of airline pilots who were aliens. The relevant FAA regulation had been published without notice and comment in January 2003; it provided that the FAA would automatically suspend certificates upon a finding by the Transportation Security Administration (TSA) that the pilot posed a security threat. If, after a further round of TSA review, the finding was confirmed, the FAA would permanently revoke the previously suspended certificate.

The court held the regulation to fall within the "good cause" exception. It found that the necessary "emergency situation" or "serious harm" from delay arose because, as TSA said, immediate promulgation of the regulation was "necessary to prevent a possible imminent hazard to aircraft, persons and property with the United States."[65] This declaration by the agency created or at least reflected, in the court's words, a "legitimate concern over the threat of further terrorist acts involving aircraft."[66] Although the court failed to note this, the Attorney General's Manual on the APA had used a threat to aviation safety as its only example of permissible emergency regulation.[67]

Both the holding and result in *Jifry* seem inevitable, in the circumstances in which the court ruled. In the post-9/11 climate, it is hard to imagine a different ruling in the very security sector whose vulnerability had been exposed by the 9/11 attacks. The court's opinion endorsed a kind of precautionary principle[68] for airline security, noting that "[t]he TSA and FAA deemed such regulations necessary in order to minimize security threats and potential security vulnerabilities to the fullest extent possible."[69] The idea that what relevant administrators "deem necessary" counts as a valid basis for applying the good-cause exception is a remarkable interpretation of the exception, one that will probably not last, or have much carrying power outside the circumstances that gave rise to it. But that is the point about adjustable parameters: dialed down in times of perceived crisis, they are dialed up again when the crisis has passed, just as in the sequence of cases decided by the Temporary Emergency Court of Appeals.

It is hard to overemphasize the importance of the good-cause exception. So-called notice-and-comment rulemaking is at the heart of modern administrative law, and at the heart of the statutory procedure for notice-and-comment rulemaking is an open-ended override for emergency situations. Such overrides are paradigmatically Schmittian. Moreover, the good-cause exception is an adjustable parameter that, in cases like *Jifry*, has been dialed down to the point where it has temporarily become as capacious as administrators "deem necessary." It has, in other words, temporarily become a legal grey hole.

ECONOMIC CRISES

So far, our examples have come principally from the arena of security and counterterror policy after 9/11. However, the dynamics are quite general in the administrative state. In the framing of the EESA, described in chapter 1, the two modes of deference we have discussed both came into play. The secretary of the Treasury's initial proposal would have excluded judicial review altogether, creating a legal black hole. The final version might be read to create standard APA-style review of the secretary's actions, if only to avoid possible constitutional questions about nondelegation. Although there is some ambiguity about what review the statute actually allows, we will indulge the assumptions least favorable to our view by stipulating that ordinary review is permitted.

The problem with APA-style review under the EESA, however, is that, as in other areas of administrative law, courts will predictably defer heavily to administrators' particular decisions in times of crisis. Courts do so both because they lack the information to second-guess those decisions in the complex circumstances of actual cases, and because they fear to be seen to thwart emergency measures. Lower courts, especially, are reluctant to challenge the decisions of the president and other high executive officials in matters of national security;[70] as we have seen, for instance in the "good cause" cases during the energy crisis of the 1970s, the same is true in economic emergencies. And the questions at issue in such cases will generally be too numerous and too fact-bound for the Supreme Court to review more than a handful of them. Crisis is not the only causal variable here; the sheer complexity and opacity of the underlying economic decisions make legislators wary of entrusting oversight to generalist judges, and the judges themselves may concur. In the most recent comparable episode, the savings-and-loan bailout of the 1980s, Congress established the Resolution

Trust Corporation (RTC) to take control of failed savings-and-loan associations and sell off their assets. Congress provided for greatly limited review[71]—no doubt because of skepticism about courts' ability to evaluate the RTC's sales decisions—and courts complied, even though there was no emergency or crisis.[72]

Whether or not such deference is desirable in the abstract, the pragmatics of a complex policymaking environment and of crisis governance give courts few alternatives. Consider the idea that courts could review the transactions the secretary might undertake, in particular the prices he offers for preferred stock in financial institutions or the prices he accepts at "reverse auctions" for mortgage-related securities. (Although the secretary has not pursued these options, they have been much discussed and we use them to illustrate the general structure of the situation). If courts subject these transactions to meaningful review, then sellers would be afraid that sales would be reversed. If courts subject these transactions to highly deferential review, then review would serve little purpose. In any event, if the secretary revives the idea of direct governmental purchases of toxic assets (as opposed to purchases effected through public-private partnerships, the current plan), it is doubtful that courts could second-guess the secretary's pricing decisions. The problem is that the mortgage-related asset market has collapsed, so there are no market prices to use as a benchmark for toxic assets. And given the likely complexity of these transactions, which would involve equity stakes, covenants of various sorts, and much else, courts would be in a difficult position if they sought to evaluate the transactions in a serious fashion.

In general, the secretary's pricing decisions under the EESA would exemplify the types of questions that courts find it difficult to review, involving as they do a combination of technicality, uncertainty about valuation, and urgency. The first two factors are also present in judicial review of rate regulation of public utilities by administrative agencies, which tends to be highly deferential; more broadly, the inability of courts to determine utility rates and common-carrier rates, through a succession of cases, was a major impetus behind the creation of early administrative agencies.[73] Beyond the features common with other regulatory schemes in which uncertain valuation is a problem, the EESA carries with it an aura of urgency, which will make courts reluctant to be seen frustrating the only major statutory mechanism for coping with the financial crisis.

The upshot is that the EESA will, in all probability, create nothing more than a series of legal grey holes, rather than genuinely independent judicial oversight. Lawyers, who are frequently obsessed with the formal question whether judicial review is technically available or not, may draw comfort from Congress's decision to provide for arbitrariness review. From another perspective, however, legal grey holes may be worse than legal black ones. The former create an illusion of oversight, whereas the latter are in a sense more candid about whether meaningful review will in fact occur.[74] Our perspective is that it is not useful to talk about whether black or grey holes are preferable. Some mix of both types is inevitable where statutes like the AUMF, the Patriot Act, and the EESA delegate administrative power to cope with an emergency. Background legalist statutes like the APA are themselves shot through with exceptions and qualifications that allow the standard pattern of crisis management to proceed without real check.

WHY SCHMITTIAN ADMINISTRATIVE LAW IS INEVITABLE

We have tried to show that black holes and grey holes are integral to the structure of American administrative law. What follows from this? For many liberal legalist theorists committed to the thick rule of law, black holes are profoundly objectionable. The term was originally coined to describe Guantánamo Bay by an English judge who saw the existence of this black hole as a "monstrous" failure of both legality and justice.[75] For some theorists, however, grey holes are even more objectionable than black holes. We have seen that liberal legal theorists like Dyzenhaus decry the existence of grey holes on the ground that preserving a facade of law-fulness is worse than outright violation of (thick) rule-of-law norms. An open violation of those norms may mobilize backlash or resistance, whereas grey holes may fool at least some of the people, some of the time.

It is not at all clear that grey holes really are worse, even from the stand-point of liberal-legalist values. Candor is not always desirable, and hypo-critical lip-service to the rule of law may even be best for the (thick) rule of law in the long run; Dyzenhaus overlooks the many virtues of preserving facades. Open creation of legal black holes may not cause backlash, but instead simply undermine norms or values that underpin the thick rule of law, where it exists. The best way to preserve those norms or values may be to draw a veil of decency over behavior that everyone knows is going on.

Relatedly, the judges who cooperate in the creation of administrative law's grey holes may be doing so because they think that is the best strategy for preserving or promoting the thick rule of law, at least under nonideal political conditions. By bringing emergency administrative action within the tent, they may hope to avoid the humiliating consequences that they fear will ensue if the executive is left outside the tent altogether—primarily that the executive will more or less ignore what the judges say. In terms of Dyzenhaus's metaphor, better to preserve the facade so that one day, when the crisis has passed, a real building may be built behind it—an option that may be lost forever if the facade is knocked down in the name of candor, or in a kind of tantrum about a temporary thinning of the rule of law.

However, the main point is that black and grey holes are inevitable for institutional reasons, whether or not desirable. Black holes arise because legislators and executive officials will never agree to subject all executive action to thick legal standards, because the inevitability of changing circumstances and unforeseen circumstances means they could not do so even if they tried—one of Schmitt's points—and because the judges would not want them to do so in any event. There are too many domains affecting national security in which official opinion holds unanimously, across institutions and partisan lines and throughout the modern era, that executive action must proceed untrammeled by even the threat of legal regulation and judicial review, no matter how deferential that review might be on the merits.

The APA's black holes—its general exclusion of uniquely presidential functions and its exceptions for military authorities and functions—are rough attempts to capture this long-standing consensus. Their content changes over time, but only within certain margins of adjustment; the black holes will never be entirely eliminated. Nor do judges of any party or ideological bent want to extend legality so far, partly because they fear the responsibility of doing so, partly because they understand the limits of their own competence and fear that uninformed judicial meddling with the executive will have harmful consequences where national security is at stake, and partly because it has simply never been done before.

The story of the original legal black hole at Guantánamo Bay illustrates these points. That black hole has now been more or less closed—the Supreme Court has held that judicial review through writ of habeas corpus is available for detainees there[76]—but this just means that attention has shifted to the base at Bagram, in Afghanistan, and to other less famous sites at which purported enemy combatants are detained. Importantly, only a handful academic theorists takes seriously a model of "global due process"[77] in which judicial review would extend to the "four corners of the earth."[78] At every step in the legalization of Guantánamo Bay, the Court's dominant civil-libertarian coalition, or at least its key member, Justice Kennedy, has refused to bind itself to a global vision of the availability of judicial review,[79] because it would be impracticable to do so, and because the consequences of doing so would be unclear and possibly grave.

As for grey holes, they arise precisely because of how administrative law is structured for ordinary cases. Grey holes arise because administrative law in any modern regulatory state cannot get by without adjustable parameters, which are the lawmakers' pragmatic response to the sheer size of the administrative state, the heterogeneity of the bodies covered by the APA, the complexity and diversity of the problems that agencies face and of the modes of administrative action, and (related to all these) the lawmakers' inability and unwillingness to specify in advance legal rules or institutional forms that will create a thick rule of law in all future contingencies, a core Schmittian theme.

This approach by the lawmakers is not a matter of logic—despite Schmitt's conceptual style of argument—but a matter of institutional capacities. Garden-variety administrative law, far removed from national security or security emergencies, recognizes that the APA's central legal standards for judicial review of administrative action—the arbitrary and capricious test, substantial evidence, reasonableness, and so on—are open-ended standards that judges can and do adjust to make review more or less intense according to circumstances. This is conventional wisdom, as witness a leading hornbook:

> Two prominent administrative law scholars once famously observed, "[T]he rules governing judicial review have no more substance at the core than a seedless grape." . . . The diversity of administrative action subject to substantive judicial review virtually rules out concrete APA standards. But something else is at work here as well. The APA's indeterminate standards of substantive review reflect Congress' recognition that it is undesirable, and perhaps impossible, to reduce this crucial judicial function to words.[80]

The final point in this passage is critical: it is inevitable, given the background conditions of the administrative state, that the norms governing judicial review of agency action will be embodied as loose standards or adjustable parameters. And those standards will be applied by judges who will defer heavily—even to the point of creating grey holes—while maintaining intact the nominal legal norms. And identified "emergencies" are not the only condition that produces this effect; a myriad of pragmatic factors or circumstances might cause judicial review to be dialed down so far as to create grey holes.

It bears repeating that the mechanisms that create this judicial deference are pragmatic rather than conceptual. It is logically possible that judges might exercise vigorous review even when the government's interests are pressing, but it is institutionally impossible for them to do so. Judges defer because they think the executive has better information than they do, and also think that this informational asymmetry or gap increases as the complexity and rate of change of the underlying policy questions increase; because (even if the judges are skeptical that the executive's information really is superior, or if they are skeptical of executive motivations) they are aware of their own fallibility and fear the harms to national security or economic well-being that might arise if they erroneously override executive policies; and because they fear the delay that may arise from judicial review, and that might be especially harmful where time is of the essence.

This overall picture reverses a stock claim, in the theory of emergency powers, that legal norms or innovations introduced during and for emergencies will spill over into the law applicable in normal times. Rather, the claim here is that a type of reverse spillover, from ordinary to extraordinary times, is inevitable in a complex administrative state. Because open-ended standards will inevitably be integral to any general framework for judicial review in such a state, adjustable parameters will arise, and these parameters will then function as grey holes when judges perceive a heightened threat and reduce the intensity of their review to a sufficiently low level. In such circumstances, the forms of judicial oversight will be retained, but the substance will be drained away.

This dynamic is not unique to emergencies; other factors can bring it into being as well. And nothing here implies that the precise black and grey holes we have now are inevitable, precisely at their current scope. There is a margin within which adjustment is possible, and indeed adjustments and fluctuations do constantly occur. The Schmittianism of American administrative law is a matter of degree; we might have black and grey holes of greater or lesser scope than we have now. Moreover, from the lawmakers' standpoint, both black holes and grey holes have a mix of costs and benefits. Black holes are more explicit, and thus produce increased legal certainty for executive officials, but create a more obvious offense to the rule of law; grey holes can accomplish some of the same ends with less visibility (as Dyzenhaus observes). Because the value of these costs and benefits will change over time, no particular set of black and grey holes is preordained.

What we do claim is that the existence of some robust set of black and grey holes is inevitable—not in a logical sense but in a pragmatic and institutional sense. The very structure of the administrative state is such that full, thick legality is infeasible. It is not conceptually impossible; nothing in the nature of things prevents legislators from specifying a code that purports to provide specific rules for all future contingencies, or prevents judges from exercising real review during perceived emergencies. But it is not in the nature of real-world institutions that they should do these things.

OF LEGISLATORS AND ASPIRATIONS

The structure of the administrative state is of course statutory, not just precedent-based.[81] This is an important point because Dyzenhaus's anti-Schmittian aspiration is addressed to legislators as much as, or more than, judges. Dyzenhaus acknowledges the poor record of judicial review of emergency executive action, so far as Commonwealth-style public law and American-style constitutional law are concerned;[82] we add that American-style administrative law is the same.

Dyzenhaus acknowledges the possibility that judges can do no better— better by his lights—than they have. But he wants legislatures to do much better than they have, internalizing the norms of the thick rule of law. And on one reading, he thinks that this is possible because "legislators and executive officials have erroneously accepted the judges' constitutional positivism as expressed in their decisions validating grey holes. Clear away the conceptual confusion, and legislators and executive officials might accept the responsibility they have for an aspirational theory of law."[83] One more focused hope is that legislatures will promote the thick rule of law through "creative institutional design"—oversight structures internal to the legislative and executive branches. Likewise, Evan Criddle argues that the "primary obstacle" to reforms that would close up the black and grey holes is not institutional, but "cultural." The problem, on Criddle's account, is that "too many legislators and judges view administrative law in static positivist terms . . . rather than in dynamic relational terms as establishing a regime in which public officials must justify all exercises of administrative powers according to public-regarding factors."[84]

We suggest, contrary to Dyzenhaus, that the inevitability of black holes and grey holes applies just as much to legislatively-formulated administrative law as it does to judge-made administrative law; and, contrary to both Dyzenhaus and Criddle, that legislators and judges create black and grey holes for quite practical reasons, not some cultural disposition, jurisprudential confusion, or high-level conceptual mistake. The black holes and grey holes of the APA are not, for the most part, interpolated into its text, as if the judges had implied a "good cause" exception for emergencies into facially mandatory administrative procedures. Rather, the black holes and the adjustable parameters that turn into grey holes during emergencies themselves have textual roots, for the most part. And perhaps it is not so surprising, as a historical matter, that the APA's drafters and enactors created those exceptions. Consider that the drafters of the APA had just lived through a global hot war and were on the verge of a global cold one. Executive power was, perhaps, near a kind of local maximum, which would decline through the Truman administration until the Supreme Court, scenting weakness, moved in for the kill in the *Youngstown* case.[85]

To be sure, a major purpose of the APA was to retrench the administrative state and to reassert legislative and judicial control over administrative action.[86] Its framers and enactors professed reverence for the rule of law, understood partly as judicial review of administrative action, and thus can only have been reluctant Schmittians (who would of course not have identified themselves as such in any event). But as is also quite clear, no one purpose entirely prevailed in the APA's drafting; rather, as Justice Jackson put it, the act "enacts a formula upon which opposing social and political forces have come to rest."[87] The framers of the APA quite deliberately left escape hatches from the administrative code of liberal legalism, recognizing that unforeseen and emergency circumstances would inevitably arise, and that no code of administrative law and procedure could hope to specify, in advance, what to do about those circumstances. Stray passages in the APA's legislative history warned against letting these escape hatches become too large. But no one thought they could be eliminated. That even the APA's framers were reluctant Schmittians just underscores the practical problems: even legislators attempting to promote (one vision of) thick legality will find a degree of Schmittianism inescapable.

The reasons that the APA's enactors created the black and grey holes were quite pragmatic, including the inability to formulate comprehensive and precise rules that would apply to the sprawling diversity of the administrative state and its problems, and a lively appreciation of the inevitability of emergencies and unforeseen circumstances. It is hard to imagine them doing otherwise, in the circumstances in which they acted; and those circumstances are if anything all the more strongly present today, as the size and diversity of the administrative state have increased and as the paradoxical inevitability of the unforeseen has become all the more salient after 9/11 and after the economic meltdown of 2008. In this respect, it is worth remembering that the APA was itself creative institutional design when enacted. It is not as though creative institutional design has not been tried;

it has been, but the practical pressures for leaving escape hatches and adjustable parameters that turn into grey holes proved insurmountable. The same forces would predictably overwhelm the vague standards of "public justification" that Criddle favors. The question is always how much justification is enough, and that is just another adjustable parameter. Criddle's basic notion is too spongy to put backbone in the rule of administrative law.[88] Given these powerful practical foundations for a Schmittian stance, the anti-Schmittian aspiration to purge administrative law of black and grey holes looks hopelessly utopian. If we understand a "Schmittian lawmaker" as a lawmaker who quite deliberately builds black and (potential) grey holes into the structure of law that is created, then the architects of our administrative state were and are Schmittian lawmakers—not liberal legalists.

STATUTORY AUTHORIZATION AND EXECUTIVE POWER: THE *YOUNGSTOWN* FRAMEWORK

A final implication involves constitutional law; although our focus in this chapter is on statutory law, there is an important idea, relevant to our thesis, that sits right on the boundary line between the two areas. The idea, which is widely popular among American legal theorists and elsewhere, is that judges should cabin the powers of the executive by requiring statutory authorization for the exercise of those powers, even in emergencies. The idea is associated with Justice Jackson's famous concurrence in the *Youngstown* case, which set out a three-part framework for evaluating executive power. If Congress has authorized the president's action, expressly or impliedly, the president's power is at its acme, while the nadir of presidential power occurs when Congress has expressly or impliedly prohibited the action. In between is a "zone of twilight" in which Congress has taken no position about the claimed executive power.[89]

Some theorists have expanded *Youngstown* into an "institutional process" view.[90] They hold that placing substantive constitutional restrictions on executive powers, through civil-libertarian judicial rulings, demands too much of the judges, especially in times of war or emergency. But what courts can successfully do, the argument runs, is to require congressional authorization for executive powers, and to enforce statutory restrictions against the executive. And in fact, the process theorists add, courts have done both of these things, even in emergencies. Requiring statutory authorization (and enforcing statutory prohibitions) ensures a legislative check on the executive and makes policies more deliberative and democratically legitimate, or so the claim runs.

The suggestion that this is what courts have in fact done is dubious. The process theorists overlook that a judicial finding of statutory authorization, or for that matter statutory prohibition, is often a conclusion rather than a premise: the judges find authorization because they wish to uphold the executive action, rather than upholding the action because they have found authorization. In a world of multiple and very vague statutory delegations bearing on national security, foreign relations, and emergency powers, judges have a great deal of freedom—not infinite freedom, of course—to assign *Youngstown* categories to support the decisions they want to reach, rather than reaching decisions based on the *Youngstown* categories.[91] The institutional process framework is only as strong as the prevailing methods of statutory interpretation, and in most of the hard cases that tend to reach the federal appellate courts, the prevailing methods will enable judges to write a straight-faced opinion putting the case in more than one of the *Youngstown* categories, and sometimes in any of them.

The problem is not or not solely that the interpretive methods available to judges are only partially determinate, and are least determinate in the skewed subset of cases that reach appellate courts. The (other) precondition for the problem to arise is that the statutory landscape of the administrative state—especially that part of the landscape bearing on war, foreign relations, national security, and economic emergencies—is itself full of highly general and vague statutory delegations, many of which contain escape-hatches or emergency exceptions. The institutional process approach implicitly imagines a highly determinate set of statutory authorizations and prohibitions covering most or all future contingencies—an un-Schmittian code of executive powers; but this is a fantasy.

As elsewhere in the administrative state, the diversity and sheer scale of the problems that Congress confronts, the highly constricted legislative agenda, the executive's proclivity to argue that it possesses unique expertise and capacity for action and so should be given a free hand (whether such arguments are right or wrong in particular cases), all cause legislators to delegate broadly and to leave the executive and the judges and themselves ample wiggle-room for unforeseen circumstances. And legislators can foresee that the unforeseen will necessarily occur, although they cannot guess what shape it will take. This is inevitably so, and its inevitable consequence is that appellate judges will have great freedom to categorize statutes, under *Youngstown*, as necessary to justify decision reached on other grounds. A central question, for both administrative law and the constitutional law of executive powers, is statutory authorization. In both domains, the work-product of de facto Schmittian lawmakers ensures that statutory authorization is at best a loose requirement.

In any case, as we emphasized earlier, the "presidential power of unilateral action" implies that in some cases, legislative action before the fact—even in the form of a prohibition—will be neither here nor there. The president may take action in the real world, if necessary in violation of restrictive framework statutes like the War Powers Resolution, and the sole question will be what Congress or the judges are able or willing to do about it after the fact. The latter question is essentially one of politics, not law, and the overall pattern is that Congress and the courts will tend to fight back only when presidents lack popularity or credibility—the key constraints on executive power that we discuss in the following chapters. The *Youngstown* framework is thus of very dubious relevance to actual political outcomes, in the dual sense that it is excessively plastic and thus follows rather than dictates results, and that even where it would yield clear results, there is a separate and serious question whether any actors will have the motivation to enforce it.

A separate problem is that *Youngstown* may produce perverse results, even from the standpoint of liberal legalism, and even where the framework does affect results.[92] Where congressional preferences are uncertain, a president deciding whether to ask Congress for permission to take an action may calculate that the costs of asking are greater than the benefits; better to act unilaterally than to ask for permission that might be refused. The courts may well count a congressional refusal as a prohibition, at least if Congress embodies its refusal in a statute, but perhaps also if Congress generates negative legislative history that the courts subsequently use. If the president doesn't ask at all, by contrast, the case will probably end up in the intermediate *Youngstown* category in which Congress has expressed no view one way or another. Depending upon presidential risk preferences and upon the probabilities and consequences of these scenarios, it is a real possibility that presidents will decide to proceed through unilateral action, including executive orders and agency action—a perverse result from the standpoint of liberal legalists whose idealized model has the president simply executing statutes that the legislature has previously deliberated and enacted. True, *Youngstown* cannot be simultaneously irrelevant (as we have argued) and bad (as this argument suggests), but it can be irrelevant in some cases and both relevant and bad in others.

CONCLUSION

Legal black holes and legal grey holes are not confined to Guantánamo Bay or to Kafkaesque literary nightmares about sham adjudication. They are integral to the administrative state. Indeed they are inevitable; no legal order governing a massive and massively diverse administrative state can hope to dispense with them, although their scope will wax and wane as time and circumstances dictate. Liberal legalist theorists of the thick rule of law are entirely correct that legal black holes and grey holes are best understood through the lens of Carl Schmitt's thought. They are only wrong in thinking that anything can be done about this state of affairs. The APA, like the Constitution, persists because of its very flexibility and reliance on open-ended standards at crucial points. Rather than constrain the executive, in practice, the APA supplies a patina of legality for most of what the executive wants to do. This is the secret of its "success," and explains the apparent contrast between the APA and the subject-specific framework statutes, whose more pointed commands have often proven ineffective. In either case, the basic aspiration of liberal legalism to constrain the executive through statutory law has largely failed.

CHAPTER 4

Constraints on the Executive

The modern executive enjoys vast discretion to govern, yet we are far from "tyranny," the outcome Madison predicted would result from the accumulation of powers in one office. Even during emergencies and war, when executive power is at a zenith, and congressional and judicial checks at their lowest ebb, tyranny is not the result. This point can be put in a number of ways. Through its long history and all of its wars and crises, the U.S. government has generally been responsive to the public interest, and has always ranked as a leader among countries around the world in protecting civil liberties. Indeed, the national government was instrumental in dismantling slavery and the Jim Crow laws in the southern states, which were the closest thing to tyranny that the United States has ever experienced. Political science indicators of various sorts confirm that, compared to the other countries around the world, the United States is a leader in democratic responsiveness and civil liberties.[1] And American practices in these respects have only improved over the decades and centuries, during the same period in which the separation of powers has eroded.

In this chapter, we discuss this puzzle. Our argument is simple: the system of elections, the party system, and American political culture constrain the executive far more than do legal rules created by Congress or the courts; and although politics hardly guarantees that the executive will always act in the public interest, politics at least limits the scope for executive abuses. After briefly making these points, we focus on the way that American political culture—which features deeply entrenched suspicion of the executive—forces the executive to adopt institutions and informal mechanisms of self-constraint that help enhance its credibility. These mechanisms are the institutional replacements for Madison's system of separation of powers.

Throughout the chapter, we focus on the presidency, because presidential power allows us to make our points about elections and political constraints in the most vivid cases. However, our points will also apply, at one remove, to agency officials appointed by an elected president. The executive includes more than the presidency, but if our argument convincingly characterizes the presidency, it characterizes the executive generally.

POPULARITY

The most common framework for thinking about presidential power is the principal-agent model.[2] The agent is the leader; it is his actions that harm or benefit the principal. The principal can be defined in various ways. One might think of it as the public; the public extended indefinitely in the future; certain segments of the public (such as voting adults); the overlapping interests of states as representatives of their populations; or agglomerations of interests produced by the interactions of individuals, institutions, and groups of various sorts such as unions and businesses. However the principal is defined, it has certain "preferences," including economic well-being, freedom, happiness, and so forth.

The principal seeks a leader who will implement its interests. The problem is that the leader has better information about his actions than the principal does. When the leader takes actions that affect outcomes such as economic growth, the principal often does not know whether positive and negative outcomes took place because of the actions or because of events outside the leader's control; this uncertainty gives the leader flexibility to take actions that produce outcomes that he prefers rather than those that the principal prefers. The challenge for constitutional design is to minimize agency costs—to design institutions that reduce the incentives of the agent to deviate from the interests of the principal.[3]

A first question is why the leader might have interests different from those of the public. A number of reasons exist. The leader might have different ideological preferences—for example, he opposes abortion while most members of the public support at least limited abortion rights. The leader might also seek wealth from the office. A further possibility is that the leader identifies with some particular group (for example, an ethnic group) and seeks to advance the group's interests. Leaders might also enjoy exercising power, and hope to remain in office as long as possible, and to have as much power as possible. They might want to start dynasties or to promote national glory. The public meanwhile might simply seek wealth or security or a healthy environment.

The major institutional mechanism for reducing the agency costs of leaders is the election.[4] The election serves two purposes. First, it serves a selection or screening function. The public learns about various politicians over time and uses the election to screen out those whose preferences are farthest from those of the public (and whose abilities are weakest). Second, it serves an incentive function. The leader will be more likely to act in the public interest if he knows that he may lose an election if he does not.

Elections are far from perfect. Under the principle of one person, one vote, everyone's preferences are given equal weight; however, some people's preferences might be more intense than those of others. Candidates advance a bundle of programs, and voters are constrained to choose one bundle or the other, so there is scope for candidates to adopt unpopular positions on some issues. In addition, people can use wealth and position to influence the outcome of elections—for example, by donating money to campaigns and paying for advertisements. Voters also have trouble keeping informed on the issues and have incentives to free ride on each other, in which case their ability to discipline wayward presidents is correspondingly limited. Elections must be periodic—they do not standardly take place on a continuous basis[5]—so a president might act badly today in the hope that people will forget by the time of the election or that other good actions will compensate for the earlier bad action.

Still, the election is a powerful mechanism for controlling agents, and this explains its ubiquity in businesses, universities, governments (in democracies), and countless other institutions. Presidents strive to maintain their popularity;[6] they clearly do so with an eye toward the election at the end of their first term and, more uncertainly, toward their legacy for the future. (Current popularity is the best evidence of future popularity, putting aside information disparities that might be resolved in the future.) By contrast, in a dictatorship the government has no reliable method of ascertaining the preferences of the people. That means that the government might fail to satisfy their interests, resulting in turmoil and revolution. Democratic elections allow for smooth transitions because they adequately aggregate preferences and provide institutional means for the transfer of power.

So far we have assumed that the leader should act so as to maximize the well-being of the public. But other values are at stake as well. The founders worried about liberty, in particular, as have many others over the centuries. A recurrent fear is that the president will maximize the interests of the majority at the expense of minorities. Originally, minorities were understood to be property holders or political elites; today, minorities are usually understood in ethnic or ideological terms. Protecting the liberty of minorities from the majority has been a constitutional commitment from the start. Liberty is sometimes understood in a general way; at other times, it is cashed out in terms of particular rights to be free from government interference—rights to property, to be notified of charges after being detained for criminal behavior, to speech and association, and so forth.

The founders believed that electoral mechanisms alone could not protect liberty. Separation of powers, federalism, and a bill of rights were therefore included in the constitutional design as auxiliary mechanisms to compensate for the deficiencies of elections. We might ask whether the founders were correct in this assessment. If elections reduce agency costs, then they should cause the president to protect liberty to the same extent that he protects the other interests and values of the public. If the public places a relatively high value on liberty, the president will do so as well. Thus, even in a pure electoral system, without separation of powers and the other protections, civil liberties could be given substantial protection.

To be sure, a recurrent worry is that the majority will direct the government to respect *its* liberties and ignore those of minority groups. Whether this will in fact occur depends on political conditions. Often there is no majority with a monolithic set of interests; instead, there are various minority groups that can join majorities by forming coalitions. If groups cycle in and out of the majority, their liberties may well be protected. If a group is permanently excluded from the majority, the liberties of its members may well be sacrificed.

As we have discussed in earlier chapters, it is not obvious how separation of powers contributes to liberty (or welfare). In the principal-agent framework, we now have three agents—president, Congress, and judiciary. Because Congress and the judiciary both consist of multiple people, the agents are similarly multiplied, though it is possible that in both institutions collective action problems can be overcome, so that it may be analytically possible to refer to each as a separate agent. We will do so for convenience.

In the economics and political science literature, scholars have struggled to provide a rational choice basis for separation of powers. In these models, the judiciary is usually put to one side, and the question is why policymaking should be divided among two agents—the executive and the legislature—rather than given to one agent such as the executive. The starting point is that a unitary system where an executive is periodically elected by the public is not necessarily ideal. The executive can extract rents from voters by adopting policies that it prefers and voters do not like. These could be policies that advance the executive's own ideological preferences, or that divert resources to the executive's supporters. Because the voters' only means of discipline is to remove the president from office, the executive will simply compare the gains from adopting self-serving policies during the current term and the cost of not being able to adopt those same policies during a later term. Ironically, if the voters have zero tolerance for rent extraction and will thus kick out any executive who adopts suboptimal policies, and the executive knows this will be their response, the executive will in fact engage in substantial rent extraction during his first term. The reason is that he does better with rents in the first term and no second term than with no rents in both terms. Voters have to tolerate enough rent extraction so that the executive will want a second term. The source of the problem is that electoral systems do not offer traditional rewards and sanctions to the agent but instead essentially offer a reward in the form of the right to engage in actions that are not optimal for the principal. By contrast, in traditional agency models addressing employer-employee relationships, better incentives can be created through the transfer of money to successful employees and the infliction of monetary and other sanctions on unsuccessful employees.

A further problem is that voters lack full information about the executive's behavior, and cannot vote for or against him simply by observing whether his actions are good or bad. Voters may be able to observe outcomes—such as general economic prosperity—but outcomes reflect contingencies partially outside of the control of the executive. If voters reelect executives solely on the basis of outcomes, they will end up reelecting bad executives who are lucky and throwing out good executives who are unlucky. Anticipating that they will not necessarily be rewarded on the basis of their efforts, executives will, at the margin, engage in actions that do not promote the public interest—for example, diverting resources to themselves, their friends, their constituents, and so forth. So, while elections are a more powerful mechanism for minimizing agency costs than alternatives such as a hereditary monarchy, they clearly will result in outcomes that fall short of the optimum.[7]

The first problem is one of agenda-setting and bargaining power; the second is one of information. Both problems are inherent in the design of elections and the nature of political competition. The question is whether separation of powers results in improvement.

One intuition might be that "competition" is good in politics, as it is in economics. We know that in markets, consumers do better when producers compete than when monopoly exists. In the standard Cournot model, consumer surplus increases when the number of sellers increases from one (monopoly) to two (duopoly) or more. Similarly, perhaps, separation of powers converts a monopolistic government into a duopolistic government, with the result that voters pay the lower duopoly "price" for public goods supplied by the executive rather than the monopoly "price" for public goods. For example, suppose that the executive supplies a single public good like national defense and charges a price in the form of a tax. In the monopolistic system, the tax would be higher than in the duopolistic system—the executive would use the revenue above what is necessary to finance the public good for its own purposes—and so separation of powers improves the welfare of the public.

In an instructive paper, Geoffrey Brennan and Alan Hamlin show that this intuition is wrong.[8] Competition for the power to tax and provide public goods can lead to good outcomes (what Brennan and Hamlin call "horizontal" separation of powers), but that has nothing to do with separation of powers in a Madisonian sense ("vertical" separation of powers). The Madisonian notion, by contrast, is that two agents must jointly consent to any policy. The proper economic analogy would be a market in which two firms must act in order to supply a good—say, a manufacturer and a distributor. Each is a monopolist within its own domain: only the manufacturer makes the good and only the distributor distributes it. If the two firms cannot cooperate, the outcome is worse for the consumer than the case of a single monopolist who both manufactures and distributes (the analogy to the single executive). The manufacturer will charge a monopoly price to the distributor who will treat this price as the cost of an input, and turn around and charge a monopoly price to the consumer. If the two firms can cooperate, then they will agree to charge the consumer the price that the single monopolist would charge and divide the profits, but there will be the extra transaction costs of cooperation—and if cooperation fails, the price will be even higher. In sum, separating powers in the Madisonian sense makes the consumer (taxpayer) no better off and probably worse off than she would be under the unitary system.

Torsten Persson, Gerard Roland, and Guido Tabellini offer a different model in which separation of powers can make the principal better off. Suppose the executive proposes the size of the budget in the first stage and the legislator can either approve or veto it; the legislature proposes the allocation of the budget in the second stage (in particular, the share of rents that goes to the executive and the legislature); and voters reelect or throw out officials in the third stage. In the second stage, the legislature will allocate the executive a minimal share of the rents, hogging the rest for itself. Because the executive anticipates this behavior in the first stage, he will propose a budget that is optimal for the public rather than a too-large budget. Voter approval ensures that he is reelected; and because the legislature cannot commit to give him a share of a large budget, he has no reason to propose one. In this model, separation of powers is superior to a system featuring a single executive because separation of powers reduces the executive's bargaining power and hence his ability to extract rents, and does so without giving the legislature agenda-setting power either.[9] However, this argument rests on some sensitive assumptions about the structure of the relationship between the executive and the legislature; as the authors acknowledge, if some of these assumptions are relaxed, the outcome could be worse than under the unitary approach. The two branches of government don't really take turns in this way—with one branch making a proposal and the other accepting or rejecting it. In fact, they bargain with each other in fluid conditions that cannot be easily modeled as moves in a sequential game. If the branches can collude, they will choose the same policies that a single executive would and divide the rents, in which case separation of powers produces no benefits.

Another argument for separation of powers is that it generates information that voters can use to evaluate elected officials. If voters know the political preferences of the executive and the legislature, then they can make inferences about their private information—the state of the world unobserved by voters—when those agents agree and disagree. This information allows them to more precisely discipline elected officials on the basis of their actions.[10] By the same token, however, separation of powers can muddy information as well. Because the agents usually must cooperate in order to achieve an outcome, the public will have trouble distinguishing each agent's contribution. Failure and success will be attributed to both, which means that the public cannot punish the agents on the basis of their performance, which is fatal in the principal-agent model.[11]

Further, it is not obvious that an institutional structure of this type is needed to generate information about the actions of elected officials. Because the executive obtains substantial rents, there is terrific competition for the office. People who seek the office have strong incentives to discover and disclose negative information about those in office. Voters also have a strong interest in obtaining information about the performance of the executive. These various incentives have given rise to powerful institutions that are not part of the constitutional structure—most prominently, the media and political parties. Indeed, a recent paper that analyzes the separation of powers ends up concluding that the optimal system would give the executive the *option* to obtain the approval of Congress, but would not require him to.[12] The logic is that it is often in the executive's interest to show that its motives are good, and obtaining the approval of agents known to have different political preferences can be a credible way to make this showing. This idea of separation of powers bears little resemblance to the Madisonian ideal, which requires the president to obtain statutory authorization except where the president has independent constitutional authority to act—a domain that Madisonians tend to construe narrowly in any event.

Then there is the problem of gridlock. The press, the political parties, and the optional system of separation of powers do not create gridlock; real or "mandatory" separation of powers does.[13] The president and Congress have different constituencies; the judiciary has no obvious constituency but may be loyal to the ideological commitments of party. To the extent that policy outcomes require the cooperation of all three institutions, the available "policy space" is narrowed to the range of outcomes that are acceptable to all three. (If transfers from winners to losers are possible, then the range is wider, but transfers are costly and create distortions.) What is optimal for the president's constituency may well not be acceptable to the people living in a few states or districts that hold the balance of power in Congress. Because the Supreme Court justices tend to linger on for decades after their appointment, their votes may reflect policy preferences from an earlier era, further constraining the choices of policymakers.

Conceivably such a system might be desirable; in practice, it has proven unworkable, and as a result Congress and the judiciary have lost power to the president. We speculate that this trend is not due solely to the advantages inherent in the executive office, but also to a general sense among the political elites that the erosion of separation of powers has not been a bad thing. Indeed, if Madison's theory were correct, then liberty and public welfare would have declined as a consequence. This does not appear to have happened; certainly, there has not been a substantial effort to limit the president's powers since the 1970s. People seem to blame Congress for gridlock, not the president, as Newt Gingrich learned to his sorrow when he tried to face down President Clinton in 1995. This suggests that elections, reflecting the public interest and the public commitment to civil liberties, have served to discipline the president, at least as well as the separation-of-powers system, but without the danger of gridlock. Extra-constitutional mechanisms such as party competition contribute to the disciplining as well.

The handful of models that find a rationale for separation of powers end up identifying trade-offs that favor separation of powers only under certain empirical conditions that are impossible to verify.[14] Putting those models aside, and the usual celebratory accounts of Madison and the founders, our conclusion that the erosion of checks and balances has promoted national welfare is relatively uncontroversial in the political science literature, though the point is rarely put in this way. On the standard account, the concentration of power in the hands of the executive that took place during and after the New Deal was necessary to address the problems of an advanced, nationwide market economy and new foreign threats that emerged from the collapse of time and distance caused by technological change. But political scientists, historians, and legal academics have been reluctant to conclude that liberty has advanced as a result of this concentration of power. Instead, they claim that the courts—preeminently during the Warren Court judicial revolution—are responsible for protecting liberty from the grasping hands of the executive. As we have explained in earlier chapters, we are skeptical of the claim that courts deserve this star treatment. The most famous Warren Court cases struck down the practices of states, usually states whose policies deviated from the national norm, and, with a few exceptions, did little to constrain national power or the power of the executive. We think that the executive has been kept in check by public attitudes.

None of this is to claim that the executive has consistently been a perfect agent. Far from it. Political scientists argue about whether the presidents represent the median voter or some other measure of the public interest. Some work argues that presidents tend to advance partisan interests.[15] Clearly, most executives choose policies somewhere between the center and the outcomes favored by their political base. But the continuity across presidencies is striking. Richard Nixon respected and advanced liberal Great Society programs. Carter supported deregulation before Reagan did; under Reagan, government spending continued its advance. Clinton's domestic policy after the 1994 Republican victory in Congress was essentially conservative. Bush's and Obama's policies toward the financial crisis were similar—with the Obama administration resurrecting the maligned Paulson plan to purchase toxic assets and appointing Timothy Geithner, one of the architects of the Bush response, as Treasury secretary. Even

Obama's health care plan resembled plans endorsed by major Republican figures at early periods. American foreign policy throughout the cold war did not exhibit partisan differences; after the cold war, partisan differences have mattered more, but they remained muted. Obama has retained the main features of virtually every counterterror tool used by the Bush administration (indefinite detention, military commissions, rendition, targeted killing, surveillance) with the exception of torture, which the Bush administration had abandoned by 2007.[16] These continuities suggest that the influence of partisan differences is muted. In any event, the empirical political science scholarship that shows partisan differences does not show that outcomes would be better—more closely aligned with those of the median voter or the public generally—if the president were more strictly constrained by Congress.

CREDIBILITY

With discretion comes distrust.[17] Voters and legislators grant the executive[18] discretion, through action or inaction, and increase executive discretion during emergencies, because they believe that the benefits of doing so outweigh the risks of executive abuse.[19] By the same token, political actors will attempt to constrain the executive, or will simply fail to grant powers they otherwise would have preferred to grant, where they believe that the risks and harms of abuses outweigh any benefits in security or other goods. The fear of executive abuse arises from many sources, but the basic problem is uncertainty about the executive's motivations. The executive may, for example, be a power-maximizer, intent on using his discretion to harm political opponents and cement his political position, or that of his political party; or he may be an empire-builder, interested in expanding his turf at the expense of other institutions.

Where the executive is indeed ill-motivated in any of these ways, constraining his discretion (more than the voters would otherwise choose) may be sensible. But the executive may not be ill-motivated at all. Where the executive would in fact be a faithful agent, using his increased discretion to promote the public good according to whatever conception of the public good voters hold, then constraints on executive discretion are all cost and no benefit. Voters, legislators, and judges know that different executive officials have different motivations. Not all presidents are power-maximizers or empire-builders.[20] Of course, the executive need not be pure of heart; his devotion to the public interest may in turn be based on concern for the judgment of history. But so long as that motivation makes him a faithful agent of the principal(s), he counts as well-motivated.

The problem, however, is that the public has no simple way to know which type of executive it is dealing with. An ill-motivated executive will just mimic the statements of a well-motivated one, saying the right things and offering plausible rationales for policies that outsiders, lacking crucial information, find difficult to evaluate—policies that turn out not to be in the public interest. The ability of the ill-motivated executive to mimic the public-spirited executive's statements gives rise to the executive's dilemma of credibility: the well-motivated executive has no simple way to identify himself as such. Distrust causes voters (and the legislators they elect) to withhold discretion that they would like to grant and that the well-motivated executive would like to receive. Of course the ill-motivated executive might also want discretion; the problem is that voters who would want to give discretion (only) to the well-motivated executive may choose not to do so, because they are not sure what type he actually is. The risk that the public and legislators will fail to trust a well-motivated president is just as serious as the risk that they will trust an ill-motivated president, yet legal scholars have felled forests on the second topic while largely neglecting the first.[21] Indeed, legal scholars assume (without evidence) that the executive's interests lead it to keep too many secrets, and thus endlessly debate how it should be compelled to disclose information that should be made public. It has not occurred to them that their premise might be wrong[22]—that excessive secrecy undermines the executive by ruining its credibility and thus does not serve its interest. Scholars of presidentialism have addressed credibility problems in general and anecdotal terms,[23] but without providing social-scientific microfoundations for their analysis.

Our basic claim is that the credibility dilemma is best explored from the perspective of *executive signaling*. Without any new constitutional amendments, statutes, or legislative action, law and executive practice already contain resources to allow a well-motivated executive to send a credible signal of his motivations, committing to use increased discretion in public-spirited ways. By tying policies to institutional mechanisms that impose heavier costs on ill-motivated actors than on well-motivated ones, the well-motivated executive can credibly signal his good intentions and thus persuade voters that his policies are those that voters would want if fully informed. We focus particularly on mechanisms of *executive self-binding* that send a signal of credibility by committing presidents to actions or policies that only a well-motivated president would adopt.

Presidents always have some credibility, at least at the start of their term. People do not vote for candidates whom they do not believe, and so the winning candidate brings to the office some amount of credibility, which he may further enhance over time by keeping his promises or making predictions that are proven correct by events. Having built up capital, some presidents find it useful to engage in deception, and some have gotten away with it, at least in the short term. Prominent examples include FDR's claim during the 1940 election that he had no intention of bringing the United States into war;[24] Eisenhower's denial that U-2 spy planes overflew the Soviet Union;[25] (probably) Johnson's description of the Gulf of Tonkin incident;[26] Nixon's statements about military incursions in Cambodia;[27] (probably) Reagan's claim that he was unaware of the arms-for-hostages scheme;[28] and Clinton's denial that he had had a sexual relationship with Monica Lewinsky.[29] But deception is potentially a costly strategy, because revelation of the deception damages the president's credibility, making it more difficult for him achieve his next set of goals.

For this reason, we focus on historical cases where the president avoids deception, where in fact he makes a true or roughly true statement about circumstances that the public cannot directly evaluate, but has trouble persuading the public to believe him. In these cases, the president needs to use mechanisms that enhance his credibility or, if he cannot, finds himself unable to act. We offer examples to illustrate the credibility dilemma, to illustrate a range of solutions to the dilemma—some successful, some otherwise—and to show that the mechanisms we will propose later in this chapter have historical precedents.

FDR: The Nazi Threat

Franklin Delano Roosevelt understood the threat posed by Nazi Germany to the United States' long-term interests long before the U.S. public did. The public was preoccupied with the Great Depression and had powerful isolationist representatives in Congress. Because of popular sentiment, FDR could not commit U.S. military assistance to Britain and France even after Germany invaded France and began bombing London.[30] Marginal economic and military assistance could be given only through complicated subterfuges and was in any event of minimal value.

Even after Japan bombed Pearl Harbor and Nazi Germany declared war on the United States, FDR had to move cautiously. The public supported war, but sought war primarily with Japan, while FDR correctly believed that Germany posed a greater threat to the United States than Japan did. In FDR's view, Japan could be, and should be, dealt with after the Atlantic alliance against Germany was solidified. Thus, although FDR had popular support on one level, he needed to devise ways to ensure support for his particular war aims and strategies, whose particular justifications would always remain at least partially obscure to the public. One of FDR's tactics for generating support was to invite prominent Republicans into his cabinet. Henry Stimson was given the post of secretary of war, and Frank Knox was made the secretary of the navy.[31] Provided with inside information, they would be able to blow the whistle if U.S. war strategy departed too much from what they believed was the public interest.

Truman: Scaring the Hell out of the Country

The Soviet Union had been the United States' ally during World War II, and many people, including FDR, expected or hoped that it would cooperate with the United States after the war as well. That the Soviet Union would have aggressive rather than pacific designs only gradually dawned on U.S. elites. By 1946, skepticism about Soviet motives was widespread in the U.S. government, but the U.S. public still labored under more genial impressions fostered by wartime propaganda. To counter the growing Soviet threat, President Harry S. Truman resolved to expend U.S. treasure to rebuild the economies of France, West Germany, Britain, and other potential allies, and to bind them together in a military defense pact. The former would require a lot of money; the latter would require the stationing of U.S. troops abroad. The U.S. public, however, was traditionally isolationist, and wished to enjoy the victory and the peace.[32] How could Truman persuade the public that further sacrifice and foreign entanglement would be necessary to defend U.S. interests against a former ally?

Truman apparently could not simply explain to the public that the Soviet threat justified the Marshall Plan and North Atlantic Treaty Organization, the United States' first permanent foreign military alliance. The problem is that the public had no way to evaluate the Soviet threat. The U.S.S.R. had not actually used military force against U.S. troops, as the Japanese had five years earlier at Pearl Harbor. The Soviet Union was instead supporting communist insurgencies in Greece and Turkey, interfering in politics in Italy, violating its promise to respect democratic processes in Poland, engaging in espionage, and so forth. Experienced and perceptive observers saw a threat, but, generally speaking, the public was in no position to do so.

To enhance the credibility of his claims about the Soviet threat, Truman did two things. First, he recast the threat as an ideological challenge. Truman gave the threat an ideological dimension so that any expression of skepticism could be construed as treachery rather than honest disagreement.[33] Second, he made an alliance with a powerful Republican senator, Arthur Vandenberg, who could assure Truman that the Republicans would not object to his policies as long as he consulted them and allowed them some influence. As a former isolationist, Vandenberg's endorsement of Truman's policy of engagement must have enhanced the credibility of Truman's claims about the Soviet threat.[34]

Both of these strategies succeeded, but neither was costless. Truman's characterization of the Soviet threat as an ideological challenge may have led to the McCarthy era and suppressed public debate about foreign policy. Truman's alliance with the Republicans meant, of course, that he would have less freedom of action.[35]

Bush I versus Bush II: The Iraqi Threat

George H. W. Bush and George W. Bush both went to war with Iraq, but they faced different threats and chose different responses. George H. W. Bush sought to drive Iraqi military forces out of Kuwait. His problem was persuading the U.S. public that a U.S. military response was justified. In retrospect it might seem that he was clearly right, but at the time the common estimation was that tens of thousands of U.S. troops would be killed.[36] This was the expected cost of a military response. On the benefit side, Bush could appeal to the sanctity of sovereign borders, but the public had little sympathy for the rich Kuwaitis. The United States' real concern was that Iraq would, with Kuwait's oil fields, become wealthy and powerful enough to expand its control over the region, threaten Saudi Arabia, dominate the Persian Gulf's oil reserves, and pose a long-term threat to the Western economies and the United States' influence in the Middle East. But all of these concerns are rather abstract, and it was never obvious that the public would accept this scenario. Indeed, the congressional authorization to use military force was far from unanimous in the House of Representatives.[37]

The credibility of Bush's claims, however, was greatly aided by international support. The public support of nations with divergent interests showed that Bush's claim about the internationally destabilizing effects of Saddam Hussein's invasion was real and not imagined. Thus any claim that a U.S. military invasion was solely in Bush's partisan political interests, or in the interests of oil companies, was seriously weakened. Formal United Nations approval and the military assistance of foreign states—which was of mainly political, not military significance—further solidified Bush's credibility.[38]

Surface similarities aside, George W. Bush faced a different kind of threat. He feared that Saddam Hussein had weapons of mass destruction, which he would give or sell to terrorist groups like Al Qaeda. It was more difficult for George W. Bush to prove that Saddam had WMDs than for his father to prove that Saddam was a threat to the region, because any WMDs were hidden on Saddam's territory while the invasion of Kuwait could be observed by all. George W. Bush followed the same strategy that his father did, albeit somewhat less enthusiastically: to enlist international support in order to bolster the credibility of his claim that Saddam continued to pose a major threat to U.S. and western interests. But George W. Bush failed to persuade foreign countries that Saddam posed a great enough threat to justify a military invasion (although they largely agreed that he either had or probably had WMDs), and he did not obtain significant international support.[39] Ironically, George W. Bush, unlike his father, had strong congressional support, in part because opposition to the first war turned out to be a political liability, and the cost of the first war (unlike the second war) turned out to be low, thanks to the financial contributions of other states and the rapid defeat of the Iraqi army.

Clinton: "Wag the Dog"

Long before the attacks of September 11, 2001, the U.S. government understood that Al Qaeda posed a threat to U.S. interests. The CIA had established a bin Laden office in 1996, and the Clinton administration was trying to develop an effective counterterrorism strategy.[40] In 1998 Al Qaeda blew up U.S. embassies in Kenya and Tanzania, whereupon Clinton ordered cruise missile strikes on targets in Afghanistan and Sudan. Just three days earlier, however, Clinton had announced on national television that he had had an affair with Monica Lewinsky. Opponents charged that he ordered the strikes in order to distract the public from his domestic problems.[41] This came to be known as the "wag the dog" strategy after a movie that featured a similar subterfuge.[42]

Clinton's credibility problem was more acute than that of earlier presidents. FDR, Truman, and George H. W. Bush (as well as, later, George W. Bush) might embark on foreign adventures in order to enhance their prestige or to pay off interest groups or to distract the public from domestic problems. George W. Bush, for example, was repeatedly accused of manipulating terrorism warnings in order to improve poll results or electoral outcomes.[43] But only in Clinton's case was it necessary for him to make an important and visible decision about foreign policy in the midst of a personal scandal in which he admitted that he engaged in deceit, with the result that his ability to conduct an effective terrorism defense was hampered by doubts about his credibility.[44] An aggressive response to Al Qaeda would have to wait until after September 11, 2001.

Bush II and Obama: The Financial Crisis

When financial crisis struck in the fall of 2008, the U.S. government needed to take dramatic action, as nearly all economists agreed. But George Bush's popularity had suffered as a result of the Iraq War, the poor response to Hurricane Katrina, and many other adverse events, as had the credibility of his administration. Nonetheless, his administration was able to persuade a hostile Congress to finance an expensive bailout plan, one that left the administration with tremendous discretion to spend money and issue loans as it saw fit, including in politically motivated ways.

The key to Bush's success was most likely the alliance that Hank Paulson, the secretary of the Treasury, forged with Ben Bernanke, the Fed chief. The Fed is an independent agency with a large reserve of credibility. Paulson and Bernanke provided a united front, never disagreeing publicly; Bernanke's participation enhanced the credibility of the Bush administration's justification of a bailout, as did, no doubt, the counterpartisan valence of Bush's policy. The incoming Obama administration, though popular at the polls, saw the value of the alliance with the Fed and maintained it. However, where it has acted alone, it has had to contend with accusations that loans have been influenced by considerations of political favor.

The examples we have discussed have a common structure. A nation or group like Nazi Germany, the Soviet Union, Iraq, or Al Qaeda—or a state of affairs like a financial crisis—threatens U.S. interests. The threat is widely understood at a general level, but the public does not understand important details: why the threat exists, its magnitude, what programs will best address it. The president believes that a particular program—NSA surveillance, unlimited detention, military preparation, lending to banks—is necessary and desirable for countering the threat, and let us assume that he is correct. At the same time, the program could be misused in various ways. It could be used to enhance the power of the president at the expense of legitimate political opponents; to pay off the president's supporters at the expense of the general public; or to spark an emotional but short-lived surge of patriotism that benefits the president during an important election but does not enhance security. The president can announce the program and justify it in general terms, but he cannot design the program in such a way that its dangers to legitimate political opposition can be eliminated.[45] As a result, his claim that the program will be used only for the public good, and not to enhance his power at the expense of political opponents, or to benefit allies, may not be believed.

Consider, for example, the policy of detaining suspected members of Al Qaeda without charging them and providing them with a trial. The public understands that Al Qaeda poses a threat to national security but lacks the information necessary to evaluate the detention policy. The public does not know the magnitude of the continuing threat from Al Qaeda: it might be the case that the group has focused its attention on foreign targets, that it no longer has the capacity to launch attacks on U.S. soil, that greater international cooperation and intelligence sharing has significantly reduced the threat, and so forth. The public also does not know whether the detainees are important members of Al Qaeda or foot soldiers or unconnected to Al Qaeda; whether the dangerous detainees could be adequately incapacitated or deterred through regular criminal processes; whether valuable intelligence is obtained from the detainees, as the Bush administration claimed, or not; whether the detainees are treated well or harshly; and numerous other relevant factors. Some of the relevant variables are public, but most are not; those that are public are nonetheless extremely difficult to evaluate. Consider the ambiguity over whether the suicides at Guantánamo Bay in June 2006 were driven by despair and harsh treatment, or were the result of a calculated effort by martyr-seeking Jihadists to score a propaganda coup.[46] As a general matter, the public does not even know whether the absence of major terrorist attacks on U.S. soil since September 11, 2001, resulted from the Bush administration's detention policy, at least partly resulted from this policy, occurred for reasons entirely independent of this policy (such as, say, the military attack on Afghanistan), or occurred *despite* the detention policy, which, by alienating potential allies, perversely made a further attack more likely than it would otherwise have been.

Described in this manner, the president's credibility problem is the result of an agency relationship, where the president is an agent and the public is the principal. In agency models, the agent has the power to engage in an action that benefits or harms a principal. In a typical version of these models, the principal first hires the agent and instructs the agent to engage in high effort rather than shirk. The agent then chooses whether to engage in high effort or shirk. High effort by the agent increases the probability that the principal will receive a high payoff, but some randomness is involved, so that the link between the agent's effort and the principal's payoff is stochastic rather than certain. If the agent's behavior can be observed and proven before a court, then the simple solution is for the two parties to enter a contract requiring the agent to engage in high effort. If the agent's behavior cannot be observed, then a contract requiring high effort is unenforceable, and instead the principal and agent might enter a contract that makes the agent's compensation a function of the principal's payoff. This gives the agent an incentive to use the high level of effort, though depending on various conditions, this incentive might be weak.[47]

Less important than the details of the agency model, and its various solutions, is the way that it clarifies the basic problem. The president is the agent and the public is the principal. The public cares about national security but also cares about civil liberties and the well-being of potential targets of the war on terror; its optimal policy trades off these factors. However, the public cannot directly choose the policy; instead, it delegates that power to the government and, in particular, the president. The president knows the range of options available, their likely effects, their expected costs and benefits—thanks to the resources and expertise of the executive branch—and so, if he is well-motivated, he will choose the best measures available.

Thus a well-motivated executive, in our sense, is an executive who chooses the policies that voters would choose if they knew what the executive knows.[48] This definition does not require that the president's deeper motives be pure; for our purposes, a well-motivated president may be concerned with his historical reputation in the long run, as many presidents are. Because presidents know that in the long run most or all of their currently private information will be revealed,[49] a concern with the judgment of history pushes presidents to make the decisions that future generations, knowing what the president knows now, will approve. To be sure, the concern with historical reputation is not perfectly congruent with doing what the current generation would approve of (with full information), because different generations have different values, as in the case of civil rights. The convergence is substantial, however, compared to far more harmful motivations a president might have, such as short-term empire-building or partisan advantage. Presidents with a concern for long-run reputation may not be disinterested leaders, but they approach the ideal of faithful agency more closely than do presidents with no such concern.

We also assume that the voters' ultimate preferences are fixed, so we put aside the possibility of presidential leadership that changes bedrock public values. However, voters' derived preferences may change as their information changes, and this further blurs the significance of changing public values over time. On this view there is still scope for leadership, in the sense that a well-motivated president might choose a policy inconsistent with voters' current ill-informed preferences, but consistent with the new preferences voters will form as their information changes, perhaps as a result of the policy itself. FDR's behavior just before World War II is the model for presidential leadership in this sense.

As this discussion suggests, the well-motivated executive may or may not keep campaign promises, or adopt popular policies. All depends on circumstances—on what the public would approve, if it knew what the president knows. A public that would condemn the president's policy P might, if it knew more, approve of P. The well-motivated president will want to adopt P in such circumstances, and will then face the problem of credibly signaling to the public that he favors the policy for good reasons that he cannot directly convey. Furthermore, we assume that the well-motivated executive will collect an optimal amount of information—up to the point where the marginal benefits of further information-gathering equal the marginal costs. This does not mean that the well-motivated executive always gets the facts right; he may turn out to be wrong. But it does mean that greater accuracy would not have been cost-justified.

Against this benchmark of faithful agency, the problem is that a given president's motivations might or might not be faithful, and the public knows this. The public fears that, for various reasons, the president might choose policies that diverge from the public's optimal policies. These include the following:

1. The president cares more about national security (or more about civil liberties, but we will, for simplicity, assume the former) than the public does. His "preferences" are different from those of the public.

2. The president cares very little about national security and civil liberties; he mainly cares about maximizing his political power and, more broadly, political success—success for himself, his party, or his chosen successor. With a view to political power and success, the president might maximize the probability of electoral success by favoring particular interest groups, voting blocs, or institutions at the expense of the public, or by adopting policies that are popular in the short term, as far as the next election cycle, but that are harmful in the long term, along with rhetoric that confuses and misleads.

The public knows that the president might have these or other harmful motivations, so when the president claims, for example, that a detention policy is essential to the war on terror but at the same time is not excessively harsh given its benefits, the public simply does not know whether to believe him.

Crucially, the risk that the public will fail to trust a well-motivated president is just as serious as the risk that it will trust an ill-motivated one. Imagine that a well-motivated president chooses the optimal policies. No terrorist attack occurs before the next election, but the public does not know whether this is because the president chose the optimal policies, the president chose bad policies and was merely lucky (as the terrorists for internal reasons focused on foreign targets), or the president chose effective but excessively harsh policies. In the election, the public therefore has no particular reason to vote for this president and could easily vote him out of office and replace him with a worse president. A president who cares about electoral success might therefore not choose the optimal policies, and even a well-motivated president might be reluctant to do so because of the risk that the uncomprehending public will replace him with an ill-motivated president. Presidents need public support even when they do not face reelection; they need the public to prod Congress to provide the president with funds for his programs and statutory authorization when necessary. A well-motivated president will abandon optimal policies if he cannot persuade the public that they are warranted.

As we noted earlier, legal scholars rarely note the problem of executive credibility, preferring to dwell on the problem of aggrandizement by ill-motivated presidents. Ironically, this assumption that presidents seek to maximize power has obscured one of the greatest constraints on aggrandizement, namely, the president's own interest in maintaining his credibility. Neither a well-motivated nor ill-motivated president can accomplish his goals if the public does not trust him.[50] This concern with reputation may put a far greater check on the president's actions than do the reactions of the other branches.

SOLUTIONS

The literature on agency models and optimal contracting provides clues for solving the problem of executive credibility. As we saw above, this literature gives two basic pieces of advice.[51] The first piece of advice is to *align preferences*. An employer will do better if her employees obtain utility from doing whatever actions benefit the employer. Suppose, for example, an employer seeks to hire someone to build furniture in a factory. The pay is good enough to attract job candidates who do not enjoy building furniture, but clearly the employer does better by hiring people who like working with their hands, and take pleasure in constructing a high-quality product, than by hiring people who do not like working with their hands. We say that the first type of person has a preference for building high-quality furniture; this person is less likely to shirk than the other type of person.

In order to align preferences, employers can use various types of *screening mechanisms* or *selection mechanisms* that separate the good types and the bad types.[52] An old idea is that job candidates who completed a training program—here, in carpentry—are more likely good types than job candidates who did not complete such a program. The reason is not that the training program improves skills, though it might; but that a person who enjoys carpentry is more likely to enter and complete such a program than a person who does not—the program, in terms of time and effort, is less burdensome for the former type of person. The employer could use other mechanisms as well, of course. She could ask for evidence that the job candidate pursues woodworking as a hobby in his free time, or, simply, that he has held other jobs in similar factories, or jobs that involve carpentry or furniture construction. Another important screening mechanism is to compensate employees partly through in-kind components or earmarked funds that are worth more to good types than to bad types. In university settings, academic salaries are partly composed of research budgets that cannot be spent on personal goods and that are worth more to good types (researchers) than to bad types (shirkers).[53]

The second piece of advice is to *reward and sanction*. This is not as simple as giving the employee a bonus if she constructs good furniture and firing her if she does not; recall that we assume that the employer does not directly observe the quality of the agent's action. Consider the following version of our example. The employees both design and construct furniture; "high-quality" furniture is both made well and pleasing to the public, so that it sells well. The employer cannot tell by looking at a piece of furniture whether it is of high quality because she does not know the tastes of the public. An employee who uses a high level of effort is more likely to produce furniture that sells well, but an employee can in good faith misestimate the public taste and produce furniture that sells poorly. Similarly, an employee who uses a low level of effort is less likely to produce furniture that sells well but nonetheless may succeed at times. Since the employer cannot observe the quality of the furniture, she cannot make the wage a function of its quality; if she pays a flat wage, then the employee does not have an incentive to engage in a high level of effort, because that involves more personal cost without producing any reward.

The main solution is to make the employee's pay a function, in part, of the quantity of the sales of the goods that the employee produces. The quantity of sales, unlike the quality of the furniture, is observable. If the pay is properly determined, then the employer will engage in a high level of effort because the expected gains from high sales exceed the cost of high effort. How closely pay should be correlated with sales depends on how risk-averse the employee is, and it may be necessary, for ordinary people who are generally risk-averse, to pay them at least a little even if sales are low, and somewhat more if sales are high.

An enormous literature develops and qualifies these results, and we will refer to relevant parts of it later as necessary rather than try to summarize it here.[54] For now, we want to briefly point out the relevance of these solutions to our problem of executive credibility.

The preference-alignment solution has clear applicability to the problem of executive credibility. To be sure, elections and other democratic institutions help ensure that the president's preferences are not too distant from those of the public, but they are clearly not sufficient to solve the executive credibility problem. Elections will never create perfect preference alignment, for well-known reasons, and in any event the well-motivated executive will do what the public would want were it fully informed, not what maximizes the chances of electoral success in the short run. Furthermore, we do not consider credibility-generating mechanisms that would require new constitutional or statutory provisions; of course the president has little or no power to redesign electoral rules in order to enhance his credibility. We will instead focus on how the president might use the existing electoral system to enhance his credibility in indirect ways—by appointing subordinates, advisors, and commission members, and by supporting certain types of candidacies for electoral office.

The reward-and-sanction solution also is applicable to the problem of executive credibility, but we think it is of less importance and will not address it in any detail. The problem that most concerns us—threats to national security—typically does not produce a clear outcome while the president is still in office. As noted above, Bush's policies in the war on terror might have been optimal, insufficient, or excessive; we will not know for many years, to whatever extent the fog of history will allow us to know at all. And the public cannot enter a contract with the president that provides that the president will receive a bonus if national security is enhanced and will be sanctioned if it is not enhanced. Consequently, Bush could not enter a contract with the public that rewarded him if his policies were good and punished him if they were bad.

However, some signaling mechanisms have a reward-or-sanction component. A good job applicant can distinguish herself from a bad job applicant by agreeing to a compensation scheme that good types value and bad types disvalue. For example, if a good type discounts future payoffs less than bad types, then good types will accept deferred compensation (such as pension contributions) that bad types reject.[55] Similarly, a well-motivated president can distinguish himself from an ill-motivated president by binding himself to a policy position that an ill-motivated president would reject. However, a president, unlike an employee, cannot bind himself by a judicially enforceable contract; therefore, this mechanism can work only if the president can engage in self-binding through informal means, as we will discuss below.

Note that either a well-motivated actor or an ill-motivated actor might use strategic devices to enhance her credibility. A bad actor might, for example, take actions to enhance the credibility of his threats. In a standard illustration, the "chicken" game occurs when two drivers race toward each other, and the loser is the one who swerves to avoid death. In that game, each driver is threatening to drive straight, and the winner will be the one who can make his threat credible, because the other driver will then know that the only choice is to swerve or die. Credibility is a valuable adjunct to many different motivations, not just to socially beneficial ones.

But this is a different type of credibility problem from the one we are interested in. In the class of problems we address, the problem that faces the well-motivated actor is that others cannot distinguish or sort him at a glance from ill-motivated actors. "Bad types" can mimic "good types" through low-cost imitation and by saying all the right things. The good type needs some device whereby he can credibly signal that he is a good type. The solution, in general, is for the good type to undertake an action that imposes greater costs on bad types than on good types. If third parties understand the cost structure of the action, then it separates the two types, because the bad type's strategy of costlessly imitating the good type no longer works. In employment screening, for example, both the lazy worker and the hard worker will claim to work hard. The employer might prefer candidates with good references, or an advanced degree, on the theory that obtaining those things will be easier for the good type than the bad type.

Let us provide a little more structure to our analysis before describing our preferred mechanisms. Suppose that a president must choose a policy that will affect national security and civil liberties; this might include asking Congress to authorize him to engage in conduct like wiretapping or the use of military force. He makes this choice at the start of his first term, and the actual effect of his choice—on national security and civil liberties—will not be revealed to the public until after the election. Terrorist attacks during the first term do not necessarily prove that he chose the wrong policies; nor does the absence of terrorist attacks during the first term prove that he chose the right policies. Only later will it become clear whether the president chose the optimal policies, perhaps many decades later. Thus, the public must vote for or against the president on the basis of the policy choice itself, not on the basis of its effect on their well-being. For expository convenience, we will assume that the president actually does make the optimal policy choice and that his problem is one of convincing the public that he has done so. Presidents who, for whatever reason, knowingly choose policies that the public would reject (if fully informed) obviously do not want to convince the public that this is what they are doing.

Our focus, then, is how the president who chooses the optimal policy, given the information available to him and the relevant institutional constraints, might use some additional mechanism to enhance the credibility of his claim that he chose the best policy.

EXECUTIVE SIGNALING: LAW AND MECHANISMS

We suggest that the executive's credibility problem can be solved by second-order mechanisms of *executive signaling*. In the general case, well-motivated executives send credible signals by taking actions that are more costly for ill-motivated actors than for well-motivated ones, thus distinguishing themselves from their ill-motivated mimics. Among the specific mechanisms we discuss, an important subset involve *executive self-binding*, whereby executives commit themselves to a course of action that would impose higher costs on ill-motivated actors. Commitments themselves have value as signals of benign motivations.

This departs from the usual approach in legal scholarship. Legal theory has often discussed self-binding by "government" or government officials. In constitutional theory, it is often suggested that constitutions represent an attempt by "the people" to bind "themselves" against their own future decision-making pathologies, or relatedly that constitutional prohibitions represent mechanisms by which governments commit themselves not to expropriate investments or to exploit their populations.[56] Whether or not this picture is coherent,[57] it is not the question we examine here, although some of the relevant considerations are similar.[58] We are not concerned with binding the president so that he cannot abuse his powers, but with how he might bind himself or take other actions that enhance his credibility, so that he can generate support from the public.

Furthermore, our question is subconstitutional; it is whether a well-motivated executive, acting within an established set of constitutional and statutory rules, can use signaling to generate public trust. Accordingly we proceed by assuming that no constitutional amendments or new statutes will be enacted. Within these constraints, what can a well-motivated executive do to bootstrap himself to credibility? The problem for the well-motivated executive is to credibly signal his benign motivations; in general, the solution is to engage in actions that are less costly for good types than for bad types.

We begin with some relevant law; then examine a set of possible mechanisms, emphasizing both the conditions under which they might succeed and the conditions under which they might not; and then examine the costs of credibility.

Law and Self-Binding

Many of our mechanisms are unproblematic from a legal perspective, as they involve presidential actions that are clearly lawful. But a few raise legal questions; in particular, those that involve self-binding.[59] Can a president bind himself to respect particular first-order policies? With qualifications, the answer is "yes, at least to the same extent that a legislature can." Formally, a duly promulgated executive rule or order binds even the executive unless and until it is validly abrogated, thereby establishing a new legal status quo.[60] The legal authority to establish a new status quo allows a president to create inertia or political constraints that will affect his own future choices. In a practical sense, presidents, like legislatures, have great de facto power to adopt policies that shape the legal landscape for the future. A president might commit himself to a long-term project of defense procurement or infrastructure or foreign policy, narrowing his own future choices and generating new political coalitions that will act to defend the new rules or policies.

More schematically, we may speak of formal and informal means of self-binding:

1. The president might use formal means to bind himself. This is possible in the sense that an executive order, if otherwise valid, legally binds the president while it is in effect and may be enforced by the courts. It is not possible in the sense that the president can always repeal the executive order if he can bear the political and reputational costs of doing so.

2. The president might use informal means to bind himself. This is not only possible but frequent and important. Issuing an executive rule providing for the appointment of special prosecutors, as Nixon did, is not a formal self-binding.[61] However, there may be political costs to repealing the order. This effect does not depend on the courts' willingness to enforce the order, even against Nixon himself. Court enforcement makes the order legally binding while it is in place, but only political and reputational enforcement can protect it from repeal. Just as a dessert addict might announce to his friends that he is going on a no-dessert diet in order to raise the reputational costs of backsliding and thus commit himself, so too the repeal of an executive order may be seen as a breach of faith even if no other institution ever enforces it.

In what follows, we will invoke both formal and informal mechanisms. For our purposes, the distinction between the authority to engage in de jure self-binding (legally limited and well-defined) and the power to engage in de facto self-binding (broad and amorphous) is secondary. So long as policies are deliberately chosen with a view to generating credibility, and do so by constraining the president's own future choices in ways that impose greater costs on ill-motivated presidents than on well-motivated ones, it does not matter whether the constraint is formal or informal.

Mechanisms

What signaling mechanisms might a well-motivated executive adopt to credibly assure voters, legislators and judges that his policies rest on judgments about the public interest, rather than on power-maximization, partisanship or other nefarious motives?

Intrabranch separation of powers

In an interesting treatment of related problems, Neal Katyal suggests that the failure of the Madisonian system counsels "internal separation of powers" within the executive branch.[62] Abdication by Congress means that there are few effective checks on executive power; second-best substitutes are necessary. Katyal proposes some mechanisms that would be adopted by Congress, such as oversight hearings by the minority party, but his most creative proposals are for arrangements internal to the executive branch, such as redundancy and competition among agencies, stronger civil-service protections, and internal adjudication of executive controversies by insulated "executive" decision-makers who resemble judges in many ways.[63] Following Katyal's lead, Bruce Ackerman argues for an "executive tribunal" of lawyers who will serve as "judges for the executive branch" and thereby "ensure the integrity of the rule of law."[64]

Katyal's argument is relevant because the mechanisms he discusses might be understood as signaling devices, but his overall approach is conceptually flawed, on two grounds. First, the assumption that second-best constraints on the executive should reproduce the Madisonian separation of powers *within* the executive branch is never defended. The idea seems to be that this is as close as we can get to the first-best, while holding constant everything else in our constitutional order. But the general theory of second-best states that approaching as closely as possible to the first-best will not necessarily be the preferred strategy;[65] the best approach may be to adjust matters on other margins as well, in potentially unpredictable ways. If the Madisonian system has failed in the ways Katyal suggests, the best compensating adjustment might be, for all we know, to switch to a parliamentary system. (We assume that no large-scale changes of this sort are possible, whereas Katyal seemingly assumes that they are, or at least does not make clear his assumptions in this regard.) Overall, Katyal's view has a kind of fractal quality—each branch should reproduce within itself the very same separation-of-powers structure that also describes the whole system—but it is not explained why the constitutional order should be fractal.

Second, Katyal's proposals for internal separation of powers are self-defeating: the motivations that Katyal ascribes to the executive are inconsistent with the executive adopting or respecting the prescriptions Katyal recommends.[66] Katyal never quite says so explicitly, but he clearly envisions the executive as a power-maximizing actor, in the sense that the president seeks to remove all constraints on his current choices.[67] Such an executive would not adopt or enforce the internal separation of powers to check himself. This is the problem with the frequently heard claim that the Justice Department's Office of Legal Counsel should exert a greater check on the executive than it has in the past (notably, when it endorsed controversial interrogation practices and warrantless wiretapping during the Bush administration). If it did, nothing would prevent the executive from marginalizing it. Indeed, presidents have established a competing office in the White House, which is more closely subject to presidential control than the Justice Department is. The White House Counsel's Office can provide advice and, if need be, legal justification, should the Office of Legal Counsel ever prove obstreperous.

Executive signaling is not, even in principle, a solution to the lack of constraints on a power-maximizing executive in the sense Katyal implicitly intends. Although an ill-motivated executive might bind himself to enhance his strategic credibility, as explained above, he would not do so in order to restore the balance of powers. Nor is it possible, given Katyal's premise of legislative passivity or abdication, that Congress would force the internal separation of powers on the executive. In what follows, we limit ourselves to proposals that are consistent with the motivations, beliefs, and political opportunities that we ascribe to the well-motivated executive, to whom the proposals are addressed. This limitation ensures that the proposals are not self-defeating, whatever their costs.

The contrast here must not be drawn too simply. A well-motivated executive, in our sense, might well attempt to increase his power. The very point of demonstrating credibility is to encourage voters and legislators to increase the discretionary authority of the executive, where all will be made better off by doing so. Scholars such as Katyal who implicitly distrust the executive, however, do not subscribe to this picture of executive motivations. Rather, they see the executive as an unfaithful agent of the voters; the executive attempts to maximize his power even where fully-informed voters would prefer otherwise. An actor of that sort will have no incentive to adopt proposals intended to constrain that sort of actor.

Independent commissions

We now turn to some conceptually coherent mechanisms of executive signaling. Somewhat analogously to Katyal's idea of the internal separation of powers, a well-motivated executive might establish independent commissions to review policy decisions, either before or after the fact. Presidents do this routinely, especially after a policy has had disastrous outcomes, but sometimes beforehand as well. Independent commissions are typically blue-ribbon and bipartisan.[68]

We add to this familiar process the idea that the president might gain credibility by publicly committing or binding himself to give the commission authority on some dimension. The president might publicly promise to follow the recommendations of such a commission, to allow the commission to exercise de facto veto power over a policy decision before it is made, or might promise before the policy is chosen that the commission will be given power to review its success after the fact. To be sure, there will always be some wiggle room in the terms of the promise, but that is true of almost all commitments, which raise the costs of wiggling out even if they do not completely prevent it.

Consider whether George W. Bush's credibility would have been enhanced had he appointed a blue-ribbon commission to examine the evidence for weapons of mass destruction in Iraq *before* the 2003 invasion, and publicly promised not to invade unless the commission found substantial evidence of their existence. Bush would have retained his preexisting legal authority to order the invasion even if the commission found the evidence inadequate, but the political costs of doing so would have been large. Knowing this, and knowing that Bush shared that knowledge, the public could have inferred that Bush's professed motive—elimination of weapons of mass destruction—was also his real motive. Public promises that inflict reputational costs on badly motivated behavior help the well-motivated executive to credibly distinguish himself from the ill-motivated one.

The more common version of this tactic is to appoint commissions after the relevant event, as George W. Bush did to investigate the faulty reports by intelligence agencies that Iraq possessed weapons of mass destruction.[69] If the president appoints after-the-fact commissions, the commissions can enhance his credibility for the next event—by showing that he will be willing, after *that* event, to subject his statements to scrutiny by public experts. Here, however, the demonstration of credibility is weaker, because there is no commitment to appoint any after-the-fact commissions in the future—merely a plausible inference that the president's future behavior will track his past behavior.

Independent agencies

Similarly, as we saw in our example of the financial crisis, the executive may be able to form alliances of convenience with independent agencies that have a reputation for expertise and integrity (or political goals different from those of the executive). It is crucial to the argument that the executive retains the option not to cooperate with the agency; otherwise, we are back to the idea of internal separation of powers. During the financial crisis, the Bush and Obama administrations chose to cooperate with the Fed even though they could (probably) have acted alone, using the Treasury's statutory authority plus possibly residual executive authority. Obama even reappointed Ben Bernanke, initially a Bush appointee, to chair the Fed.

Bipartisan appointments

In examples of the sort just mentioned, the signaling arises from public position-taking. The well-motivated executive might produce similar effects through appointments to office.[70] A number of statutes require partisan balance on multimember commissions; although these statutes are outside the scope of our discussion, we note that presidents might approve them because they allow the president to commit to a policy that legislators favor, thus encouraging legislators to increase the scope of the delegation in the first place.[71] For similar reasons, presidents may consent to restrictions on the removal of agency officials, because the restriction enables the president to commit to giving the agency some autonomy from the president's preferences.[72]

Similar mechanisms can work even where no statutes are in the picture. As previously mentioned, during World War II, FDR appointed Republicans to important cabinet positions, making Stimson his secretary of war. Clinton appointed William Cohen, a moderate Republican, as secretary of defense in order to shore up his credibility on security issues. Obama retained Robert Gates, a moderate Republican holdover from the Bush administration, as his secretary of defense and appointed Ray LaHood, a Republican congressman, as secretary of transportation. Bipartisanship of this sort might improve the deliberation that precedes decisions, by impeding various forms of herding, cascades, and groupthink;[73] however, we focus on its credibility-generating effects. By (1) expanding the circle of those who share the president's privileged access to information, (2) ensuring that policy is partly controlled by officials with preferences that differ from the president's, and (3) inviting a potential whistleblower into the tent, bipartisanship helps to dispel the suspicion that policy decisions rest on partisan motives or extreme preferences, which in turn encourages broader delegations of discretion from the public and Congress.

A commitment to bipartisanship is only one way in which appointments can generate credibility. Presidents might simply appoint a person with a reputation for integrity, as when President Nixon appointed Archibald Cox as special prosecutor (although plausibly Nixon did so because he was forced to do so by political constraints, rather than as a tactic for generating credibility). A person with well-known preferences on a particular issue, even if not of the other party or widely respected for impartiality, can serve as a credible whistleblower on that issue. Thus presidents routinely award cabinet posts to leaders of subsets of the president's own party, leaders whose preferences are known to diverge from the president's on the subject; one point of this behavior is to credibly assure the relevant interest groups that the president will not deviate (too far) from their preferences.

The Independent Counsel Statute institutionalized the special prosecutor and strengthened it. But the statute proved unpopular and was allowed to lapse in 1999.[74] This experience raises two interesting questions. First, why have presidents confined themselves to appointing lawyers to investigate allegations of wrongdoing; why have they not appointed, say, independent policy experts to investigate allegations of policy failure? Second, why did the Independent Counsel Statute fail? Briefly, the statute failed because it was too difficult to control the behavior of the prosecutor, who was not given any incentive to keep his investigation within reasonable bounds.[75] Policy investigators would be even less constrained since they would not be confined by the law, and at the same time, without legal powers they would probably be ignored on partisan grounds. A commission composed of members with diverse viewpoints is harder to ignore, if the members agree with each other.

More generally, the decision by presidents to bring into their administrations members of other parties, or persons with a reputation for bipartisanship and integrity, illustrates the formation of *domestic coalitions of the willing*. Presidents can informally bargain around the formal separation of powers[76] by employing subsets of Congress, or of the opposing party, to generate credibility while maintaining a measure of institutional control. FDR was willing to appoint Knox and Stimson, but not to give the Republicans in Congress a veto. Truman was willing to ally with Arthur Vandenberg but not with all the Republicans; Clinton was willing to appoint William Cohen but not Newt Gingrich. George W. Bush likewise made a gesture toward credibility by briefing members of the Senate Intelligence Committee—including Democrats—on the administration's secret surveillance programs, which provided a useful talking point when the existence of the programs was revealed to the public.

Counterpartisanship

Related to bipartisanship is what might be called counterpartisanship: presidents have greater credibility when they choose policies that cut against the grain of their party's platform or their own presumed preferences.[77] Only Nixon could go to China, and only Clinton could engineer welfare reform. Voters and publics rationally employ a political heuristic: the relevant policy, which voters are incapable of directly assessing, must be highly beneficial if it is chosen by a president who is predisposed against it by convictions or partisan loyalty.[78] Accordingly, those who wish to move U.S. terrorism policy toward greater security at the price of less liberty might do well to support the election of a Democrat.[79] Obama has maintained the major features of Bush's counterterror approach, involving reliance on military tools such as indefinite detention, military commissions, and domestic surveillance, albeit not torture, and criticism has been muted. But when he sought to close Guantánamo Bay and try suspected terrorists in civilian courts, he ran into a storm of political opposition. Because Obama is on the left, and is therefore assumed to give heavy weight to civil liberties, he can credibly take tough measures against terrorists but cannot credibly offer them greater protections against abuse. By the same logic, George W. Bush was widely suspected of nefarious motives when he rounded up alleged enemy combatants, but not when he created a massive prescription drug benefit.

Counterpartisanship can powerfully enhance the president's credibility, but it depends heavily on a lucky alignment of political stars. A peace-loving president has credibility when he declares a military emergency but not when he appeases; a belligerent president has credibility when he offers peace but not when he advocates military solutions. A lucky nation has a well-motivated president with a belligerent reputation when international tensions diminish (Ronald Reagan) and a president with a pacific reputation when they grow (Abraham Lincoln, who opposed the Mexican War). But a nation is not always lucky.

Transparency

The well-motivated executive might commit to transparency, as a way to reduce the costs to outsiders of monitoring his actions.[80] FDR's strategy of inviting potential whistleblowers from the opposite party into government is a special case of this; the implicit threat is that the whistleblower will make public any evidence of partisan motivations. The more ambitious case involves actually exposing the executive's decision-making processes to observation. To the extent that an ill-motivated executive cannot publicly acknowledge his motivations or publicly instruct subordinates to take them into account in decision making, transparency will exclude those motivations from the decision-making process. The public will know that only a well-motivated executive would promise transparency in the first place, and the public can therefore draw an inference as to credibility.

Credibility is especially enhanced when transparency is effected through journalists with reputations for integrity or with political preferences opposite to those of the president. Thus George W. Bush gave Bob Woodward unprecedented access to White House decision making, and perhaps even to classified intelligence,[81] with the expectation that the material would be published. This sort of disclosure to journalists is not real-time transparency—no one expects meetings of the National Security Council to appear on C-SPAN—but the anticipation of future disclosure can have a disciplining effect in the present. By inviting this disciplining effect, the administration engages in signaling in the present through (the promise of) future transparency.

There are complex trade-offs here, because transparency can have a range of harmful effects. As far as process is concerned, decision makers under public scrutiny may posture for the audience, may freeze their views or positions prematurely, and may hesitate to offer proposals or reasons for which they can later be blamed if things go wrong.[82] As for substance, transparency can frustrate the achievement of programmatic goals or policy goals themselves. Where security policy is at stake, secrecy is sometimes necessary to surprise enemies or to keep them guessing. Finally, one must take account of the incentives of the actors who expose the facts—especially journalists who might reward presidents who give them access by portraying their decision making in a favorable light.[83]

We will take up the costs of credibility shortly. In general, however, the existence of costs does not mean that the credibility-generating mechanisms are useless. Quite the contrary: where the executive uses such mechanisms, voters and legislators can draw an inference that the executive is well-motivated, precisely because the existence of costs would have given an ill-motivated executive an excuse not to use those mechanisms.

Multilateralism

Another credibility-generating mechanism for the executive is to enter into alliances or international institutions that subject foreign policy decisions to multilateral oversight. Because the information gap between voters and legislators, on the one hand, and the executive, on the other, is especially wide in foreign affairs, there is also wide scope for suspicion and conspiracy theories. If the president undertakes a unilateral foreign policy, some sectors of the domestic public will be suspicious of his motives. All recent presidents have faced this problem. In the case of George W. Bush, as we suggested, many have questioned whether the invasion of Iraq was undertaken to eliminate weapons of mass destruction, or to protect human rights, or instead to safeguard the oil supply, or because the president has (it is alleged) always wanted to invade Iraq. In the case of Bill Clinton, some said that the cruise missile attack on Osama bin Laden's training camp in Afghanistan was a "wag the dog" tactic intended to distract attention from Clinton's impeachment.

A public commitment to multilateralism can close or narrow the credibility gap. Suppose that a group of nations have common interests on one dimension—say, security from terrorism or from proliferation of nuclear weapons—but disparate interests on other dimensions—say, conflicting commercial or political interests. Multilateralism can be understood as a policy that in effect requires a supermajority vote, or even unanimity, among the group to license intervention. The supermajority requirement ensures that only interventions promoting the security interest common to the group will be approved, while interventions that promote some political agenda not shared by the requisite supermajority will be rejected. Knowing that multilateralism raises the threshold of action, domestic audiences can infer that interventions that gain multilateral approval do not rest on disreputable motives.

It follows that multilateralism can be either formal or informal. Action by the United Nations Security Council can be taken only under formal voting rules that require unanimity among its five permanent members and a supermajority of all its members. Informally, in the face of increasing tensions with Iran, George W. Bush's policy involved extensive multilateral consultations and a quasi commitment not to intervene unilaterally. Knowing that his credibility was thin after Iraq, Bush presumably adopted this course in part to reassure domestic audiences that there is no nefarious motive behind an intervention, should one occur.

It also follows that multilateralism and bipartisan congressional authorization may be substitutes, in terms of generating credibility. In both cases the public knows that the cooperators—partisan opponents or other nations, as the case may be—are unlikely to share any secret agenda the president may have. The substitution is only partial, however; the Madisonian emphasis on bipartisan authorization has proven insufficient. The interests of parties within Congress diverge less than do the interests of different nations, which makes the credibility gain greater under multilateralism. In eras of unified government, the ability of the president's party to put a policy through Congress without the cooperation of the other party (ignoring the threat of a Senate filibuster, a weapon that the minority party often hesitates to wield) often undermines the policy's credibility even if members of the minority go along; after all, the minority members may be going along precisely because they anticipate that opposition is fruitless, in which case no inference about the policy's merits should be drawn from their approval. Moreover, even a well-motivated president may prefer, all else equal, to generate credibility through mechanisms that do not involve Congress, if concerned about delay, leaks, or obstruction by small legislative minorities. Thus Truman relied on a resolution of the United Nations Security Council rather than congressional authorization to prosecute the Korean War.[84]

The costs of multilateralism are straightforward. Multilateralism increases the costs of reaching decisions, because a larger group must coordinate its actions, and increases the risks of false negatives—failure to undertake justified interventions. A president who declines to bind himself through multilateralism may thus be either ill-motivated and desirous of pursuing an agenda not based on genuine security goals, or well-motivated and worried about the genuine costs of multilateralism. As usual, however, the credibility-generating inference holds asymmetrically: precisely because an ill-motivated president may use the costs of multilateralism as a plausible pretext, a president who does pursue multilateralism is more likely to be well-motivated.

Strict liability

For completeness, we mention that the well-motivated executive might in principle subject himself to strict liability for actions or outcomes that only an ill-motivated executive would undertake. Consider the controversy surrounding George W. Bush's telecommunications surveillance program, which the president claimed covered only communications in which one of the parties was overseas; domestic-to-domestic calls were excluded.[85] There was widespread suspicion that this claim was false.[86] In one poll, 26 percent of respondents believed that the National Security Agency listened to their calls.[87] The credibility gap arose because it is difficult in the extreme to know what exactly the NSA does, and what the costs and benefits of the alternatives are.

Here the credibility gap might be narrowed by creating a cause of action, for damages, on behalf of anyone who can show that domestic-to-domestic calls were examined.[88] Liability would be strict, because a negligence rule—did the agency exert reasonable efforts to avoid examining the communication?—requires too much information for judges, jurors, and voters to evaluate, and would just reproduce the monitoring problems that gave rise to the credibility gap in the first place. Strict liability, by contrast, would require a much narrower factual inquiry. Crucially, a commitment to strict liability would only be made by an executive who intended to minimize the incidence of (even unintentional and non-negligent) surveillance of purely domestic communications.

However, there are legal and practical problems here, perhaps insuperable ones. Legally, it is hardly clear that the president could, on his own authority, create a cause of action against himself or his agents to be brought in federal court. It is well within presidential authority to create executive commissions for hearing claims against the United States, for disbursing funds under benefit programs, and so on; but the problem here is that there might be no pot of money from which to fund damages. The so-called Judgment Fund, out of which damages against the executive are usually paid, is restricted to statutorily specified lawsuits. For this reason, statutory authorization for the president to create the strict liability cause of action would probably be necessary, as we discuss shortly.[89] Practically, it is unclear whether government agents can be forced to "internalize costs" through money damages in the way that private parties can, at least if the Treasury is paying those damages.[90] And if it is, voters may not perceive the connection between governmental action and subsequent payouts in any event.

The news conference

Presidents use news conferences to demonstrate their mastery of the details of policy. Many successful presidents, like FDR, conducted numerous such conferences.[91] Ill-motivated presidents will not care about policy if their interest is just holding power for its own sake; thus, they would regard news conferences as burdensome and risky chores. The problem is that a well-motivated president does not necessarily care about details of policy, as opposed to its broad direction, and journalists might benefit by tripping up a president in order to score points. Reagan, for example, did not care about policy details, but is generally regarded as a successful president.[92] To make Reagan look good, his handlers devoted considerable resources trying to prepare him for news conferences, resources that might have been better used in other ways.[93]

"Precommitment politics."

We have been surveying mechanisms that the well-motivated executive can employ once in office. However, in every case the analysis can be driven back one stage to the electoral campaign for executive office. During electoral campaigns, candidates for the presidency take public positions that partially commit them to subsequent policies, by raising the reputational costs of subsequent policy changes.[94] Under current law, campaign promises are very difficult to enforce in the courts.[95] But even without legal enforcement, position-taking helps to separate the well-motivated from the ill-motivated candidate, because the costs to the former of making promises of this sort are higher. To be sure, many such promises are vacuous, meaning that voters will not sanction a president who violates them, but some turn out to have real force, as the first President Bush discovered when he broke his clear pledge not to raise taxes.

The possibility of statutory commitments

So far we have proceeded on the austere assumption that no constitutional or statutory changes are allowed. We have confined ourselves to credibility-generating mechanisms that arise by executive signaling—commitments that the executive could initiate by legal order or by public position-taking, without the permission of other institutions.

However, this restriction may stack the deck too heavily against the solutions we suggest. A central example of the credibility problem, after all, arises when voters and legislators want to enact statutes transferring further discretion to a well-motivated executive, but are not sure that that is the sort of executive they are dealing with. In such cases, there is no reason to exclude the possibility that the executive might ask Congress to provide him with signaling mechanisms that he would otherwise lack. In the surveillance example, Congress was considering amendments to relevant statutes.[96] It is possible to imagine a well-motivated executive proposing that Congress explicitly ratify his authority to examine overseas communications, while also proposing—as a demonstration of credibility—that the ratification be bundled with a statutory cause of action imposing strict liability for prohibited forms of surveillance.

THE COSTS OF CREDIBILITY

The mechanisms we have discussed generate credibility, which is a benefit for voters and legislators who would like to increase the discretion of the well-motivated executive. What of the cost side? In each case, there are costs to generating credibility, although the character and magnitude of the costs differ across mechanisms.

Signaling is by definition costly; the presence of a cost is what distinguishes ill-motivated mimics, who are unwilling to incur the cost, from good types. In this context, the inherent costliness of signaling means that the president must use time or resources to establish credibility with the public when, if voters were perfectly informed, that time and those resources could be expended directly on determining and implementing policy. But costs can be reflected in more subtle ways as well. Many of these mechanisms rely on the participation of agents who themselves may be ill-motivated. Whistleblowers can cry wolf when there is no partisanship, merely substantive disagreement; journalists might offer not transparency but translucency, images distorted by their own biases and strategies. Miscellaneous costs arise in other ways as well. Multilateralism raises decision costs; transparency can harm deliberation; and so on.[97]

Often the basic trade-off facing presidents is that *credibility is gained at the expense of control*. Mechanisms such as creating independent commissions and pursuing multilateralism illustrate that to gain credibility, presidents must surrender part of their control over policy choices, partially constraining executive discretion in the present in return for more trust, which will then translate into more discretion in the future. The loss of control is a cost, even to the well-motivated executive. To be sure, the well-motivated executive may be more willing than the ill-motivated one to trade some loss of present control for increased future discretion, if the ill-motivated executive tends to be myopic or to discount the future more heavily; but it is not clear that that is so—many terrifying dictators have been quite farsighted—and in any event everything depends upon the particular trade-off inherent in the particular case.

Presidents are sometimes willing to pay the costs of credibility; often they are not.[98] However, there is no general reason to assume that they will always do so when it is optimal to do so, and not otherwise. Presidents, like others, make mistakes, or overlook useful political tactics, or fail to choose the best means to serve their ends; that is what makes advice about policy mechanisms potentially useful. We do not urge that presidents should use credibility-generating mechanisms in every case, nor do we claim that the mechanisms we have offered are good for all times and places. Rather we have tried to indicate, at least in a general way, the conditions under which the benefits will outweigh the costs, from the standpoint of the well-motivated executive and of the voters and legislators who wish to confer authority upon him.

A general objection to our approach might emphasize the cost side, as follows. Whether the benefits outweigh the costs under particular circumstances is very hard for voters and legislators to judge. The ill-motivated executive can always claim that he has not adopted the credibility-generating mechanisms because of these costs; in that respect he can mimic a well-motivated executive who does genuinely believe that the costs exceed the benefits in the case at hand. Because of this second-order information gap, voters and legislators will still be unable to distinguish the good executive from the bad.

This critique is overblown. For one thing, the very availability of these mechanisms, once generally known, indirectly provides the public with information even if they are not used, and indeed because they are not used. The failure to invite members of the other political party, or foreign nations, to participate in a crucial decision of foreign policy might cause voters to increase their skepticism about executive motivations. Relatedly, there is an asymmetry we have emphasized above: where the benefits really do exceed the costs, the well-motivated executive will employ the mechanisms, whereas the ill-motivated executive is less likely to do so, depending on whether use of the mechanisms happens to coincide with his strategic interests. Use of these mechanisms thus provides some evidence from which voters can infer that the executive is well-motivated. If the executive does not adopt (any of) the mechanisms, he might or might not be ill-motivated, but if he does adopt (some of) them, he is more likely to be well-motivated, so the mechanisms help voters and legislators to sort the bad from the good. The inference is evidential, not a logical necessity, but it is useful nonetheless.

More generally, we do not deny that there will always be difficult cases in which the well-motivated executive should adopt a particular policy but has no way to persuade people that his motivations are public-spirited, because the costs of generating credibility really do exceed the benefits. All we claim is that there is a substantial range of cases in which use of the mechanisms make all concerned better off. So long as voters have some information, the well-motivated executive has the right incentives. The credibility mechanisms lie on a sliding scale: their value is lower the less voters can understand them, higher the more voters can understand them.

Overall, it is sensible to think that there is a middle range in which voters' information and competence are high enough that the credibility mechanisms are useful, but not so high that voters can just directly assess whether the executive has good motivations and is adopting optimal policies. Plausibly, the median of the electorate in the United States, and in other advanced democracies, falls in this middle range, most of the time. To be sure, it is hard to demonstrate, for each of the mechanisms we have surveyed, that the benefits exceed the costs under a significant range of circumstances. On the other hand, it is hard to demonstrate the contrary as well. Presidents and others have used them, or near relatives, at many points in the past, which gives some grounds for optimism that these mechanisms have real-world resonance.

CREDIBILITY IS POWER

For presidents, credibility is power. With credibility, the formal rules of the separation-of-powers system can be bargained around or even defied, as Lincoln and FDR demonstrated. Without credibility, the president is a helpless giant. Even if legal and institutional constraints are loose and give the president broad powers, those powers cannot effectively be exercised if a sufficiently large supermajority of the public believes that the president lies or has nefarious motives. It is here that we depart from Madison. Madison believed that the unchecked president would adopt abusive policies; our view is that the unchecked president is generally too weak to adopt abusive policies. That president must develop mechanisms that enhance his credibility or exploit features of the institutional and political environment that allow him to do the same.

But presidential credibility can benefit all relevant actors, not just presidents. The decline of congressional and judicial oversight has not merely increased the power of ill-motivated executives—the typical worry of civil libertarians. It also threatens to diminish the power of well-motivated presidents, with indirect harms to the public. Such presidents would, if credibly identified, receive even broader legal delegations and greater informal trust—from legislators, judges, and the public—than presidents as a class actually have. Absent other credibility-generating mechanisms, such as effective congressional oversight, presidents must bootstrap themselves into credibility through the use of signaling mechanisms.

The mechanisms we survey, and no doubt others, represent the de facto system of self-imposed constraints that have emerged as a substitute for the separation of powers.

CHAPTER 5
Global Liberal Legalism

The failure of Madison's theory and its various epicycles have featured prominently in public debate about the Bush administration's response to the 9/11 attack. Many critics of that response have groped for another perspective that would give force to their qualms, and what has emerged can be given the label *global liberal legalism*. Global liberal legalism is a cosmopolitan version of Madison's theory. It departs from the structure of Madison's thought—the founders, although knowledgeable about and respectful of international law, never described it as an institutional check—but it reflects Madisonian values and concerns.

What is global liberal legalism? Like traditional separation-of-powers thinking, it proposes a constraint on the executive. (More broadly, global liberal legalism proposes a constraint on national governments, but in foreign relations the executive takes the lead, and for that reason we will generally refer to the executive.) Because Congress does not adequately check the executive, the constraint on the executive must come from without—from international law—rather than from within. Domestic judges, drawing on international law, take up some of the slack left by Congress. Domestic courts compel the executive to comply with international law, including norms of international law to which the executive has not explicitly consented. Meanwhile, international institutions, especially international courts, put pressure on the executive from outside the country. The belief, or at least hope, is that international law—acting through both domestic and international courts—can check the American executive and compel it to respect liberal norms.

Global liberal legalism does not address the United States in particular. It reflects an attitude about international order in general—sometimes called a commitment to the "international rule of law." But because the United States in recent years has been seen in many quarters as a kind of rogue state that ignores established international rules, arguments about global liberal legalism have focused on the United States. And because many people attribute recent American behavior to the whims of an unconstrained executive, global liberal legalism has suggested itself as a possible substitute for the internal Madisonian checks that have failed.

The argument has a number of steps, all of them vulnerable to criticism. First, international law must be "liberal"—but is it? Second, international courts and other institutions, and perhaps foreign countries as well, must have the motivation and capacity to force the United States to comply with international law, or at least those portions of international law that reflect liberal norms. Third, American courts must have the motivation and capacity to force the executive to comply with liberal norms in international law. We express skepticism about all three of these claims in this chapter, and then conclude with additional skepticism about the normative basis for global liberal legalism.

INTERNATIONAL LAW

International law consists of the rules that govern the relationships between states. It has always stirred the imagination of reformers and utopians, but the day-to-day reality of international law is rather pedestrian. A range of treaties and customary norms govern important aspects of the relationships between states—their embassies and the extradition of criminals, the transportation and communication standards that link states together, navigation on the seas, the treatment of migrants and other aliens, international trade, and more. International law rests on state consent. The treaties and customary norms are carefully constructed by states to serve their national interests. Thus, international law is only as liberal as the states that make it or the goals that they happen to pursue.

Most international law is not particularly liberal. Bilateral treaties adjust borders, resolve disputes, and arrange for limited forms of cooperation. They have always been useful for illiberal as well as liberal nations. The great multilateral treaties required the consent of all nations, or nearly all of them, and most nations are not liberal. Consider the UN charter. It does not respect democratic ideals but instead gives most of the power to the five permanent members of the Security Council—Russia, China, the United States, France, and the United Kingdom. The General Assembly, which does respect the principle of one state, one vote—but not one person, one vote—has no power to make international law under the UN charter. The charter respects the right of territorial integrity; it does not interfere with domestic institutional arrangements, however inconsistent they may be with liberal norms. The Security Council has no authority to intervene in order to advance the rule of law in authoritarian states even in the unlikely event that its members wanted to. And the Security Council itself combines executive, legislative, and judicial powers. Its mission—to maintain collective security—is committed to it alone; no institution checks it. It is a political body that maintains its legitimacy by issuing judgments that states can live with.[1] The International Court of Justice, which was created at the same time, does not have the power of judicial review or any other source of authority to constrain the Security Council.

The relationship between the UN charter and an international rule of law, then, is tenuous at best. The charter does contain rules that could in principle constrain powerful states—notably, restrictions on the use of military force—but these rules are consistent with a wide range of ideologies and do not seem particularly liberal. Restrictions on the use of military force, if obeyed, reduce interstate violence, but also enforce the status quo—a system of independent states that can use violence against their own people, and enforce illiberal norms domestically. The institutional structure of the UN, as noted, is essentially an unchecked oligarchy of powerful states,[2] far from the Kantian federation of free states, to say nothing of the modern global representative institutions of which Kant's descendants dream.

A common response to this point is that the UN can be reformed. Its representativeness can be improved, its powers enhanced.[3] However, the idea of international governance reproduces the problem that occupied the earlier chapters of this book, except at the international rather than national level. International governance, such as it is, mainly involves responding to crises—wars and threats of war, natural disasters, economic and financial collapses. Just as liberal political systems have proven unable to generate norms that adequately provide for national crises and constrain the executive in times of crisis, international law has failed in its similar goal of guiding and constraining national governments. The United Nations system has not stopped war—dozens of unauthorized wars have taken place since the system began in 1945.[4] The drafters of the charter's simple rules—no war except in self-defense or with Security Council authorization—could not envision and account for the tremendous variety of conflicts that would ensue, and the complicated political and moral issues that they would pose. The violent civil conflicts that accompanied decolonization, for example, were largely regarded as legitimate in the third world, as it was then called, and illegitimate in the first world; the United Nations charter had nothing to say about them. The problem has appeared in its most acute form in connection with humanitarian intervention. In 1999, the United States and its allies launched a military intervention in Serbia to stop Serbian forces from engaging in ethnic cleansing in Kosovo. The Security Council refused to authorize this military intervention, yet the humanitarian case for the intervention was compelling, leading a group of notables to declare the intervention "illegal but legitimate,"[5] as if to quote Carl Schmitt. The legal norms ran out. No international executive exists, but a group of powerful countries implicitly declared a state of exception and acted so as to preserve the legitimacy of the international order despite itself.

The failure of international law to constrain powerful states like the United States, which leaves freedom of action for national executives, cannot be attributed to some minor remedial defect in international law, one that can be corrected in due course. It results from the very nature of crisis governance.

THE HUMAN RIGHTS REGIME, THE LAWS OF WAR, AND *JUS COGENS* NORMS

The most important source of liberal norms in international law is the group of human rights treaties and, to a lesser extent, the laws of war. The human rights treaties include the Genocide Convention, which outlaws genocide; the Torture Convention, which outlaws torture; the International Covenant on Civil and Political Rights; the International Covenant on Economic, Social and Cultural Rights; and other treaties governing subjects such as the rights of women, children, and the disabled. The ICCPR contains so-called negative rights to political and civil freedom, of the sort contained in the U.S. Bill of Rights and constructed in subsequent judicial opinions—to wit, rights to speech, to privacy, to political participation, to association, to judicial process, to humane punishment, and so forth. The ICESCR contains certain positive rights to government assistance or protection, including rights to medical care, education, social security, and work. Most of the world's nations belong to most of these treaties. The United States is an outlier. It belongs to the ICCPR and the genocide and torture conventions, but it has refused to ratify the ICESCR and the treaties related to women, children, and people with disabilities, as well as a number of others.

The laws of war also embody some liberal norms. Among other things, this body of law requires armed forces to give process to captured enemy soldiers and especially to enemy soldiers who are tried for war crimes. Occupying armies must protect the rights of citizens within occupied territories. Liberal legalist scholars and critics argued that the laws of war required the Bush administration to grant process rights to members of Al Qaeda, and American courts have tended to agree.

The human rights treaties, the laws of war, and other treaties as well can be regarded as a source of liberal norms in international law. These treaties protect basic rights of individuals to be free of government interference, in areas central to human autonomy and political participation. The treaties do not simply ratify the U.S. Bill of Rights, of course, and one might argue about whether many of their terms are truly liberal or not. The treaties permit certain types of prohibitions, such as bans on political parties, that few would regard as liberal; may even compel certain illiberal outcomes, such as restrictions on defamation of religion; and sometimes go beyond what liberalism would require. Indeed, international human rights treaties put far less emphasis on the protection of property rights than the Bill of Rights does, reflecting the more collectivist orientation of many countries. But their overall effect is to limit the discretion of nation states, and thus of the governments that control them, to mistreat their own people as well as foreigners.

But, as constraints on executives, the human rights treaties and related sources of international law have significant limitations. The treaties permit certain derogations in emergencies, but, more important, cannot prevent de jure or de facto withdrawal. In practice, states do not formally withdraw from human rights treaties but that is almost certainly because states face no penalty for violating the treaties, which they do frequently, sometimes without any real justification but more commonly on the basis of tendentious interpretations—most famously, the Sharia-based interpretations favored by some Muslim countries. A recent empirical literature confirms that states that enter human rights treaties rarely improve their human rights practices except for states already undergoing transitions from authoritarian to democratic regimes.[6] The usual explanation for this pattern is that the human rights treaties do not create effective mechanisms for enforcement; instead, they create committees or commissions that can issue reports but have no authority to issue binding legal orders. The deeper problem is that states have limited interest in stopping human rights violations in foreign countries, and so do not expend significant resources to punish states that engage in those violations.

The frailty of the treaty regime has led some scholars to argue that human rights norms exist not only in treaties but also in an area of non-derogable customary international law known as *jus cogens*. Customary international law consists of nontreaty norms that states observe out of a sense of legal obligation. Most international legal scholars believe that states cannot merely withdraw from customary international law and thus are bound to it.[7] However, it is clear that customary international law changes as state practice changes, which means that violations must be acceptable as long as they are sufficiently widespread. Be that as it may, *jus cogens* norms are said to be specifically non-derogable. States may not withdraw from or change them; nor may they agree by treaty that those norms do not apply to their relationship. *Jus cogens* norms are thought to prohibit aggressive war, genocide, torture, and perhaps to protect certain other personal and political rights.

Yet *jus cogens* is a foggy idea, even by the standards of international law. States have agreed on a number of occasions that *jus cogens* norms exist, but if they rest on the consent of states, then states can withdraw their consent, in which case *jus cogens* norms cannot be non-derogable. If *jus cogens* norms do not rest on consent, where do they come from? How does one determine what they are? The unavoidable conclusion is that they rest on natural law—international morality. But natural law ideas lost their influence in international law in the first place because states could not agree on what natural law required, and so natural law norms could not provide a stable basis on which to conduct international relations. Indeed, while states agree that *jus cogens* norms exist, they have had a great deal of trouble agreeing on what they are. Torture perhaps. Genocide, but genocide is defined in many different ways. Aggressive war, but states cannot agree on what aggressive war means. Numerous other *jus cogens* norms have been proposed, but the debates seem irrelevant to state action.

For all its defects, *jus cogens* provides the springboard to a more aggressive type of global liberal legalism, which goes under the name of world constitutionalism.[8] This view releases human rights norms from the dungeon of treaty law, and claims that they bind all states regardless of their positions on the treaties or customary international law. Advocates of world constitutionalism have cobbled it together from wisps of doctrine; the idea has no basis in law but is an aspiration.[9] Nonetheless, it has a following among some European and American academics who see it as the only logical basis of a "rule of law" at the international level.

These academics argue that states must comply with the world constitution, for example, that international trade law must be interpreted so as to comply with human rights law—an argument that states and international institutions so far have resisted. The argument was also considered by the European Court of Justice in the *Kadi* case.[10] In that case, an individual whose assets were frozen by order of the Sanctions Committee of the Security Council brought a lawsuit arguing that the order violated human rights norms. The ECJ held for the petitioner on the ground that EU member states had to give European human rights law priority over international law. It declined to hold, to the disappointment of many, that the Security Council had acted illegally by violating international (as opposed to European) human rights norms.

So we are left with two alternative conceptions of international law: a more limited and not particularly liberal version centered around the United Nations; and a more ambitious and authentically liberal version centered around the human rights treaties. Neither system has much coercive force. The Security Council has never shown interest in advancing liberal rights, and even if it were to do so, the United States, operating through the executive branch as always, can simply veto Security Council resolutions that do not serve its interests. And, as we have seen, foreign nations have little interest in compelling other nations to live up to their human rights obligations—and with respect to the United States, no capacity for doing so even if they have an interest.

INTERNATIONAL COURTS

The failure of states, either individually or in the United Nations, to impose significant constraints on the United States or, for that matter, virtually any country that violates liberal norms embodied in international law, has led scholars to look elsewhere for enforcement of liberal international norms. In recent years, attention has been directed to international courts. If nothing else, courts are supposed to be devoted to the rule of law. International courts, then, can advance the international rule of law and force states to bow to it.

Such is the theory. The reality deflates the theories. The preeminent international court is the International Court of Justice, the judicial organ of the UN. This 15-member court, which sits in The Hague, has jurisdiction over all international law disputes between states. Its founders hoped that this court would have mandatory jurisdiction, and established a mechanism that would allow states to commit to using the court to resolve their disputes.

Since its founding, the ICJ has been a marginal institution. It has heard very few cases—about one hundred over almost 65 years—and many of the cases were of little lasting significance. It has had some trouble persuading states, especially powerful states, to comply with its judgments. Indeed, over the years states have shown less and less enthusiasm for this court and have increasingly deprived it of jurisdiction so that it cannot hear cases in the first place. The United States, one of its early champions, has refused to comply with a couple notable adverse judgments, and after one of them, the Nicaragua case of 1986,[11] withdrew from mandatory jurisdiction. Rather than treat the ICJ as the court of last resort, states have increasingly resorted to arbitration and to newly established courts with more limited jurisdictions and defined missions.[12]

The ICJ is in a particularly bad position to defend liberal rights because individuals have no power to bring cases to it. Kadi, the subject of the Security Council's sanction order, had no right to complain to the ICJ, so he brought his case in national courts instead. Although the human rights treaties fall under the ICJ's jurisdictions, it has rarely addressed them and has produced no notable or influential decisions that advance human rights or the rule of law.

As noted above, states have constructed a variety of institutions that address human rights norms. These institutions are not courts; they are essentially investigative bodies that have the power to monitor and report on the human rights practices of states. The most prominent is the UN Human Rights Council, which commissioned the controversial Goldstone report on the conflict between Israel and Hamas in Gaza in 2008–2009. The Council replaced the UN Commission on Human Rights in 2006. The General Assembly dismantled the Commission because of complaints that its membership was dominated by human-rights-abusing nations that had no interest in advancing or even respecting human rights, and used the Commission as a platform for attacking Israel. The Council has performed no better. It has made some reluctant noises about the genocide in Sudan, complained vociferously about Israel, and mostly ignored the rest of the world.

Experience with the Council, the Commission, and the ICJ reflects a basic fact about international institutions: that they either act in the interests of the states that operate them or they are ignored. In the case of the Council and the Commission, the majority of states have reasons, both political and moral, for objecting to Israel's behavior. But because their ideological and strategic approaches to other countries conflict, they cannot agree to condemn the human rights abusers among them.

The latest international court is the International Criminal Court, which went into operation in 2002. As its name indicates, this court, unlike most other international courts, is a criminal court with a prosecutorial arm that has the power to investigate, and a judicial arm that can conduct trials. It does not have jurisdiction over human rights treaties; its jurisdiction covers international criminal law, but this body of law does overlap with human rights norms. Certain grievous violations of human rights such as torture are illegal and can be prosecuted. Further, the ICC itself must comply with basic liberal norms of judicial process.

The United States initially supported the ICC but ultimately refused to ratify the treaty that authorized it. The major disagreement involved the question whether the ICC would obtain jurisdiction "automatically," whenever serious international crimes took place and the nation with jurisdiction over them refused to prosecute them in good faith, or only after a referral from the Security Council. The United States advocated the latter position because it was unwilling to permit its own citizens to be the subject of the jurisdiction of an international court, and its veto would ensure that the Security Council would never grant a referral to investigate Americans. The United States envisioned the ICC as a permanent successor to the criminal tribunals set up during the civil war in Yugoslavia and in the aftermath of the genocide in Rwanda—as a kind of tribunal in waiting that can be invoked on a case-by-case basis when justified by violence in *other* countries. The U.S. position was rejected.

The result, of course, is that the ICC does not have jurisdiction over U.S. citizens, although it claims that power if U.S. citizens commit crimes on the territory of ICC members—a claim that the United States rejects. It is too soon to evaluate the ICC's powers and capacities with much confidence, but the prospect that it will be a major force for liberal norms is dim. Three African countries—Uganda, the Central African Republic, and the Democratic Republic of Congo—have asked the ICC to launch investigations against various rebels and guerillas, and the ICC has complied. Here, it has served as a kind of judicial development agency, and it has done so under the most propitious conditions because of governmental cooperation. Yet in Uganda, a conflict has already emerged between the government, which wants to grant an amnesty to the rebels in the hope that they will lay down their arms, and the ICC, which sees amnesties as inimical to its mission. Meanwhile, the Security Council has referred the international crimes in Sudan to the ICC, which promptly indicted its head of state. But the African Union has announced that its members will not extradite him to The Hague amidst a great deal of bickering and confusion. If this announcement is taken at face value, then most of its 53 members states, those which are parties to the ICC, have already declared their readiness to disregard their painstakingly wrought treaty obligations.

The ICC, the ICJ, and the other international courts and institutions are simply too weak and poorly motivated to advance liberal norms. Their weakness is by design. The nonliberal states that joined these institutions never had any interest in being held to liberal norms, and the liberal states that provided the leadership also realized—or have come to realize—that the institutions are only as good as their judges, which are to a large extent people from illiberal or semiliberal states, and not always devoted to the rule of law.

FOREIGN COURTS AND UNIVERSAL JURISDICTION

Another claimed source of the international rule of law comes from an unexpected place: Spain and other countries that have adopted universal jurisdiction statutes. These statutes give courts jurisdiction over certain international crimes that are committed anywhere in the world. Traditionally, courts exercised jurisdiction only over crimes committed on the soil of the nation in which the courts sit or, less commonly, over crimes committed on foreign soil involving that nation's citizens as perpetrators or (even more unusually) victims. However, certain treaties such as the Genocide Convention obligated states to take action against international criminals, whatever their nationality and wherever their crimes took place, and over time states have tried to comply with these treaties by enacting universal jurisdiction statutes.

The significance of this type of statute was always questionable. Many states denied that international law permitted such prosecutions. Trials under these statutes were extremely unusual because states had virtually no interest in prosecuting foreigners for crimes committed in other countries. The courts could rarely obtain personal jurisdiction over those foreigners, foreign countries would virtually never turn them over, and a trial would involve formidable logistical difficulties because the victims, evidence, and witnesses would all be far away, often under the control of a government with no interest in cooperation. The usual expectation was that those foreign countries would request extradition—but of course this never happened when the governments of those foreign countries were responsible for the crimes. All this changed—or appeared to change—in 1998, when Spain's energetic and controversial investigating judge, Baltasar Garzón, brought charges against the former dictator of Chile, Augusto Pinochet, and sought his extradition from Britain, where Pinochet had traveled for medical treatment, winning a judgment from the House of Lords. Although the British government ultimately returned Pinochet to Chile for health reasons, the precedent was set, and Garzón and others set about investigating other government officials allegedly responsible for international crimes—including Israeli generals and politicians, American generals and politicians, and the president of China.

Here, then, was another way that international legal norms might be brought to bear against governments and government officials inclined to ignore them. It was not to be. As long as the universal jurisdiction statutes sat on the books and did not lead to prosecutions, the states whose nationals might be put in jeopardy could ignore them. But in 2003, Belgium watered down its statute when the United States threatened to pull NATO headquarters from Brussels, and more recently Spain has moved to place prosecutions under its universal jurisdiction statute under political control. Garzón awaits trial for turning his attention to Spain's own history of atrocities; he opened an investigation into the Franco era, allegedly in violation of Spanish law. Whatever the merits of the charges against Garzón, this episode illustrates the hazards of judicial efforts to enforce international legal norms against national governments without their permission.

There is a trivial sense in which the American executive is subject to checks from foreign states and international institutions. If some U.S. project requires international cooperation, then other states can check the U.S. executive by refusing to cooperate. This type of constraint has nothing to do with the Madisonian view, which does not advocate checking the executive for arbitrary reasons or in the interest of foreign countries. Madison sought to check the executive in order to reduce agency costs; his followers emphasize the importance of checking the executive in order to protect rights. International pressure that performs this function is, in fact, weak and sporadic, and can hardly counter domestic and international pressure in the other direction, when states' interests are inconsistent with liberal norms.

Global liberal legalists offer another approach, one that involves American courts. On this view, American courts force the executive to comply with liberal international norms. The involvement of domestic courts is a crucial element of the argument, for two reasons. First, unlike international courts and other international institutions, American courts have the power, both de jure and de facto, to check the executive. Second, unlike the various international institutions, American courts have a traditional allegiance to liberal norms. Thus, they can filter out the bad of international law and let in the good. Global liberal legalism, then, performs its checking function by harnessing the authority of the domestic judiciary, which has both de jure and de facto power to constrain the executive.

The argument is trickier than it first appears. The move to global legalism followed from worries about insufficient domestic checking of the executive. The concern was not just about Congress's failure to exercise its checking function. American courts tend to defer to the executive during emergencies and times of war, precisely the time—according to this argument—when those courts should be vigilant about executive abuse. Even apart from emergencies and wars, a supine judiciary has permitted power to collect in the executive over a half century period that saw the rise of the executive's domestic administrative powers in parallel with the rise of its foreign relations powers.

So why would American courts compel the executive to comply with international law? Until recently, few would have agreed with the premise of this question—that, in fact, American courts can compel the executive to comply with international law or have any interest in doing so.[13] The history of foreign relations law—the relevant area of legal doctrine—suggests a contrary thesis. The Constitution declares that treaties are the "law of the land," but they hardly ever constrain the executive. Courts have permitted the executive to withdraw the United States from a treaty unilaterally, without seeking the consent of the Senate, as is required to ratify a treaty. Even when the executive does not so act, courts frequently defer to the executive's interpretation of a treaty. Tendentious interpretations that maximize the executive's freedom of action are acceptable as long as they do not go too far. And courts interpret many treaties so that they do not have the force of domestic law. Moreover, even when they do, treaties have equal status with statutes, which means that later-enacted statutes take precedence over them, and when those statutes authorize presidential action, the executive can act in violation of a treaty. And beyond all this, the executive decides in the first place whether the United States shall enter a treaty (with the Senate's consent). If the treaty seems likely to constrain his actions—either on its face, or as a predictable result of aggressive judicial interpretation—he will be reluctant to enter it, or he will water down its terms during negotiations.

Consider a human rights treaty like the ICCPR. The United States entered this treaty but added reservations and understandings to make clear that, in the U.S. view, the treaty does not create any rights not already recognized by the U.S. Constitution. For good measure, the United States declared that the treaty was not self-executing, that is, did not create any legal rights enforceable by courts. The source of this declaration in this instance was southern senators who feared that the ICCPR might bar Jim Crow laws, and cold warriors who feared that international institutions might fall under the influence of the Soviets,[14] but non-self-execution has since then become a mantra of the executive. The courts have respected these statements, and the ICCPR has had a correspondingly miniscule effect on domestic rights. In a handful of cases, courts have relied on the ICCPR to help interpret ambiguous statutes under a sporadically applied canon of interpretation requiring that ambiguous statutes be construed consistently with international law. But these cases are rare.

Customary international law has played an even smaller role in domestic adjudication. The Constitution gives Congress, not the courts, the power to introduce norms of customary international law into domestic law. Federal courts sometimes rely on customary international law to develop certain areas of federal common law, such as admiralty, but they have always permitted the executive to override these rules where the executive has authority, such as in the laws of war. Like treaties, customary international law can influence the interpretation of ambiguous statutes that affect foreign relations, but again this is rare.

Foreign relations law, then, reflects a strong commitment to executive primacy. Courts are largely deferential and, under traditional foreign relations doctrine, very rarely force the executive to comply with liberal (or any) international law except when Congress has specifically incorporated it into a statute, which has not happened very often. *Hamdan v. Rumsfeld*,[15] where the Supreme Court struck down the system of military commissions set up by the Bush administration, is an outlier. The Court found that the commissions violated a provision of the Geneva Conventions that had been incorporated into a statute. Aside from this case, however, deference to the executive is the rule. The reason—the one given by judges and commentators—is that the executive has special expertise for conducting foreign relations, and foreign relations require speed, secrecy, centralized authority, and other characteristics the judicial system lacks.

The claim that domestic courts have the capacity and interest to check the executive for the sake of the international rule of law rests on two relatively new developments in foreign relations law: alien tort statute litigation and the use of foreign and international law to interpret the U.S. Constitution.

The alien tort statute gives courts jurisdiction over suits brought by aliens for torts that violate international law. It was enacted in 1789 but its modern importance dates back only to 1980, when a court held that the statute covered a human rights violation committed by an alien, against an alien, in a foreign country. That case involved a police officer who tortured and murdered the person whose family brought the claim;[16] since then, cases involving an enormous range of behavior have been brought. Plaintiffs have sued multinational corporations for doing business with the apartheid regime of South Africa, for constructing pipelines in Indonesia with the protection of government security forces that engaged in human rights abuses, for paying ransom money to right-wing paramilitaries in Columbia, for selling armored tractors to Israel, for providing financial services to Palestinian militants, and much else. Cases have also been brought against former heads of state and government officials.

Alien tort statute litigation is unique throughout the world. No other country offers civil remedies for international law violations; American-style damages awards, including punitive damages, hold the promise of real deterrence. And although the alien tort statute is theoretically available to the (alien) victim of any international law violation that constitutes a tort, in practice it is attractive only to victims of human rights violations. Human rights violations injure individuals, not states; and they are easily characterized as torts. So alien tort litigation frequently draws on international human rights treaties, the very treaties that, according to the U.S. government, do not have domestic effect.

In a general sense, then, alien tort statute litigation has raised the profile of the human rights treaty regime. But the proponents of global liberal legalism have gone farther, claiming that judicial enforcement of the alien tort statute can impose a Madisonian check on the American executive. This claim is implausible.

For one thing, alien tort litigation cannot be brought against the U.S. government or officials in the U.S. government because of immunity doctrines. Nor is it likely that it can be brought against former heads of state or government officials. In general, alien tort statute litigation has not resulted in money changing hands; foreign defendants can avoid paying damages simply by keeping their assets out of the United States. All this changed when plaintiffs began suing multinational corporations, claiming that they are complicit in the human rights violations of the governments with which they do business. But these suits have been a hard slog, with virtually no success. At best, they might cause some independent contractors to think twice before doing business with an American government bent on using those contractors—say, security firms—to violate human rights. But chances are that the benefits of doing business with the American government outweigh these still very remote risks.

The constitutional cases present a different set of issues. In a small number of cases decided in the late 1990s and early 2000s, the Supreme Court struck down laws using a controversial style of constitutional interpretation that incorporated foreign and international law. In one such case, the Court struck down a law that prescribed the death penalty for people who committed certain crimes as juveniles.[17] The law violated the Eighth Amendment prohibition on cruel and unusual punishment, the Court said. In the course of interpreting "cruel and unusual," the Court cited practices in foreign countries (which had no similar law) and international treaties (which appeared to condemn such a law).

These cases generated enormous controversy but also confusion about what was at stake. For supporters of the practice, the Court was merely gathering information from other countries, no different from reading and citing Locke. Citations to the high courts of foreign countries could also enhance comity and American judicial influence. Critics argued that the Court violated the U.S. Constitution by allowing itself to be influenced by foreign law.[18] The deeper question was whether liberal international and foreign legal norms should constrain the U.S. government. This would be a new type of global liberal legalism: international norms would provide a check on the U.S. government and hence the executive.

It is unlikely that this line of cases will amount to much. The political controversy that the cases engendered indicates that the use of foreign and international law to interpret the U.S. Constitution lacks political legitimacy, and so its widespread use would be dangerous for the courts' authority. Justices have already backed away from the practice. Further, the cases so far have been, as defenders of the practice have emphasized, relatively minor—mostly tied to the Eighth Amendment. Indeed, they have had nothing to do with abuses by the U.S. executive; the focus has been state laws.

Even if judges pursue this approach, it does not necessarily lead to global liberal legalism. As discussed earlier, international law and foreign law consist of illiberal as well as liberal norms, and so the interpretive method, faithfully applied, could lead to the curtailment of liberal rights rather than their enhancement. Since judges would need to exercise discretion in picking and choosing among international norms, global liberal legalism would go only as far as American judges—frequently provincial, and not always liberal—let it.

FROM IS TO OUGHT? THE NORMATIVE BASIS OF GLOBAL LIBERAL LEGALISM

Global liberal legalism—the theory that international law places Madisonian checks on the U.S. executive—does not describe the world as it exists today. Its proponents have scraped together a handful of tubers from the infertile soil of international law and called it a feast. One might argue that global liberal legalism is a normative vision, not a descriptive hypothesis, and should not be criticized just because it has not yet come to pass. But even normative visions must rest on a plausible account of how the world operates. Global liberal legalism lacks such a account. It does not explain how an anarchical world system populated by illiberal as well as liberal states, all of them oriented toward their national interests, would demand that the American president refrain from violating the rights of American citizens.[19] Recall in this regard that the foreign indignation stirred up by American counterterrorism policies centered on the U.S. government's treatment of foreigners, not Americans, who were never sent to Guantánamo Bay.

The defects of global liberal legalism come into full view when one considers that some person or institution must be charged with the task of putting global liberal legalism into operation. We have seen the candidates: foreign states; their prosecutors and judges; international courts; and U.S. domestic courts. The claim that foreign states, collectively or individually, could enforce global liberal legalism just assumes away the problem: what compels those states to respect liberal ideals and impose them on the United States? Foreign judges enforce foreign law, which is made by foreign states. As we have seen, those states have no interest in trying Americans for human rights abuses and have deprived their judges of that power. International judges are similarly appointed by foreign states and remain beholden to them and occupy a creaky, slow, and mostly ineffectual judicial system. Domestic judges cannot enforce liberal norms of international law except by picking and choosing, which has already caused political trouble. Also consider that "liberalism" is not, and never has been, a self-defining concept. If global liberal legalism is understood broadly, many elements of American policy are ceded to foreign or domestic judges, or international lawmaking bodies. There can be controversies over what liberalism demands, and if those controversies are to be decided by foreign institutions, then democracy in the United States is poorer for it.[20]

Indeed, if anything can rouse Congress from its torpor, it is the prospect of foreign interference with domestic political processes. We have mentioned the political controversy engendered by the occasional judicial practice of relying on foreign and international law; members of Congress proposed banning this interpretive method. In response to the claim that the ICC has jurisdiction over American citizens who commit international crimes on the territory of ICC members, Congress passed a law dubbed the "Hague Invasion Act," which, in language normally used to authorize military invasions, empowered the president to extract American citizens from the clutches of that tribunal. Whatever their differences, Congress and the executive are united in their opposition to what they regard as infringements on American sovereignty. This is the main reason the judiciary has always treaded carefully in this area; one suspects as well that the judiciary shares this attitude. In such circumstances, global liberal legalism has a long way to go before it will be able to provide meaningful checks on the American executive.

LIBERAL LEGALISM IN FOREIGN DEMOCRACIES

Our focus has been the United States, but if we are correct that the decline of liberal legalism in the United States reflects general economic and technological trends, then one might expect similar patterns in other liberal democracies. Separation of powers, and related institutional constraints on government, such as judicial supremacy and parliamentary control, should be eroding in countries around the world. Executive power should be on the march. If this is the case, the prospect that foreign countries, acting through their executives, will provide a substitute for Madisonian checking of the U.S. executive is poor indeed.

We do not have the space or expertise to test this hypothesis in a rigorous fashion, but we do want to address some of the issues it raises. Initially, our arguments do not entail that every country in the world follows the same path as the United States, starting at some point of origin with a government excessively burdened with liberal legalism and then experiencing a monotonic trend in the direction of executive dominance. Other countries have followed different trajectories. Most European countries were monarchies at the time of the American Revolution and, after many ups and downs, settled into a pattern of liberal democracy that exists today. Many Latin American countries have cycled between periods of dictatorship and democracy since their independence in the nineteenth century. Most African countries gained independence only after World War II and still lack full capacity to control their populations; with a few exceptions, they have suffered from authoritarianism. Russia is a quasi-authoritarian country. Middle Eastern countries are mostly authoritarian. India is an entrenched democracy. Japan is a longtime democracy albeit for the most of its modern history subject to one-party control. A number of smaller countries (South Korea, Taiwan) have democratic institutions; others (Vietnam) do not.

Our major claim is that, in the United States, executive power is undervalued for ideological reasons, while at the same time being essential to peace and prosperity. Recent trends, including globalization, have increased executive power, thanks to acquiescence on the part of the other branches and the implicit support of the people and the elites. This does not imply anything about the optimal level of executive power in other countries. Countries that started off with very strong executive institutions could certainly experience the opposite trajectory. The trends we identify are compatible with the flourishing of both authoritarian systems (which can respond vigorously to challenges because leaders need not worry about elections, but which may be hampered by lack of democratic legitimacy) and democracies (which can respond vigorously to challenges, but only as long as popular support exists). Indeed, we do not make any general claims about whether the "optimal" institutional arrangements will prevail, so that executive power rises when countries face significant economic and security threats and declines when they do not.

Still, our claims about the United States may seem in tension with recent events in other countries. There have been several waves of democratic transformation over the last century, culminating in the collapse of the Soviet Union and the establishment of liberal democracies in many of its former satellite states.[21] Democracy also made headway in South Africa, Indonesia, the Philippines, and Latin America. Although we have taken pains to argue that executive power is compatible with democracy, it might seem that authoritarian systems have more effective executives, and so the collapse of authoritarian systems implies that executive primacy in democracies is doomed as well. In addition, American-style judicial review has spread to many countries that traditionally had no judicial review or only weak forms of judicial review. Ran Hirschl has documented this process, although in his view this pattern is liberal in form but not in substance—it reflects efforts by elites to shortcut democracy and entrench norms that are unpopular with the masses.[22]

It may well be the case that in certain European countries the courts have obtained greater power, but the story is complex, and mainly a sideshow. The main event is the transfer of power from legislatures to executives. European integration has played a central role in this process. As Philipp Kiiver explains:

> Conventionally, the national parliaments are seen as the losers of European integration, having underestimated the European dimension and having allowed the governments to escape effective democratic accountability. Since the Council [of Europe] as such is indeed not accountable to the European parliament, the only formal accountability link there remains the individual ministers' reliance on parliamentary confidence at home. Most national parliaments, however, are widely perceived to be rather modest and ineffective in exercising scrutiny over their ministers concerning European policy.[23]

The Council of Europe is the main decision-making body for the European Union. It consists of the prime ministers of the member states. Yet the parliaments of the member states do not have the capacity to supervise their prime ministers' participation in the Council.

There are several reasons for this.[24] The EU's legislative programs are ambitious and technical. The prime minister can rely on the national bureaucracy's expertise; the parliament can keep apprised of developments in European law only with difficulty. Further, because the prime minister of a particular member state can be outvoted in the Council in a range of matters, the parliament may not be able to exercise control over policy outcomes even if it manages to keep tight rein on the prime minister. For this reason, parliament has weaker incentives to monitor European affairs and the European policy of the prime minister than it has to monitor other aspects of the prime minister's performance. Although technically the parliament has another chance to exert control when directives are handed down from the EU, in reality it must either follow those directives and enact the necessary legislation or put the nation at risk of legal action for violating European law.

The upshot is that national parliaments have lost power to the executive in the realm of European affairs. They cannot exercise their checking function as effectively as in the past. Nor have checks and balances been reproduced at the European level. The European Parliament is weak. Policy is made by the Council and the European Commission—two bureaucracies not known for their transparency. The main court of the European system—the European Court of Justice—does not take petitions from individuals and does not directly protect individual rights, although in a few significant cases it has encouraged member states to recognize certain fundamental rights. The ECJ is most famous for its role in facilitating integration by insisting that European law take precedence over the national law of member states, not for protecting individual rights.

Executive power has increased in Europe for other reasons as well.[25] The weak, unstable executive of the Fourth Republic of France was a major cause of its collapse and replacement in 1958 with a quasi-parliamentary regime that featured a strong presidency. The strong executive in Italy today owes much to the long postwar experience with unstable governments as well. Concerns about secrecy and national security have contributed to a weakening of judicial control over the executive in Germany, though judicial control remains significant in that country.[26] Executive power seems to be flourishing in Canada and Australia.

The major (possible) counterexample among the rich liberal democracies is the United Kingdom. In the United Kingdom, Parliament and the courts have in recent years proved somewhat more assertive in checking ministerial action even in matters affecting national security.[27] However, the United Kingdom started from a baseline different from that of the United States. While the United States is notionally committed to the separation of powers, the status quo ante in the United Kingdom was complete fusion of executive and legislative power, with the fused institution dominated by the executive. In matters of national security, Parliament and the courts gave near-total deference to the ministry, as evidenced by the famous 1942 *Liversidge* decision, in which "national security was held to be 'par excellence a non-justiciable question,' which was 'clearly a matter for executive discretion and nothing else.'"[28] Against that baseline, any positive level of oversight or review by Parliament and the courts is an improvement from the standpoint of liberal legalism, but does not show that the UK system diverges from our analysis of the U.S. system; it is quite possible that the latter is becoming ever less legalist while the former is becoming slightly more so, resulting in convergence. But these trends are complex and one should draw conclusions from them only with caution.

Indeed, the larger pattern is that in Britain "executive power has been growing steadily for more than a century."[29] A short-term retrenchment should not mask the long-term trend.

European countries did ratify a European Convention on Human Rights and establish a European Court of Human Rights (ECtHR) to interpret and enforce it. Unlike the ECJ, the ECtHR accepts petitions from individuals, and has the power to award damages to victims (which states usually pay) and order states to repeal repressive laws (which states do not always do). The significance of the ECtHR is open to question. The treaty that it enforces simply ratifies the norms that EU members already endorsed. Non-EU members such as Russia have not been constrained by the ECtHR; indeed, Russia has slid further into authoritarianism since it joined the ECtHR system in 1998.[30] The court has an enormous backlog of more than 100,000 cases. A court of 47 judges, which has jurisdiction over hundreds of millions of people in 47 countries, does not have the resources to address more than a tiny fraction of human rights abuses.

We do not want to draw strong conclusions from such complex events. But, at a minimum, trends in European and other major democracies do not contradict our argument that liberal legalism is ailing in the United States.

GLOBALIZATION AND THE EXECUTIVE

Conventional wisdom holds that globalization has favored national executives. This view was reflected in Kiiver's comments, quoted above, about the way that European integration has favored the executives of the member states and weakened the parliaments. But the point extends beyond Europe. Executives have always had the leading role in foreign affairs because of the fast-changing nature of international relations and the importance of secrecy and unity. It was in the arena of domestic policy that the legislature and judiciary were supposed to be dominant. With globalization, many topics that had been matters of domestic policy became issues of foreign relations and hence presumptively within the control of the executive. Legislatures and judiciaries could only lose out. International organizations, which are so adored by global liberal legalists, turned out to be dominated by executives, who appoint national representatives to international organizations, negotiate with them, and otherwise deal with them on a day-to-day basis. When international organizations, including courts, try to act independently, they discover that national governments can work around them by creating new organizations that fragment international law.[31]

In this light, global liberal legalism seems like a rearguard action—an ideological effort to reconcile the new era of executive power with traditional notions of rule of law. This may explain why people can be persuaded by grandiose claims about the international rule of law that are built on such weak foundations. In fact, the many gains that have come with globalization have required Americans and other people around the world to give up some of their cherished commitments to legalism.

CHAPTER 6

Tyrannophobia

So far we have attempted to show that the administrative state relaxes legal constraints on the executive, but generates political constraints in the form of public opinion. In this chapter we fit this picture together with the fear of unbridled executive power that is such a prominent strand in liberal legalism. We suggest that liberal legalists overlook the importance of de facto constraints arising from politics, and thus equate a legally unconstrained executive with one that is unconstrained *tout court*. The horror of dictatorship that results from this fallacy and that animates liberal legalism is what we call "tyrannophobia."

Tyranny looms large in the American political imagination. For the framers of the Constitution, Caesar, Cromwell, James II, and George III were antimodels; for the current generation, Hitler takes pride of place, followed by Stalin, Mao, and a horde of tyrants both historical and literary. Students read *1984* and *Animal Farm* and relax by watching Chancellor Palpatine seize imperial power in *Star Wars*. Unsurprisingly, comparisons between sitting presidents and the tyrants of history and fiction are a trope of political discourse. Liberals and libertarians routinely compared George W. Bush to Hitler, George III, and Caesar. Today, Barack Obama receives the same treatment, albeit in less respectable media of opinion. All major presidents are called a "dictator" or said to have "dictatorial powers" from time to time.[1]

Yet the United States has never had a Caesar or a Cromwell, or even come close to having one, and rational actors should update their risk estimates in the light of experience, reducing them if the risk repeatedly fails to materialize. By now, 235 years after independence, these risk estimates should be close to zero. Why then does the fear of dictatorship—tyranno-phobia—persist so strongly in American political culture? Is the fear justi-fied, or irrational? Does tyrannophobia itself affect the risk of dictatorship? If so, does it reduce the risk or increase it?

We will begin with some definitions and conceptual distinctions, prin-cipally to identify the varieties of tyrannophobia that we will consider. We then examine fears of dictatorship in American history and some compar-ative evidence on the causes of dictatorship and on the relationship, across countries, between dictatorship and tyrannophobia. We find no evidence that tyrannophobia prevents dictatorship.

We then turn to a broader evaluation of the relationship between tyran-nophobia and dictatorship in American history. As to the original constitu-tional design, we suggest that the framers' choice of an independently elected executive may have created a risk of dictatorship in an earlier day, but that in the present day elections and independent demographic fac-tors, notably the wealth of its population, now ensure that the United States is unlikely to lapse into dictatorship. The very economic and polit-ical conditions that have created powerful executive government, in the modern administrative state, have also strengthened informal political checks on presidential action. The result is a president who enjoys sweeping de jure authority, but who is constrained de facto by the reaction of a highly educated and politically involved elite, and by mass opinion.

Overall, our argument is in the alternative. One possibility is that tyran-nophobia has no effect on the risk of dictatorship; we provide some evi-dence for that hypothesis. Alternatively, tyrannophobia might both reduce the risk of dictatorship (a benefit) and also block desirable grants of authority to the executive (a cost). If so, we suggest that the benefit is min-imal, because demographic factors and the basic framework of elections provide an independent and sufficient safeguard against dictatorship; hence the cost of tyrannophobia exceeds the benefit.

CONCEPTS AND DISTINCTIONS

Tyrannophobia is the fear of dictatorship, but what is dictatorship? The term is slippery in a family-resemblance sort of way, with many competing definitions and a great deal of vague usage. One recent treatment distin-guishes "tinpot" dictators, who maximize personal consumption, from "totalitarian" dictators, who maximize power.[2] In general usage, "dictator-ship" takes many forms. In one version, dictatorship is the end point of a continuum that runs from fully autocratic rule by one person alone, through oligarchy, to democracy. In this version, talk of democratic dictatorship, or perhaps even constitutional dictatorship, would be oxymoronic. In another version, dictatorship refers to the nature of the policies that government institutes; a "democratic" or populist government that violated civil liberties and arbitrarily confiscated property could coherently be called dictatorial. A third theme, especially pronounced in Anglo-American discourse, focuses on the executive and equates dictatorship with unchecked executive power, in which case legislative dictatorship would be the oxymoron.

Rather than attempting to identify a natural kind of dictatorship, which probably does not exist anyway, we will combine the first and third accounts by stipulating that dictatorship is a political system of legally unchecked rule by one person or an identified small group of persons. Legal checks can be divided into two categories: the requirement that the leader obtain the consent of other government officials (for example, legislators) before acting; and the requirement that the leader submit to periodic popular elections. Dictatorships tend to exist when both types of checks are weak or nonexistent. On this account, dictatorship lies on a continuum and is thus a matter of degree, so usage implicitly varies: the fewer the checks, the more plausible the "dictator" label becomes, but some people use the label to refer narrowly to unelected leaders, some to elected leaders who need no consent from others, and some to an (elected) executive who is subject to some legal checks yet commits abuses. On our definition, this last usage is hyperbolic and erroneous, yet there is an important substantive issue here about the risk of abuses short of dictatorship; we address the issue below.

As intensional definitions of "dictatorship" are so slippery, extensional definition may help indicate our interests. The paradigm cases we have in mind include absolute monarchies (but not constitutional monarchies), fascist dictatorship based on leader-worship, military dictatorships and juntas, and most of the stock tyrannies mentioned above. We mean to exclude various large-scale oligarchies and systems of collective rule, such as the Chinese Communist Party. Dictatorship is fully consistent with the existence of de facto political checks on the ruler; there will almost always be political forces the dictator(s) must be careful to reward or appease, such as the military or security services, mass public opinion, or an elite "selectorate"[3] that influences the choice of dictators.

Indeed, it is common in the political economy literature on dictatorships to assume that a dictator stays in power by satisfying the preferences of some group—a subgroup such as the elites but potentially the entire population.[4] If the dictator fails to satisfy this group, it will overthrow him. A democratic government is assumed to satisfy the preference of the median voter;[5] if it does not, the median voter will select a different government. Accordingly, the dictator and the democratic government may act identically when the dictator needs the support of a majority of the entire population. The only difference is that the democratic government is constrained by the de jure power of the median voter, while the dictator is constrained by the de facto power of the median citizen.

Given this definition of dictatorship, one of our major aims is to identify several varieties of tyrannophobia, and to do this several distinctions are necessary. The tyrannophobe may fear dictatorship in the extreme sense we have identified—the endpoint of the continuum, where the leader faces no legal checks at all, neither elections nor the consent of others for lawmaking—or else the tyrannophobe may fear dictatorship in a weaker sense, such as abuses by an elected executive. In general, our claims will be stronger as the tyrannophobe's fears are more extreme, weaker as the tyrannophobe is more moderate; the problems have a sliding-scale quality.

Another key distinction involves the nature of the fear that occurs in tyrannophobia. Some fears are rationally warranted by the evidence and can be described as justified fear. Alternatively, fear may be an emotional response that short-circuits rational consideration of the evidence, and thus constitutes an unjustified fear. Tyrannophobia is intrinsically ambiguous, and can refer to either variety of fear, so we will discuss both. We should note, however, that if tyrannophobia is rational—if it refers to a belief about the probability of dictatorship that reflects Bayesian updating—then the label has no explanatory value. In understanding (for example) why constitutional framers put constraints on the executive, we would refer to their justified beliefs rather than the emotion of fear. Tyrannophobia is interesting to the extent that it reflects irrational beliefs, in which case one wants to understand why people have these irrational beliefs, and what effect these beliefs have on constitutions and other political outcomes. Although we will discuss both versions of tyrannophobia, our focus will be on the irrational version.[6]

Furthermore, risks are a product both of the probability that an event will materialize—here, that a dictator will take power—and of the harms that will occur if the risk does materialize. On the margin of probability, the unjustified variety of tyrannophobia takes the form of exaggerated perception of the risk that a dictatorship will occur, through the creeping expansion of executive power, through a sudden seizure of executive power in a crisis, or through some other sequence. We consider versions of these claims below.

On the margin of harm, the question is whether the tyrannophobe rationally considers the evidence about the costs and benefits of dictatorship.[7] Liberal legalists sometimes imply that dictatorship has catastrophic effects on welfare, but this is a caricature, not supported by the evidence. It is not even clear whether authoritarian governments systematically offer different public policies than democracies do. A comparison of democracies and non-Communist nondemocracies between 1960 and 1990 finds that the two regime-types offer very similar substantive public policies; they differ principally in terms of policies related to winning or maintaining public office, in that nondemocracies are more likely to select leaders through violence.[8] More generally, "Although some studies have established a significant positive link between measures of political freedom and [income] growth . . ., others have found that authoritarian regimes have better growth records."[9] Likewise, a recent survey finds that "there is no evidence that constraints on the executive predict growth."[10] Yet the most recent study finds that dictatorships do produce fewer public goods than democracies do.[11] Some of these findings can be reconciled by the hypothesis that dictatorial regimes exhibit higher variance than democratic regimes and a higher dispersion of growth rates;[12] perhaps democracy has both a lower downside and a lower upside.[13] Whether that trade-off is desirable depends upon the nature of the status quo ante, the risk aversion of the population, and the absolute level of performance under the democratic alternative.[14]

It is not our contention that dictatorship is superior to democracy. Among other problems, political freedom and equality are themselves components of welfare. Certainly, in the developed world, where democracies function well, dictatorship has little to recommend it. The cross-country evidence we have cited suggests more ambiguity about the developing world. It may be that a dictatorship that keeps order and delivers a few other public goods is superior to a democracy that quickly degenerates into anarchy. Our more modest point is just that institutional design of democratic institutions should not assume that the loss of well-being caused by a transition from democracy to dictatorship is higher than it in fact is.

Another distinction involves different types of safeguards against dictatorship. Even if dictatorship is a real risk, and even if it would be harmful if it occurred, the requisite precautions might be either institutional or else political and cultural. The former typically arise through deliberate constitutional design, involving familiar institutions such as legislative oversight, judicial review for statutory authorization or constitutionality, and (in some systems) the separation of powers. Political and cultural precautions arise, if at all, through decentralized action by many individuals. They can be arranged on a continuum from relatively formal modes of political organization, such as political parties capable of resisting dictatorship, to unwritten constitutional norms and conventions,[15] such as the long-standing convention that that no president should stand for a third term (until Roosevelt did so), to a loosely defined ethos of libertarianism. We will examine the relationship between institutional and noninstitutional constraints in later sections.

A last type of tyrannophobia has a temporal dimension. There is a long history of *time-limited dictatorships*.[16] In the ancient Roman republic, for example, a dictator could be appointed to address an emergency for a term that typically expired after six months. Some renaissance Italian republics had a similar position. And many modern constitutions grant executives special (although usually not absolute) powers during emergencies. By our definition, time-limited dictatorships are not true dictatorships because the dictator derives his authority from the people or from elected officials.[17] But time-limited dictatorships loom large in the imagination of the tyrannophobe because many time-limited dictators have refused to step down.

TYRANNOPHOBIA IN THE FOUNDING ERA

The Declaration of Independence is the ur-text of tyrannophobia in the United States. Britain at the time had a constitutional monarchy, and the king was by no means the sole or even leading figure in determining colonial policy but shared power with Parliament. Yet the Declaration focuses not on Parliament, or the British people, but on the king, and his supposedly tyrannical methods.

> The history of the present King of Great Britain is a history of repeated injuries and usurpations, all having in direct object the establishment of an absolute Tyranny over these States. To prove this, let Facts be submitted to a candid world.[18]

A long list of the king's outrages end in this climax:

> In every stage of these Oppressions We have Petitioned for Redress in the most humble terms: Our repeated Petitions have been answered only by

repeated injury. A Prince, whose character is thus marked by every act which may define a Tyrant, is unfit to be the ruler of a free people.[19]

Parliament receives only a passing reference in the next paragraph. British policy toward the American colonies, although very much a joint product of king and Parliament, is personified in the king, a tyrant.

Why did Jefferson employ this rhetorical strategy? Parliament, whatever its defects, was a quasi-representative body. If Parliament is to be blamed for the injuries suffered by the American colonies, then so must the British people. Yet Americans had deep ties with the British—not just by consanguinity, as noted by the Declaration, but also commercial, religious, and ideological. Given Britain's mastery of the seas, it would have been difficult to imagine that the colonies, after independence, could flourish without some sort of accommodation with the British. Indeed, the Declaration's references to the British people are notably gentle:

> Nor have We been wanting in attentions to our British brethren. We have warned them from time to time of attempts by their legislature to extend an unwarrantable jurisdiction over us. We have reminded them of the circumstances of our emigration and settlement here. We have appealed to their native justice and magnanimity, and we have conjured them by the ties of our common kindred to disavow these usurpations, which, would inevitably interrupt our connections and correspondence. They too have been deaf to the voice of justice and of consanguinity. We must, therefore, acquiesce in the necessity, which denounces our Separation, and hold them, as we hold the rest of mankind, Enemies in War, in Peace Friends.[20]

The effort to separate out the king for special obloquy, and to distinguish him from the British people and their parliament, exploited British historical memory and political currents in Britain at that time. British hostility to its own monarchy extended back to the seventeenth century, culminating in the regicide of Charles I. By the eighteenth century, there was an uneasy compromise between Crown and the people, but George III was not a popular figure. He was the target of a powerful political movement that accused him and the parliamentary leadership of corruption. "Country" critics of the king and Parliament argued that the Crown used offices and revenues at its disposal to bribe members of Parliament who would therefore no longer serve as a counterweight to executive power.[21] Many Americans shared these views.[22] Although Americans greatly respected, even idealized, the king earlier in the eighteenth century, while having only a vague notion of what Parliament was, by the revolutionary period he had attracted intense hostility on the ground that he had violated the social contract.[23] The exaggerated beliefs about the king's power, and the correspondingly vague sense of parliamentary power, may explain why the king was blamed for British colonial policy. It was thus an obvious strategy to blame the king for the injuries that made the American Revolution necessary, and absolve the British people as much as possible, in this way exploiting divisions in the British political class and laying the foundations for a return to friendly relations in the future. The leaders of the revolution were also deeply read in the classics, and received classical wisdom emphasized the threat to liberty at the hands of tyrants, culminating in the person of Julius Caesar, who put the finishing touches on Rome's moribund republican institutions.

These ideas did not just supply rhetoric. American political institutions during and after the Revolution were notable for the weakness of the executive office. State legislatures inherited the executive powers of royal governors; state governorships were mostly weak, ministerial offices.[24] The Articles of Confederation failed to establish an executive office for the national government. Suspicion of the executive ran deep. Yet as state legislatures used their newfound powers to cancel debts, redistribute wealth, and persecute dissenters, it soon became clear that "legislative tyranny," a term that came into use at that time, was just as dangerous as executive tyranny.[25] Meanwhile, at the national level, the absence of a powerful executive hampered the war effort, limited the ability of the national government to respond to internal rebellions, and put the American people at a disadvantage in commercial disputes with foreign nations.

Hence one of the chief motivations for holding a constitutional convention was to strengthen the national executive.[26] The Federalists were pragmatists who were willing to abandon their earlier opposition to a strong executive because intervening experience had taught them that a weak executive spelled ruin.[27] But they ran into a strong tide of opposition. Indeed, the Antifederalists could simply cite the Revolution-era criticisms of George III. Again, the names of Caesar, Cromwell, and other historical tyrants were invoked.[28] Republics are often weak and internally divided, hence vulnerable to a charismatic leader who can promise unity and who controls the military. Once powerful figures obtained the office of the executive, institutional barriers against abuse would fall away. Antifederalists adopted the Country Party's rhetorical "logic of escalation," "by which it tended to see in every limited act of government a larger plan aiming to subvert popular liberty."[29] For the Country critics, Britain was constantly in danger of sliding back into the royal absolutism from which the Glorious Revolution had only temporarily and imperfectly saved the nation. For the Antifederalists, a powerful executive office in the United States would pose similar dangers. They imitated the tyrannophobic rhetoric of the Country Party even after the United States was no longer threatened by Britain's monarchical institutions and even though circumstances in the United States differed from those in Britain. Thus did tyrannophobic tropes enter American political discourse at an early stage, transplanted from a country that had experienced real tyrants in its recent past, but taking root in the soil of a country for which royal absolutism had no party. The rhetoric persisted after its foundation had vanished.

The debate about executive abuse was not resolved in the Constitution. The founders created a presidency and vested it with undefined executive powers. A handful of more specific powers that would turn out to be consequential did not have a clear meaning at the time of negotiations. The veto power might be understood just to mean the right to veto unconstitutional legislation, not legislation that the president rejected on policy grounds. The commander-in-chief power could refer only to tactical control, not military strategy and foreign policy in general. The power to receive ambassadors could refer to a ceremonial role, not (as it was later interpreted) the power to recognize states and governments. It was possible to conceive of the presidency as a ministerial position, similar to that of any number of weak governorships that existed in the American states, or as a much more important figure.[30] Ambiguous language papered over these disputes and the debate continued into the Washington administration.[31]

POSTFOUNDING AMERICAN HISTORY

The trend of presidential power over two centuries resembles a graph of GDP or the stock market—a gradual trend upward but with cyclical peaks and valleys along the way. The canonical list of powerful presidents includes Washington, Jackson, Polk, Lincoln, Theodore Roosevelt, Wilson, Franklin Delano Roosevelt, and Nixon.[32] Each powerful president was followed by one or more weak presidents, at least if we include among the weak Truman, who cemented American dominance of world institutions and ran an essentially unilateral war in Korea, but who also became highly unpopular and (thus) lost a major showdown with the Supreme Court.[33] Each powerful president was accused, at one time or another, of Caesarism (as were many weak presidents). Discomfort with the concentration of power in the hands of one man may well have led to a political backlash in each case, hampering the ability of the successors to exercise power. Many of these presidencies were also followed by formal constitutional and legislative changes designed to limit the power of future presidents.[34] In other cases, the weakness of succeeding presidents may have owed more to the hostile political climate toward executive power that the powerful president left in his wake.

FDR's administration was the watershed.[35] Many of the presidencies that followed it were powerful—Truman's for a time, Eisenhower's, Johnson's, Nixon's, Reagan's. Of these, only Nixon's abuses created a backlash, leading to the weak presidencies of Ford and Carter and to a series of framework statutes intended to check executive power. As we have seen in chapter 3, however, those framework statutes have for the most part failed to constrain presidential government.

Historians usually invoke the cold war and the rise of the administrative state as the explanatory factors giving rise to the imperial presidency. The United States was, for the first time in its history, continuously engaged in a life-or-death struggle with a foreign power, over decades rather than years. A powerful executive was always thought necessary for planning and conducting military operations; accordingly, the powerful executive was institutionalized.[36] Meanwhile, the United States had developed a true national market that required regulation at a national level. The technological problems in the modern era seemed to require continuous monitoring and adjustment, tasks that only an executive bureaucracy can handle.[37]

But if American presidents have gained more legal and political power over time, they remain vastly more constrained, at least politically, than the Caesars and the Cromwells that the founders feared. Indeed, the United States—unlike many other countries, including Germany, of course—has never had a dictator—in the sense of unchecked rule by one person for an indefinite period.[38] Every president has humbly submitted to quadrennial elections and respected their results. George Washington, in many respects a model of the constrained executive, devoted much of his Farewell Address to warning his fellow citizens about the risks and evils of tyranny.[39] Lincoln violated the law at the start of the Civil War but felt that he needed to obtain congressional ratification of his actions after the fact, and stood for election at the end of his first term. Wilson and Roosevelt also had tremendous power to conduct war, but presidential power has always contracted with the return to peace. Peacetime dictatorships have never taken place.

The peculiar danger reflected by Caesar and Cromwell, and later Napoleon, was that a charismatic military leader would become a dictator by popular acclimation. This never happened in the United States. The closest example is Andrew Jackson, and while he used his powers aggressively—notably, by ignoring a Supreme Court ruling and by refusing to comply with a statute that required the Treasury to deposit funds with the Bank of the United States—no historian considers him a dictator. Although Jackson's impact on the presidency was large in the long term—he was the first charismatic, populist president, and helped establish the modern party system—like so many other strong presidents, he provoked a backlash[40] and was followed by a string of mediocrities (aside from Polk, who, however, served only one term). A few historians think that Douglas MacArthur could have staged a coup d'état after being fired by Truman. This judgment is questionable; MacArthur quickly became a figure of ridicule.[41] Eisenhower, while arguably a strong president, used his powers moderately. Americans admire the military but the culture is not militaristic; aside from Washington, Eisenhower, and Jackson, no great military leader has had any success as a politician.[42]

The worst decade for democracy was the 1930s, when global economic upheaval produced dictatorships around the world. Conditions were worse in the United States than in many of these countries. For a very brief period, some Americans admired Mussolini, who seemed to be able to get things done. In 1927, Studebaker even named one of its cars the "Dictator."[43] But the rise of dictatorship in Europe and elsewhere, especially when it took an ugly turn in the 1930s, spurred a backlash in the United States. The only serious American politician who could even remotely seem to fit the fascist mold was Huey Long, the governor of Louisiana from 1928 to 1932, and senator from 1932 to 1935. As governor and leader of a political party, Long advanced a populist platform of redistribution and public works. He was a charismatic leader who some believe sought to create a cult of personality and to obtain dictatorial powers.[44] Whether or not he had this goal, he never came close to achieving it at the national level. He was assassinated before he had any serious prospect of obtaining national power.

Stepping back from the details, two points stand out. The most powerful, quasi-dictatorial presidents are often the very presidents who have obtained the approval of history; Lincoln and Roosevelt are exemplars. Such presidents overcame the gridlock of ordinary politics and supplied new policies that made them enduringly beloved. If there is consensus about anything in American history, it is that Lincoln and Roosevelt were great presidents. Moreover, even the quasi-dictatorial presidents have obeyed basic constraints, such as the need to stand for election and respect the results. These two features plausibly flow from the same source, presidential sensitivity to public opinion and the judgment of fellow citizens.

HYPOTHESES

This quick historical sketch suggests several hypotheses about the role of tyrannophobia in American history. The first is that the inheritance of tyrannophobia, as reflected in the Declaration of Independence and founding debates, has served Americans well by providing a bulwark against abuse of executive power—either by motivating de jure constraints on the executive or popular skepticism toward demagogues who sought executive office. Such people could not gain traction at a national level or for any amount of time because they awoke historical memories of Caesar and Cromwell. Popular presidents like FDR faced similar tyrannophobic resistance.[45] Tyrannophobia damaged FDR's standing when he tried to pack the Supreme Court, and tyrannophobia would lead to the enactment of institutional constraints on the executive after FDR's administration ended, such as the Twenty-second Amendment, which limited the president to two terms, and the Administrative Procedure Act, which imposed procedural constraints on executive administration.[46] On this view, a central feature of American political psychology—fear of executive power—serves as a constraint on the executive every bit as important as the separation of powers and other institutional constraints.

The second hypothesis is that American tyrannophobia has been a fundamentally irrational phenomenon that has interfered with needed institutional development. Caesar took control of a highly militarized and hierarchical society. The seventeenth-century England of Cromwell and the Stuarts was also profoundly different from that of the United States— agrarian, poorly educated, riven by violent religious conflicts, aristocratic, and centered around a hereditary monarchy. What relevance could these examples have for the United States—relatively educated, egalitarian, and religiously peaceful from the founding, and then industrialized, highly educated, and secular over time? We might think of tyrannophobia as similar to other prejudices that perhaps had some social function under radically different circumstances in the distant past, but that have no place in modern times, and only retard institutional change that is needed to address modern challenges.[47] Indeed, if the aim is to minimize the risk of dictatorship, or just to take optimal precautions against it, tyrannophobia might be counterproductive, for reasons we will discuss.

The first two hypotheses treat tyrannophobia as a causal factor; another possibility is that it is epiphenomenal. Americans fear the executive, but this fear does not make the risk of dictatorship greater or less. Tyrannophobia is an effect, not a cause. We will take up these hypotheses both from a comparative perspective and as applied to the United States.

DOES TYRANNOPHOBIA PREVENT DICTATORSHIP?

One way to evaluate the hypotheses mentioned above is by doing cross-country comparisons. We begin by attempting to test the hypothesis that tyrannophobia helps to prevent dictatorship. We find no evidence for that effect. Across polities, tyrannophobia is no safeguard of democracy. The literature attributes dictatorship to general demographic variables; our own look at the evidence leaves this conclusion undisturbed.

The hypothesis is that public fear of dictatorship—tyrannophobia—explains why some states never become dictatorships, while others do. To test this hypothesis, one needs a measure of tyrannophobia. In our discussion of American history, we appealed to documentary sources. We do not have the expertise to conduct a similar analysis for other countries; nor is it obvious how one could convert documentary evidence into a quantifiable variable.

Indeed, tyrannophobia might be a culturally specific phenomenon, unique to the United States. It is difficult to think of another country where fear of the executive is such an important part of political discourse (although, as we will see, American tyrannophobia appears to be an elite phenomenon, not shared by the general population). Many countries are, of course, authoritarian, and people in authoritarian countries rarely criticize the government openly. Consider China and Russia. Among democracies, some have an authoritarian streak, such as France with its Gaullist tradition. In Germany, the touchstone for political discourse is not dictatorship but nationalism. Britain, not threatened by dictatorship since the seventeenth century, is comfortable with its ceremonial monarchy, powerful Parliament, and (hence) exceptionally powerful prime minister. One might think that tyrannophobia would flourish in countries that have recently moved from dictatorship to democracy, such as Brazil, Argentina, Chile, and Indonesia, but one must recall that in many of those countries, partisans of the defunct authoritarian regime remain and wield substantial influence. By contrast, the United States kicked out its Tories after the Revolution.

We have searched for quantitative proxies for tyrannophobia, and the best we have found are results from the World Values Survey.[48] We focus on two questions. The first question asks whether having a "strong leader" is very good, fairly good, bad, or very bad.[49] The second question asks whether "democracies are indecisive and have too much squabbling" and gave respondents the choice of answering: agree strongly, agree, disagree, and strongly disagree.[50] We assume that tyrannophobes are more likely to answer the first question with "very bad" and the second question with "strongly disagree."

We put together a dataset that includes the survey results (in both cases, the variable equals the sum of the percentages of the two positive responses), along with the Polity IV democracy score for 2000 (from 0 to 10, reflecting increasing democratization), per capita GDP for 2000, and information regarding whether the country was governed by a dictatorship at any time after 1950.[51] Table 6.1 provides the information for 22 countries.

Our dataset is cross-sectional, so we cannot directly test whether a democracy with a tyrannophobic population is less likely to become a dictatorship. Instead, we simply looked for correlations. We do not find statistically significant correlations that support the psycho-cultural hypothesis.[52] A tyrannophobic public (as measured by answers to the survey questions) is just as likely to live in a nondemocracy as in a democracy. There is thus no evidence that tyrannophobia prevents the rise of dictatorships.

ALTERNATIVE EXPLANATIONS FOR THE ABSENCE OF DICTATORSHIP

If tyrannophobia does not prevent dictatorship, what does?

Demographics

Probably the most robust result of cross-country empirical work on dictatorship is that the best safeguard for democracy is wealth. No democracy has collapsed in a nation whose average per capita income was greater than a little over $6,000 in 1995 dollars.[53] (In Weimar Germany in 1933, average per capita income was $3,556, down from $4,090 in 1928).[54] Stated in 2008 dollars, average per capita income in the United States is no less than $39,751.[55] If this pattern reflects causal forces, the United States is

Table 6.1. SURVEY RESULTS FOR SELECTED NATIONS

Country	"Strong Leader"	"Democracies Indecisive"	Polity IV Democracy (2000)	Per Capita GDP (2000)	Period of Dictatorship (1950–2007)
Australia	24%	—	10	$23,200	—
Belgium	33%	61%	10	$25,300	—
Brazil	64%	—	8	$6,500	1964–1984
Canada	22%	50%	10	$24,800	—
China	36%	35%	0	$3,600	1950–2007
Colombia	31%	—	7	$6,200	1950–1956
Egypt	16%	29%	0	$3,600	1952–2007
France	33%	74%	9	$24,400	—
Germany	17%	35%	10	$23,400	—
India	64%	66%	9	$2,200	—
Indonesia	24%	25%	7	$2,900	1957–1998
Iran	74%	28%	4	$6,300	1950–1996
					2004–2007
Japan	24%	43%	10	$24,900	—
Mexico	58%	62%	8	$9,100	1950–1987
Nicaragua	19%	—	8	$2,700	1950–1983
Russia	57%	72%	7	$7,700	1950–1991
South Africa	44%	52%	9	$8,500	—
Spain	33%	36%	10	$18,000	1950–1975
Sweden	18%	48%	10	$22,200	—
United Kingdom	28%	45%	10	$22,800	—
United States	33%	39%	10	$36,200	—
Vietnam	9%	—	0	$1,950	1954–2007

Sources: World Values Survey, http://www.worldvaluessurvey.org (last visited July 15, 2009); Polity IV Annual Time-Series 1800–2007: Excel time-series data, http://www.systemicpeace.org/inscr/p4v2007.xls (last visited July 30, 2009); Central Intelligence Agency World Factbook, http://cia.gov/library/publications/download/download-2001/factbook_2001.zip (last visited July 30, 2009) (all values in 2000 dollars.). Data were obtained through the Online Data Analysis feature using both the fourth wave (1999–2004) and the fifth wave (2005–2008) of the World Values Survey. The primary survey data used were from the responses to "Political system: Having a strong leader (E114)," and "Future changes: Greater respect for authority (E018)" from the fifth wave. These data were supplemented with fourth wave data from those two questions and "Democracies are indecisive and have too much squabbling (E121)." Where there were data from both waves, only the most recent survey results were used. When the survey results had two options for positive responses, the response rates were aggregated. The Polity IV Democracy score "is an additive eleven-point scale (0–10). The operational indicator of democracy is derived from codings of the competitiveness of political participation (variable 2.6), the openness and competitiveness of executive recruitment (variables 2.3 and 2.2), and constraints on the chief executive (variable 2.4)." Monty G. Marshall & Keith Jaggers, *Polity IV Project: Political Regime Characteristics and Transitions, 1800–2007 Dataset Users' Manual* 13, http://www.systemicpeace.org/inscr/p4manualv2007.pdf (last visited July 30, 2007). The period of dictatorship was determined by looking at both the Democracy score and the actual Polity IV score, which is the composite of the Democracy score and the Autocracy score. *Id.* at 15.

unlikely to become a dictatorship in the foreseeable future, simply because of its enormous wealth.

What causes the association between wealth and the stability of democracy? The causes are uncertain, even if the pattern itself is robust. One account is that "the intensity of distributional conflicts is lower at higher income levels."[56] On this model, as income rises, the marginal utility of further increases in income declines, so the relatively poor will have less to gain (in utility terms) from subverting the democratic order in order to redistribute wealth to themselves, while the relatively rich will have less to lose from majoritarian redistribution under democracy. The poor will accept less redistribution, the rich will accept more, the set of policies that are politically acceptable to both sides expands, and no social group thinks it is worthwhile to gamble on a bid for dictatorship.

A different but compatible model focuses on inequality between elites and masses.[57] Democracy, in the sense of the electoral franchise, arises when masses can credibly threaten to revolt and to expropriate the wealth of rich elites. The elites want to buy off the masses with a measure of redistribution, but a promise to make direct transfers is not credible; the masses realize that once the revolutionary crowd has dispersed, elites will have no incentive to redistribute. Understanding this, elites offer the masses voting power so as to credibly commit to share the wealth.[58] In a majoritarian democracy with a skewed distribution of wealth, the median voter will vote for transfers from rich to poor. The model implies that democracy will come into existence only when inequality is neither too high nor too low; if inequality is very high, the elites will have too much to lose from redistribution and will choose to fight it out, while if inequality is very low, the masses will have too little incentive to organize for revolution in the first place.

So both wealth in the absolute sense and the distribution of wealth are relevant, to both the emergence of democracy and its stability over time. Empirically, factors besides wealth and moderate redistribution can also help to create or sustain democracy, although these factors appear less important.[59] A higher average level of education lowers the costs to citizens of mobilizing en masse to create a credible threat against elites, lowers the costs of obtaining and processing information about government action, and socializes citizens in the putative virtues of the democratic order in which they live. Ethnic and linguistic homogeneity are positively correlated with the stability of democracy,[60] perhaps because homogeneity lowers the costs of mass organization. Finally, where there is heterogeneity, the existence of "overlapping cleavages"—cross-cutting social structures rather than unified and hostile subgroups—helps democracy as well.[61]

The upshot is that most factors favor democracy in the United States, including wealth, education, and "overlapping cleavages." Although the United States is a heterogeneous country, it has been uniquely effective at assimilating immigrants with different backgrounds. The most worrisome factor is inequality: the United States in recent years has achieved levels of inequality higher than that of most countries (for which there are calculations), placing it in an uncomfortable group consisting mostly of developing countries with weak political institutions.[62]

Institutional Design

The institutional design hypothesis is that constitutional structure and rights prevent dictatorship. A central controversy in the literature involves a possible connection between presidentialism and the failure of democracy. A number of scholars have argued that presidential systems are more brittle than parliamentary ones, in the sense that presidential systems are more likely to collapse into authoritarian rule.[63] A key mechanism behind this result is that presidential systems "are highly vulnerable to legislative-executive deadlocks."[64] In times of economic or political crisis especially, such deadlocks create public demand for the strong hand of a dictator, and an elected president can more easily meet that demand by staging an *autogolpe* than can any other official.

On this view, presidentialism is especially risky in the presence of a fragmented party system.[65] Where parties multiply, gridlock follows, and an independently elected executive can appear to stand above party, offering decisive action while facing little in the way of organized countervailing power. The framers failed to anticipate the development of the modern political party,[66] and in America's early history parties were fluid, fragmentary and ill-defined, so this path to dictatorship was a live possibility—at least if the theory is correct. However, an alternative view is that the empirical pattern is an artifact of selection effects: presidential systems collapse into dictatorships because presidential systems are selected in unstable countries.[67] At present, there is no scholarly consensus on the issue.

Where does this leave us? The demographic hypothesis looks stronger than ever in light of the weak or ambiguous results for the competitors. To be sure, our data analysis has been extremely tentative and crude. We think there is enough here, however, to justify skepticism toward the psychological hypothesis that tyrannophobia preserves democracy against the threat of dictatorship.

Against this historical and comparative background, we turn to the relationship between tyrannophobia and dictatorship in the United States. If tyrannophobia were a crucial safeguard against dictatorship, it would have benefits. However, we believe that tyrannophobia is either not a safeguard against dictatorship, or is at best an unnecessary and costly one, akin to placing one's house underground to guard against the risk of a meteor strike. In the administrative state that flowered in the twentieth century, demographic factors and the basic constraint of elections jointly provide an independent and sufficient buffer against dictatorship. The contemporary United States is too wealthy, with a population that is too highly educated, to slide into authoritarianism. An implication is that even if tyrannophobia reduces the risk of dictatorship, it must also constrain grants of power to the executive that are otherwise desirable. The former effect is a benefit, the latter a cost; but the benefit is minimal, because demography and elections, taken together, independently prevent dictatorship. Accordingly, either tyrannophobia has no effect on the risk of dictatorship, or else it produces social costs for little in the way of offsetting benefits.

Causes of Tyrannophobia

As we saw above, tyrannophobic rhetoric, possibly rational, played an important role in the American founding. The puzzle is that, even if it was justified in that period as a prophylactic against dictatorship (and it may well not have been), it has persisted across two hundred years of political stability.

Bounded rationality

Psychologists have offered a number of hypotheses for why people have incorrect beliefs about the risk of an event. These hypotheses center around bounded rationality, particularly cognitive biases and reliance on mental shortcuts called heuristics.[68] People exaggerate risks of events that inspire them with dread (cancer deaths rather than ordinary illnesses), that they have no control over (nuclear accidents rather than car accidents), and that have unusual salience. The first tendency is related to loss aversion, the attribution of greater weight to losses than to identical gains against an arbitrary reference point. People are also imperfect Bayesians: they update probability estimates in light of new information as they should, but they do not do this very well or very quickly. Instead they give too much weight to their initial estimates and discount new information that conflicts with it. Past probability estimates are stickier, over time, than would be the case with unbounded rationality.

Let us compare a relatively unconstrained executive and an executive who takes orders from a legislature. There is a straightforward trade-off: the first executive can adopt policies very easily; the second must obtain the consent of a majority of the legislature. Accordingly, the first executive can more easily act to advance and undermine the public good; the second executive will have to choose from a narrower range of policy outcomes, with a limited upside and downside for the public.

We can immediately see that the executive's ability to inflict worse as well as better outcomes will engage the public's loss aversion. People will irrationally overweight the bad outcome, and hence they will exaggerate the downside of the strong executive relative to the upside. The limited executive, with its limited downside, will therefore be more appealing. More speculatively, it is possible that people feel that they have less control over the executive—a remote figure with a national constituency—than over the legislature, by virtue of their representation by an individual with whom they are more likely to have contact (or to know someone who knows him or her, etc.). Further, the president is a salient figure, the personification of government and the focus of the national media. It follows that the risks and consequences of executive power are also more salient than the risks of legislative and judicial power. Finally, and even more speculatively, imperfect Bayesian updating implies that possibly justified fears of executive overreaching that existed in earlier periods, including the founding, could outlast changes in circumstances.[69] Bayesian updating is an attribute of individual decision-making of course, but perhaps such a phenomenon could take place at a collective level. Successive generations inherit attitudes toward the executive held by previous generations; attitudes that might be justified at an earlier time are not adjusted by later generations in light of changed circumstances, such as the improved education of the citizenry.

One might even suggest that in a country such as the United States with strong traditions of equality and individualism, the president will frequently be the target of strong feelings of resentment and envy. The pomp of the office sits uneasily with republican sensibilities. The suspicion that any president will secretly attempt to obtain dictatorial powers might help resolve cognitive dissonance between these feelings and the evident inability of presidents to do much more than respond to crises and implement a tiny portion of their political agenda.[70] Tyrannophobia is an element of the broader paranoid style in American politics, which attributes vast, wrenching social changes to the machinations of individuals or small groups thought to have extraordinary power.[71]

Overall, then, the suggestion is that ongoing tyrannophobia in the United States can be explained by cognitive biases and other psychological phenomena. Just as a single nuclear accident can cause people to overestimate the risks of nuclear energy and hence demand that government shut down that industry, with the result that no further accident can ever occur, the prefounding brush with executive tyranny—followed by the dictatorships of such figures as Mussolini, Hitler, Stalin, and Mao—has caused Americans to overestimate the risk of executive power and hence recoil against even reasonable moves toward greater executive authority. Even though dictatorship has never existed in the United States, Americans fear dictators and refuse to support anyone who seems to have dictatorial ambitions, and are reluctant to support legislative and constitutional changes that could increase executive power; this reluctance persists even though circumstances have changed, and the actual risks of dictatorship are far lower than in the past.

Rational updating

There is a second and related possibility, which resonates with American political culture; we will state it only briefly. On this account, the relaxation, over time, of de jure checks on the presidency has fed tyrannophobia, because the growth of de facto checks on the presidency is ignored. Tocqueville observed that Americans are legalistic,[72] and it is still a striking fact of American political discourse that even elites tend to equate the absence of *legal* checks on the executive with the absence of *any* checks on the executive. Political checks on the executive are more amorphous and vague than legal checks; they do not often produce the sort of salient constitutional showdowns that occur when presidential power is tested and constrained by a decision of the Supreme Court. The epistemic costs of acquiring and processing information about political checks are higher than for legal checks, so even rational citizens might underestimate the extent and strength of the former relative to the latter. The consequence is that as legal checks erode, the populace will increase its estimate of the risks of dictatorship, while the actual risk may remain constant or even decline, depending on the actual strength of the political checks.

On this account, tyrannophobia need not rest upon bounded rationality in the sense of psychological quirks. It is merely an overestimate of the risks of dictatorship arising from positive information costs—more precisely, differences in the cost of acquiring information about different types of constraint on the executive. An implication is that if the costs of political information fall because of the Internet and other technological advances, the public will know more about political checks on the executive, and tyrannophobia will abate.[73]

The Effects of Tyrannophobia

Tyrannophobia and the risk of dictatorship

Tyrannophobia might itself affect the risk of dictatorship. This effect, if it exists, might run in either of two directions: widespread tyrannophobia among the public or elites might either reduce the risk of dictatorship or actually increase it. A third possibility is that tyrannophobia has no independent causal force at all. We will consider these possibilities in turn.

On the first possibility, tyrannophobia is a fear that provides its own remedy. Perhaps the United States has never come close to dictatorship in part because tyrannophobia is widespread, causing political actors to take stringent precautions against executive abuses, including hyperbolic assertions that any increase in executive power is the harbinger of dictatorship. In the most optimistic version of this account, the framers premised central institutions of American constitutional law on the fear of dictatorship and geared them to minimize the risk, but this is desirable because the risk is high; eternal vigilance is the price of liberty. If the risk has never materialized, that is because our vigilance has never lapsed. Moreover, the longer the period with no dictatorship—where dictators have occasionally materialized in other nations, even seemingly liberal and democratic ones—the more the framers' fears of dictatorship seem justified, in a cycle of self-confirming expectations.

Unfortunately, that optimistic possibility is observationally equivalent to two other possibilities: (1) dictatorship is not observed in the United States because it was never a real risk in the first place, even without the institutions erected to guard against it; (2) the precautionary institutions actually had the perverse effect of increasing the risk of dictatorship, but by fortuity that risk never materialized. In either case, the elaborate safeguards against dictatorship built into the constitutional structure are costs that create no expected benefit or that even create expected harm. A firm that hires expensive security guards and then experiences no robberies should realize that several different inferences are possible: the guards' presence prevents the robberies (the optimistic scenario); or the risk was lower than initially feared and the guards are an unnecessary expense; or the guards' presence actually exacerbates the risk of robberies, by signaling that the firm has valuables it needs to protect, but luckily none has yet taken place. The available information does not discriminate among these possibilities. A symptom of unjustified tyrannophobia is the assumption that the optimistic story simply must be correct.

In the worst possible case, tyrannophobia might actually increase the risk of dictatorship and thus prove self-defeating. Two mechanisms might bring this about. In the first, tyrannophobic constitutional designers set up elaborate vetogates, legislative and judicial oversight, and other checks and balances, all with an eye to minimizing the risks of executive dictatorship. However, these checks and balances create gridlock and make it difficult to pass necessary reforms. Where the status quo becomes increasingly unacceptable to many, as in times of economic or political crisis, the public demands or at least accepts a dictator who can sweep away the institutional obstacles to reform.[74] Here the very elaborateness of the designers' precautions against dictatorship creates pent-up public demand that itself leads to dictatorship. Comparative politics provides (contested) evidence for this story,[75] and if Lincoln or Roosevelt had become a genuine dictator, a similar account would be natural. On this view, the United States was lucky not to have experienced dictatorship during earlier periods of its history; we return to this point shortly.

In another mechanism, tyrannophobic constitutional designers create oversight bodies to check the executive, yet these oversight bodies themselves become tyrannical. In this way, tyranny sneaks up behind the back of the tyrannophobe, who is gazing vigilantly in the wrong direction. In Honduras in 2009, a democratically elected president proposed a constitutional amendment to abolish presidential term limits. Citing the risk of executive dictatorship, legislators and soldiers dragged him from his bed and hustled him into exile—a classically dictatorial move. There are no such lurid cases in the United States, but mechanisms of legislative oversight have sometimes produced a kind of legislative tyranny writ small, as in the case of Joe McCarthy, many of whose abuses were effected through committee oversight of executive branch personnel and decision making. The fear of "Government by Judiciary"[76] is best understood as a fear that judicial checks, intended to prevent legislative or executive tyranny, will themselves produce either judicial tyranny or, more plausibly, judicial gerontocracy.

Both these mechanisms suggest that precautions against tyranny can create the risks they aim to avert.[77] Institutional design must then trade off two competing risks of tyranny, which can arise either because there are no institutional checks in place, or because the very institutions set up to guard against it produce unintended effects. Checks against tyranny embody a kind of precautionary principle. Here as elsewhere, however, precautionary principles can be self-defeating if precautions exacerbate the risk itself, so precautions must be entered on both sides of the cost-benefit ledger.[78]

So in the abstract, it is plausible that tyrannophobia prevents dictatorship, but also plausible that it exacerbates the risks. Finally, tyrannophobia might simply have no effect on the risk of dictatorship at all. The comparative evidence surveyed earlier clearly suggests this, although it does not conclusively demonstrate it. Across a large set of democracies and nondemocracies, levels of tyrannophobia, defined as the inverse of support for a strong executive, are not significantly correlated with the type of political regime. Tyrannophobic publics are as likely to live in nondemocracies as in democracies. Tyrannophobia probably does not constitute a safeguard against dictatorship, in the United States or elsewhere.

Alternative explanations

If tyrannophobia has not protected America from dictatorship, what has? We will examine two competing hypotheses: that America has avoided tyranny through the excellence of its constitutional design, and that America has avoided tyranny by virtue of its demographics. The second hypothesis has much more support.

Institutions: Of presidentialism and luck

One theory is that America has never experienced dictatorship because of the foresight of the framers. Fearing Caesarism, Cromwellism, and monarchical prerogative, the framers on this account set up an elaborate system of separated powers accompanied by checks and balances. The premise of the system was that the union of executive, legislative, and judicial powers in the same hands "may justly be pronounced the very definition of tyranny."[79] The framers also limited the executive's emergency powers, in part by providing safeguards against suspension of the writ of habeas corpus, whose central function is to ensure judicial review of executive detention.[80]

Perhaps these institutional devices have succeeded in some broad sense, even considering the rise of the so-called imperial presidency in the twentieth century. Roosevelt failed to pack the Court, in part because of widespread fear of executive dictatorship;[81] the Administrative Procedure Act, forced through despite a reluctant executive, created procedural and judicial checks on executive power; Nixon was forced from office by the threat of impeachment; and Congress set up the framework statutes of the 1970s, such as the War Powers Resolution[82] and the National Emergencies Act,[83] in order to constrain future abuses. In each of the cases, the basic separation of powers—implying a powerful and independent legislature—hampered executive aggrandizement because the legislature resisted it. Although the separation of powers in the legal sense has undoubtedly been weakened in the twentieth century, in part by the death of the nondelegation doctrine and the grant of massive rulemaking powers to the executive, its functions have been taken up, in part, by competition between political parties.[84]

Viewed in terms of comparative constitutional design, however, the framers' choices seem in hindsight to have been poor ones, at least from the standpoint of minimizing the risk of dictatorship. The central decision to create an independently elected executive—although rationalized in the Federalist Papers as a tyranny-prevention measure—was in fact adopted *faute de mieux*, after a protracted stalemate at the convention, which came very close to adopting a parliamentary model in which the executive would be selected by the majority party in Congress.[85] In comparative perspective, the choice of a presidential system turns out to have been risky, although, to be fair, the framers lacked the information needed to understand the effects of their choice.

As we saw above, some scholars believe that presidential systems are more likely to collapse into authoritarian rule than parliamentary systems are, at least at low levels of wealth and especially in the presence of fragmented parties. If these scholars are correct, the separation of powers in the American sense of a separately elected executive is a risk factor for dictatorship, rather than a precaution against it; to the extent that this is true, and if tyranny-prevention was the framers' major aim, the framers blundered.[86] By a happy accident of history, however, America inherited the first-past-the-post electoral system from Britain, and that system has a well-documented tendency to create, over time, two dominant parties,[87] in turn reducing the risks of presidentialism. Thus the risks that a fragmented party system may create, under presidentialism, were avoided.[88] Here again the framers acted from ignorance, but their choices were fortuitous. In addition, the decision to give emergency powers to Congress (in the suspension clause), rather than the president, probably did not help forestall a dictatorship. Lincoln violated the clause, and Congress acquiesced.

This is not to say that institutional choice did not matter at all. After all, the founders could have, but did not, establish a dictatorship. One could plausibly argue that the federalist structure of the Constitution helped deter the formation of a *national* dictatorship. Anyone who aspired to absolute power would have to contend with independent power centers in the states even after subjugating Congress and the federal judiciary. Federalism also weakens incentives to form a dictatorship in a state: ease of exit would deprive the dictator of rents. An independent judiciary, as opposed to one maintained and funded by the executive, also would be a nuisance to an aspiring dictator. All that said, however, it is plausible that the United States has avoided tyranny largely despite its constitutional design, not because of that design.

Demography and the administrative state

The best explanation for the lack of dictatorship in America—at least in America today, as opposed to the nineteenth century—is neither psychological nor institutional, but demographic. Comparative evidence suggests that wealth is the best safeguard for democracy. Equality, homogeneity, and education matter as well. How does the United States, circa 2011, fare on these dimensions? Ethnic, religious, and linguistic homogeneity have declined, and inequality has risen, but because of its high performance on other margins, there is little cause for concern about American democracy. The United States has an enormously rich, relatively well-educated population and multiple overlapping cleavages of class, race, religion, and geography. Simply by virtue of its high per capita income, the likelihood of dictatorship in the United States is very low, at least if the historical pattern reflects causation. The high-water mark of the modern presidency's approach to domestic dictatorship—Nixon's "third-rate burglary" of the offices of his political opponents—was pathetic stuff in historical and comparative perspective, and immediately put Nixon on the path to disgrace. Likewise, comparisons between Weimar Germany and the United States of the Bush administration[89] were, to say the least, exaggerated.

We add a less obvious point. Legal scholars, especially those of a libertarian or civil-libertarian bent, often express concern that the formal separation of powers has atrophied over the course of the twentieth century. On this account, economic and security crises, the rise of the administrative state, the death of the nondelegation doctrine, the imperial presidency, the ineffectual character of the War Powers Resolution and the other framework statutes of the 1970s, all mean that in many domains presidents operate without substantial legal checks, although they have political incentives to cooperate with Congress and to seek statutory authorization for their actions. Among the framers' miscalculations was their failure to understand the "presidential power of unilateral action"[90]—the president's power to take action in the real world, with debatable legal authority or none at all, creating a new status quo that then constrains the response of other institutions. In the most overheated version of this view, such developments are taken to pose a real risk of executive tyranny in the United States.[91]

We suggest, however, that the same large-scale economic and political developments that have caused a relaxation of the legal checks on the executive have simultaneously strengthened the nonlegal checks. Legal checks on the presidency have been relaxed largely because of the need for centralized, relatively efficient government under the complex conditions of a modern dynamic economy and a highly interrelated international order. Yet those economic and political conditions have themselves helped to create de facto constraints on presidential power that make democracy in the United States stable.

The modern economy, whose complexity creates the demand for administrative governance, also creates wealth, leisure, education, and broad political information, all of which strengthen democracy and make a collapse into authoritarian rule nearly impossible. Modern presidents are substantially constrained, not by old statutes or even by Congress and the courts, but by the tyranny of public and (especially) elite opinion. Every action is scrutinized, leaks from executive officials come in a torrent, journalists are professionally hostile, and potential abuses are quickly brought to light. The modern presidency is a fishbowl, in large part because the costs of acquiring political information have fallen steadily in the modern economy, and because a wealthy, educated, and leisured population has the time to monitor presidential action and takes an interest in doing so. This picture implies that modern presidents are both more accountable than their predecessors and more responsive to gusts of elite sentiment and mass opinion, but they are not dictators in any conventional sense.

More tentatively, we also suggest that the relaxation of legal checks may *itself* have contributed to the growth of the political checks, rather than both factors simply being the common result of a complex modern economy. On this hypothesis, the administrative and presidential state of the New Deal and later has, despite all its inefficiencies, plausibly supplied efficiency-enhancing regulation, political stability, and a measure of redistribution, and these policies have both added to national economic and cultural capital and dampened political conflict. The administrative state has thus helped to create a wealthy, educated population and a supereducated elite whose members have the leisure and affluence to care about matters such as civil liberties, who are politically engaged, and who help to check executive abuses. However, while the direct effects of wealth, education, and other factors on the stability of democracy are clear in comparative perspective, there is more dispute about the overall economic effects of regulation and the administrative state.[92]

THE COSTS AND BENEFITS OF TYRANNOPHOBIA

We have suggested that the framers' tyrannophobia, combined with the lack of dictatorship in later periods, plausibly fuels contemporary tyrannophobia, insofar as contemporary actors infer that the framers' design choices are what has allowed democracy to endure. However, the inference is invalid, for the key choice of presidentialism may itself have been a risk factor for dictatorship; if it was, then the framers inadvertently put self-government at risk, but were favored by fortune. Likewise, while it is possible that tyrannophobia has an endogenous tyranny-preventing effect, it is equally possible that it perversely increases the risk, and the most plausible conclusion of all is that it has no effect in either direction; to ignore the latter two possibilities is itself a major symptom of tyrannophobia. Tyrannophobia in the United States is real, and it may well be the result of the psychological and informational factors discussed above, but there is no evidence that it contributes to the absence of dictatorship in the United States, and some affirmative evidence that it does not do so.

Even if tyrannophobia has a weak effect of that sort, it seems clear that wealth and other demographic factors in all likelihood prevent dictatorship in the United States, quite apart from its tyrannophobic political culture. So even if tyrannophobia once checked dictatorship, that check is unnecessary today, in light of the exceptional stability of advanced democratic polities like the United States. The main possible benefit of tyrannophobia is therefore illusory. On the other hand, if tyrannophobia hampers useful grants of power to the executive, it creates social costs, namely an entrenched reluctance to transfer necessary powers to the executive. Elsewhere, we have described a range of institutions and policy initiatives that would increase welfare by increasing executive power, especially in the domain of counterterrorism, but that are blocked by "libertarian panics" and tyrannophobia.[93] Overall, then, the cost-benefit ledger of tyrannophobia shows real costs and illusory benefits.

To be sure, even if tyrannophobia is not needed to prevent dictatorship, it might usefully prevent executive abuse that falls short of dictatorship. Consider the possibility, for example, that executives are naturally inclined to use their powers to spy on and otherwise harass political opponents—not to establish dictatorship, but just to obtain a marginal advantage in the next election.[94] This is harmful behavior that should be deterred. If institutions can deter this behavior only with difficulty because executive officials all answer to the president, perhaps tyrannophobia can deter it. The executive, expecting overreaction by the public if word leaks out, does not engage in the abusive behavior in the first place.

This is certainly possible, and if the choice is between tyrannophobia and a completely inert and indifferent public, tyrannophobia might seem preferable. Better still, however, would be a rational and informed public that would express the appropriate amount of outrage when the executive engages in abuse, and that could distinguish gradations of abuse rather than treat all such actions as steps on the road to dictatorship. Modern economies, which feature falling information costs and a leisured elite, tend to create such publics, although for the reasons we have discussed, tyrannophobia persists as well.

This version of the case for tyrannophobia—as a deterrent to low-level executive abuses—is more plausible than the more ambitious argument that tyrannophobia is justified because it deters dictatorship. Low-level executive abuse has taken place in the United States in living memory, and so one might want to nourish tyrannophobia so that executives fear that even minor abuses will lead to a harsh public reaction and are deterred. But this weaker argument is vulnerable to the same kinds of objection as the stronger argument. There is no evidence that tyrannophobia deters low-level executive abuse; it is equally plausible that overheated rhetoric limits beneficial grants of power to the executive. As before, the benefit side of this trade-off is likely to be illusory at least in part, for an educated and leisured population, and the regular cycle of elections, will themselves check executive abuses—as evidenced by the 2006 and 2008 elections in the United States. The problems here have the same structure as the problem of whether tyrannophobia deters dictatorship proper, but with all the costs and benefits diluted to an uncertain degree.

There is one last case for tyrannophobia. Suppose that rational members of the public would free ride on each other, with the result that actual public scrutiny of the presidency falls short of the optimal. Instilling people with tyrannophobia might give them the emotional impetus to overcome the collective action problem. But the presidency already has intrinsic interest for the public. "As the parties wasted away, the Presidency stood out in solitary majesty as the central focus of political emotion, the ever more potent symbol of national community."[95] On this account, presidents already receive close public scrutiny; judiciaphobia and legislatophobia would be healthier political emotions.

CONCLUSION

Tyrannophobia is a central element of American political culture, and has been since the founding. We have offered several claims and hypotheses to illuminate its origins and importance. We suggest that tyrannophobia arises from the interaction between history and the quirks of political psychology, or from the differential costs of information about legal and political checks on the executive; that dictatorship in the strong sense is not a real possibility in the United States today because of demographic factors and the electoral constraint; that dictatorship in the weak sense of executive abuse is not a problem that overheated rhetoric about tyranny can successfully address;[96] and that tyrannophobia therefore has little social utility in modern circumstances. Either tyrannophobia produces no benefits (as the evidence suggests), or it produces minimal benefits and substantial costs.

The theoretical significance of tyrannophobia is that it is betrays a central fallacy of liberal legalism: the assumption that the only possible constraints on the executive are de jure constraints. Because of this fallacy, liberal legalists see the legally unconstrained executive as a tyrant. Yet the executive is buffeted by political winds and the criticism of elites, and is thus highly sensitive to shifts in public opinion. In one version of tyrannophobia, liberal legalists fear a "plebiscitary presidency," but this is if anything too weak a description of the executive in the administrative state; rather than responding merely to periodic plebiscites, the executive is constantly buffeted by the latest poll numbers and opinion cascades. Ironically, the plebiscitary presidency is constrained, not tyrannical. But law is not what provides the constraint.

Conclusion

We do not yet live under a plebiscitary presidency. In such a system, the president has unchecked legal powers except for the obligation to submit to periodic elections. In our system, Congress retains the formal power to make law. It has subjected presidential lawmaking to complex procedures and bureaucratic checks,[1] and it has created independent agencies over which the president in theory has limited control. The federal courts can expect the executive to submit to their orders, and the Supreme Court retains certain quasi-lawmaking powers, which it exercises by striking down statutes and blocking executive actions. The federal system is still in place. State legal institutions retain considerable power over their populations.

But these legal checks on executive authority (aside from the electoral constraint) have eroded considerably over the last two hundred years. Congress has delegated extensive powers to the executive. For new initiatives, the executive leads and Congress follows. Congress can certainly slow down policymaking, and block bills proposed by the executive; but it cannot set the agenda. It is hard to quantify the extent of congressional control over regulatory agencies, but it is fair to say that congressional intervention is episodic and limited, while presidential control over both the executive and independent agencies is strong and growing stronger. The states increasingly exercise authority at the sufferance of the national government and hence the president. The federal courts have not tried to stop the erosion of congressional power and state power.

Some commentators argue that the federal courts have taken over Congress's role as an institutional check. It is true that the Supreme Court has shown little compunction about striking down statutes (although usually state statutes), and that it rejected some of the legal theories that the Bush administration used to justify its counterterrorism policies. However, the Court remains a marginal player. The Court ducked any legal rulings on counterterror policies until the 2004 *Hamdi* decision, and even after the *Boumediene* decision in 2008, no detainee has been released by final judicial order, from Guantánamo or elsewhere, except in cases where the government chose not to appeal the order of a district judge. The vast majority of detainees have received merely another round of legal process. Some speculate that judicial threats to release detainees have caused the administration to release them preemptively. Yet the judges would incur large political costs for actual orders to release suspected terrorists, and the government knows this, so it is unclear that the government sees the judicial threats as credible or takes them very seriously. The government, of course, has many administrative and political reasons to release detainees, quite apart from anything the courts do. So the executive submits to judicial orders in part because the courts are careful not to give orders that the executive will resist.

In general, judicial opposition to the Bush administration's counterterrorism policies took the form of incremental rulings handed down at a glacial pace, none of which actually stopped any of the major counterterrorism tactics of that administration, including the application of military power against Al Qaeda, the indefinite detention of members of Al Qaeda, targeted assassinations, the immigration sweeps, even coercive interrogation. The (limited) modifications of those tactics that have occurred resulted not from legal interventions but from policy adjustments driven by changed circumstances and public opinion, and by electoral victory of the Obama administration. However, the Obama administration has mostly confirmed and in some areas even expanded the counterterrorism policies of the Bush administration. Strong executive government is bipartisan.

The 9/11 attack provided a reminder of just how extensive the president's power is. The executive claimed the constitutional authority to, in effect, use emergency powers. Because Congress provided redundant statutory authority, and the Supreme Court has steadfastly refused to address the ultimate merits of the executive's constitutional claims, these claims were never tested in a legal or public forum. But it is worth trying to imagine what would have happened if Congress had refused to pass the Authorization for Use of Military Force and the Supreme Court had ordered the executive to release detainees in a contested case. We think that the executive, backed up as it was by popular opinion, would have refused to obey. And, indeed, for just that reason, Congress would never have refused its imprimatur and the Supreme Court would never have stood in the executive's way. The major check on the executive's power to declare an emergency and to use emergency powers is—political.

The financial crisis of 2008–2009 also revealed the extent of executive power. Acting together, the Fed, the Treasury, and other executive agencies spent hundreds of billions of dollars, virtually nationalizing parts of the financial system. Congress put up a fuss, but it could not make policy and indeed hardly even influenced policy. Congress initially refused to supply a blank check, then in world-record time changed its mind and gave the blank check, then watched helplessly as the administration adopted policies different from those for which it said the legislation would be needed. Courts played no role in the crisis except to ratify executive actions in tension with the law.[2]

What, then, prevents the executive from declaring spurious emergencies and using the occasion to consolidate its power—or for that matter, consolidating its power during real emergencies so that it retains that power even after normal times return? In many countries, notably in Latin America, presidents have done just that.[3] Citing an economic crisis, or a military threat, or congressional gridlock, executives have shut down independent media, replaced judges with their cronies, suppressed political opposition, and ruled by dictate. Could this happen in the United States? The answer is, very probably, no. The political check on the executive is real. Declarations of emergency not justified by publicly visible events would be met with skepticism. Actions said to be justified by emergency would not be approved if the justification were not plausible. Separation of powers may be suffering through an enfeebled old age, but electoral democracy is alive and well.

We have suggested that the historical developments that have undermined separation of powers have strengthened democracy. Consider, for example, the communications revolution, which has culminated (so far) in the Internet Age. As communication costs decrease, the size of markets expand, and hence the scale of regulatory activity must increase. Localities and states lose their ability to regulate markets, and the national government takes over. Meanwhile, reduced communication costs increase the relative value of administration (monitoring firms and ordering them to change their behavior) and reduce the relative value of legislation (issuing broad-gauged rules), favoring the executive over Congress. At the same time, reduced communication costs make it easier for the public to monitor the executive. Today, whistleblowers can easily find an audience on the Internet; people can put together groups that focus on a tiny aspect of the government's behavior; gigabytes of government data are uploaded onto the Internet and downloaded by researchers who can subject them to rigorous statistical analysis. It need not have worked out this way. Governments can also use technology to monitor citizens for the purpose of suppressing political opposition. But this has not, so far, happened in the United States. Nixon fell in part because his monitoring of political enemies caused an overwhelming political backlash, and although the Bush administration monitored suspected terrorists, no reputable critic suggested that it targeted domestic political opponents.

Our main argument has been methodological and programmatic: researchers should no longer view American political life through the Madisonian prism, while normative theorists should cease bemoaning the decline of Madisonianism and instead make their peace with the new political order. The center of gravity has shifted to the executive, which both makes policy and administers it, subject to weak constraints imposed by Congress, the judiciary, and the states. It is pointless to bewail these developments, and futile to argue that Madisonian structures should be reinvigorated. Instead, attention should shift to the political constraints on the president and the institutions through which those political constraints operate—chief among them elections, parties, bureaucracy, and the media.

As long as the public informs itself and maintains a skeptical attitude toward the motivations of government officials, the executive can operate effectively only by proving over and over that it deserves the public's trust. The irony of the new political order is that the executive, freed from the bonds of law, inspires more distrust than in the past, and thus must enter ad hoc partnerships with political rivals in order to persuade people that it means well. But the new system is more fluid, allowing the executive to form those partnerships when they are needed to advance its goals, and not otherwise. Certain types of partnership have become recurrent patterns—for example, inviting a member of the opposite party to join the president's cabinet. Others are likely in the future.

In the place of the clockwork mechanism bequeathed to us by the Enlightenment thinking of the founders, there has emerged a more organic system of power sharing and power constraint that depends on shifting political alliances, currents of public opinion, and the particular exigencies that demand government action. It might seem that such a system requires more attention from the public than can reasonably be expected, but the old system of checks and balances always depended on public opinion as well. The centuries-old British parliamentary system, which operated in just this way, should provide reason for optimism. The British record on executive abuses, although hardly perfect, is no worse than the American record and arguably better, despite the lack of a Madisonian separation of legislative and executive powers.

ACKNOWLEDGMENTS

We would like to thank the people who have helped us with this project, directly or indirectly. They include Yun Soo, Emily and Spencer Vermeule, John Carey, David Dyzenhaus, Jack Goldsmith, Michael Kenneally, Sanford Levinson, Martha Minow, Adam Tomkins, Mark Tushnet, and an anonymous reviewer for Oxford University Press. We benefited from a conference on executive power organized by Sandy Levinson at the University of Texas at Austin in the spring of 2010. We give particular thanks to Bill Scheuerman, who provided very helpful comments on the entire manuscript, as well as to other participants at the Austin conference. Also thanks to our editor, Dave McBride, for his advice and encouragement.

The book incorporates heavily revised material from the following articles:

Chapter 1: Eric A. Posner & Adrian Vermeule, "Crisis Governance in the Administrative State: 9/11 and the Financial Meltdown of 2008," 76 *University of Chicago Law Review* 1613 (2009); Eric A. Posner & Adrian Vermeule, "Constitutional Showdowns," 156 *University of Pennsylvania Law Review* 991 (2008); Adrian Vermeule, "Emergency Lawmaking after 9/11 and 7/7," 75 *University of Chicago Law Review* 1155 (2008).

Chapter 2: "Constitutional Showdowns."

Chapter 3: Adrian Vermeule, "Our Schmittian Administrative Law," 122 *Harvard Law Review* 1095 (2009); Adrian Vermeule, "Posner on Security and Liberty: Alliance to End Repression v. City of Chicago," 120 *Harvard Law Review* 1251 (2007).

Chapter 4: Eric A. Posner & Adrian Vermeule, "The Credible Executive," 74 *University of Chicago Law Review* 865 (2007).

Conclusion: Adrian Vermeule, "States of Detention," *The New Republic* (available at http://www.tnr.com/book/review/states-detention).

We thank the journals that published these papers and the many colleagues who gave us comments on them.

NOTES

INTRODUCTION

1. *See generally* BRUCE ACKERMAN, THE DECLINE AND FALL OF THE AMERICAN REPUBLIC (2010). Ackerman's book is only the most recent of a stream of works that detail the decline of the separation of powers and, more broadly, the decline of liberal legalism and the rule of law. *See, e.g.*, PETER M. SHANE, MADISON'S NIGHTMARE: HOW EXECUTIVE POWER THREATENS AMERICAN DEMOCRACY (2009); THEODORE LOWI, THE END OF LIBERALISM (1969). Curiously, these books then usually go on to offer a series of prescriptions for reviving (some version of) liberal legalism and the Madisonian separation of powers. We believe that the diagnoses of decline are so convincing that the prescriptions for revival are futile; the very motivations, beliefs, and opportunities that these authors ascribe to political actors in their diagnoses, if true, rule out their prescriptions.

2. *See generally* Richard A. Epstein, *Why the Modern Administrative State Is Inconsistent with the Rule of Law*, 3 NYU J. LAW & LIBERTY 491 (2008). The term "liberal legalism" does not use "liberal" in the debased vernacular sense in which, say, Nancy Pelosi is a liberal. Liberal legalism certainly includes self-de-scribed "classical liberals" such as Richard Epstein, who loathe delegation, fear the executive's emergency powers, and long for a return to congressional control of executive power. *See* Richard A. Epstein, *Executive Power on Steroids*, WALL ST. J., Feb. 13, 2006, at A16, *available at* http://www.cato.org/pub_display. php?pub_id=5557 ("The Constitution gives Congress the power to set policy; it gives to the president the right, and the duty, to execute it").

3. *See generally* A.V. DICEY, INTRODUCTION TO THE STUDY OF THE LAW OF THE CONSTITUTION (8th ed. 1915).

4. *See generally* DAVID DYZENHAUS, THE CONSTITUTION OF LAW: LEGALITY IN A TIME OF EMERGENCY (2006).

5. William E. Scheuerman, *The Economic State of Emergency*, 21 CARDOZO L. REV. 1869, 1887 (2000). Scheuerman expands upon this point in an important book, LIBERAL DEMOCRACY AND THE SOCIAL ACCELERATION OF TIME 107–27 (2004).

6. An illuminating exception is NOMI CLAIRE LAZAR, STATES OF EMERGENCY IN LIBERAL DEMOCRACIES (2009). Lazar argues that legal constraints on the executive are merely of instrumental value and that informal constraints

can substitute for them, and to that extent we agree. Lazar, however, remains committed to liberalism, and in this respect we think she flinches from the logic of her own conclusions. Once formal constraints on the executive are abandoned and everything is remitted to politics, there is little that is distinctively "liberal" about the resulting arrangements; it is not obvious what is gained by defining liberalism so capaciously.

7. In 2007, there were some 1.2 million civilian employees outside the Department of Defense, and another 651,000 civilian employees within. *See* John Yoo, *Administration of War*, 58 Duke L.J. 2277, 2282 & nn. 26–28 (2009).

8. *See* Shane, *supra* note 1, at 150–58.

9. *See* Neal Devins & David E. Lewis, *Not-So Independent Agencies: Party Polarization and the Limits of Institutional Design*, 88 B.U. L. Rev. 459 (2008).

10. *Compare Myers v. United States*, 272 U.S. 52 (1926) (stating that all officials exercising executive power must be removable at will by the president), *with Humphrey's Executor v. United States*, 295 U.S. 602 (1935) (confining *Myers* to "purely executive officers" as opposed to officers exercising "quasi-legislative" and "quasi-judicial" powers).

11. *See* Elena Kagan, *Presidential Administration*, 114 Harv. L. Rev. 2245 (2001).

12. For some mechanisms that support agency autonomy, and some early case studies, *see* Daniel Carpenter, The Forging of Bureaucratic Autonomy: Reputations, Networks and Policy Innovation in Executive Agencies, 1862–1928 (2001).

13. *See* Ackerman, *supra* note 1; Shane, *supra* note 1.

14. On the questions whether delegation gives de jure lawmaking authority to the executive, and whether delegation is socially beneficial, *see* Eric A. Posner & Adrian Vermeule, *Interring the Nondelegation Doctrine*, 69 U. Chi. L. Rev. 1721 (2002); and Eric A. Posner & Adrian Vermeule, *Nondelegation: A Post-Mortem*, 70 U. Chi. L. Rev. 1331 (2003).

15. *J.W. Hampton Co. v. United States*, 276 U.S. 394 (1928).

16. For a list of open-ended delegations the Court has upheld since the New Deal, *see Whitman v. Am. Trucking Ass'n*, 531 U.S. 457 (2001) (upholding a delegation to the Environmental Protection Agency of authority to set air quality standards as "requisite to protect the public health . . . with an adequate margin of safety").

17. *See Panama Ref. v. Ryan*, 293 U.S. 388 (1935) (invalidating a provision of the National Industrial Recovery Act on nondelegation grounds); *A.L.A. Schechter Poultry Corp. v. United States*, 295 U.S. 495 (1935) (invalidating other provisions of the National Industrial Recovery Act on nondelegation grounds). *See also Carter v. Carter Coal*, 298 U.S. 238, 311 (1936) (suggesting, while invalidating a statute as exceeding Congress's power over commerce, that delegation to private persons is constitutionally suspect).

18. Daryl J. Levinson & Richard H. Pildes, *Separation of Parties, Not Powers*, 119 Harv. L. Rev. 2311 (2006).

19. *See* Dyzenhaus, *supra* note 4.

20. *See* Francis E. Lee, Beyond Ideology: Politics, Principles, and Partisanship in the U. S. Senate (2009).

21. Terry M. Moe & William G. Howell, *The Presidential Power of Unilateral Action*, 15 J.L. Econ. & Org. 132 (1999); William Howell, Power without Persuasion: A Theory of Presidential Action (2003). For a recent overview of the burgeoning literature, see Kenneth R. Mayer, *Going Alone: The Presidential Power of Unilateral Action*, in The Oxford Handbook of the American Presidency 427–454 (2009).

22. Jide O. Nzelibe & Matthew Stephenson, *Complementary Constraints: Separation of Powers, Rational Voting, and Constitutional Design*, 123 Harv. L. Rev. 617 (2010).

23. *See* Arthur M. Schlesinger, Jr., The Imperial Presidency (1973). For other works in this vein, *see* Ackerman, *supra* note 1; Gene Healy, The Cult of the Presidency (2008); Charlie Savage, Takeover: The Return of the Imperial Presidency and the Subversion of American Democracy (2007); Andrew Rudalevige, The New Imperial Presidency (2005); Peter Irons, War Powers: How the Imperial Presidency Hijacked the Constitution (2005).

24. See Mayer, *supra* note 21, at 449–50.

25. To some degree, we attempt here to generalize and modify Mark Tushnet's important claim that emergency powers are subject to political regulation in addition to, and sometimes instead of, legal regulation. *See* Mark Tushnet, *The Political Constitution of Emergency Powers: Some Lessons from Hamdan*, 91 Minn. L. Rev. 1451 (2007); Mark Tushnet, *The Political Constitution of Emergency Powers: Parliamentary and Separation-of-Powers Regulation*, 3 Int'l J. L. in Context 275 (2008). The differences are that Tushnet's category of political controls includes legislative as well as executive institutions (in a separation-of-powers system), and addresses only emergency powers, whereas we take emergencies to be merely the extreme on a continuum of policy problems.

26. For political science literature on the "plebiscitary presidency," *see, e.g.,* Craig A. Rimmerman, Presidency by Plebiscite: The Reagan-Bush Era in Institutional Perspective (1993); Theodor J. Lowi, The Personal President: Power Invested, Promise Unfulfilled (1985). The foundation of this literature is Max Weber's argument for a plebiscitary president in Weimar Germany. *See* Max Weber, *The President of the Reich*, in Weber: Political Writings 304 (Peter Lassman & Ronald Speirs eds., Ronald Speirs trans., 1994).

CHAPTER 1

1. The Federalist No. 47 (James Madison).

2. *See* Matthew McCubbins & Thomas Schwartz, *Congressional Oversight Overlooked: Police Patrols versus Fire Alarms*, 28 Am. J. Pol. Sci. 16–79 (1984).

3. For the congressional dominance thesis, and a critique of its logical and evidentiary failings, see Terry M. Moe, *An Assessment of the Positive Theory of 'Congressional Dominance,'* 12 Legislative Studies Quarterly 475 (1987).

4. Daryl J. Levinson, *Empire-Building Government in Constitutional Law*, 118 HARV. L. REV. 915 (2005).

5. ALEXANDER M. BICKEL, THE LEAST DANGEROUS BRANCH ch. 4 (2d ed. 1986).

6. Howard Gillman, *How Political Parties Can Use the Courts to Advance Their Agendas: Federal Courts in the United States, 1875–1891*, 96 AM. POL. SCI. REV. 511 (2002); Jack M. Balkin & Sanford Levinson, *Understanding the Constitutional Revolution*, 87 VA. L. REV. 1045 (2001).

7. ADAM FERGUSON, AN ESSAY ON THE HISTORY OF CIVIL SOCIETY 187 (1767).

8. Bruce Ackerman, *The Emergency Constitution*, 113 YALE L.J. 1029, 1042 (2004).

9. John O. McGinnis, *Constitutional Review by the Executive in Foreign Affairs and War Powers: A Consequence of Rational Choice in the Separation of Powers*, LAW & CONTEMP. PROBS., Autumn 1993, at 303.

10. JON ELSTER, EXPLAINING SOCIAL BEHAVIOR: MORE NUTS AND BOLTS FOR THE SOCIAL SCIENCES (2007).

11. Edna Ullmann-Margalit, *Invisible-Hand Explanations*, 39 SYNTHESE 263 (1978).

12. FRIEDRICH A. HAYEK, THE USE OF KNOWLEDGE IN SOCIETY (1945).

13. Becker suggests that interest-group pressures on legislatures produce efficient legislation. *See* Gary S. Becker, *A Theory of Competition among Pressure Groups for Political Influence*, 98 Q.J. ECON. 371 (1983). But even if this is true, taken in isolation, there is no guarantee that the outputs of the whole lawmaking system will be efficient; that further thesis requires that the interaction of the branches conduces to efficiency.

14. Levinson, *supra* note 4.

15. *See* Adrian Vermeule, *Foreword: System Effects and the Constitution*, 123 HARV. L. REV. 4, 28–30 (2009).

16. Kenneth A. Shepsle, *Congress Is a They, Not an It: Legislative Intent as Oxymoron*, 12 INT'L REV. L. & ECON. 239 (1992).

17. Jon Elster, *Unwritten Constitutional Norms* (citing ARTHUR M. SCHLESINGER, JR., THE IMPERIAL PRESIDENCY 74–75 (1973)(unpublished manuscript 2010); DANIEL LAZARE, THE FROZEN REPUBLIC: HOW THE CONSTITUTION IS PARALYZING DEMOCRACY (1996)).

18. *See* KEITH KREHBIEL, INFORMATION AND LEGISLATIVE ORGANIZATION 254–57 (1991).

19. The quotation in the subhead comes from Daryl J. Levinson & Richard H. Pildes, *Separation of Parties, Not Powers*, 119 HARV. L. REV. 2311, 2312–16 (2006).

20. WILLIAM G. HOWELL & JON C. PEVEHOUSE, WHILE DANGERS GATHER (2007).

21. Levinson & Pildes, *supra* note 19; Justin Fox & Richard van Weelden, *Partisanship and the Effectiveness of Oversight* (unpublished).

22. *See* 5 U.S.C. § 2954 (permitting minorities of House and Senate committees that oversee governmental affairs to require executive agencies to produce documents).

23. United States Office of Personnel Management, Employment and Trends: Table 14—Federal Civilian Employment by Branch, Selected Agency, Pay System and Area, December 2005 and January 2006, http://www.opm.gov/feddata/html/2006/january/table14.asp (last visited Apr. 23, 2006).

24. *See* United States Department of Labor, Bureau of Labor Statistics, *Job Opportunities in the Armed Forces, in* OCCUPATIONAL OUTLOOK HANDBOOK, 2006–2007 EDITION, *available at* http://www.bls.gov/oco/ocos249.htm (visited Apr. 23, 2007) (listing military active duty personnel for 2005).

25. *See* NEIL K. KOMESAR, IMPERFECT ALTERNATIVES: CHOOSING INSTITUTIONS IN LAW, ECONOMICS, AND PUBLIC POLICY 141–42 (1994).

26. *See* Richard H. Fallon, Jr., *Legitimacy and the Constitution*, 118 HARV. L. REV. 1787, 1795 (2005).

27. *Youngstown Sheet & Tube Co. v. Sawyer*, 343 U.S. 579, 588–89 (1952).

28. *New York Times Co. v. United States*, 403 U.S. 713 (1971).

29. *Boumediene v. Bush*, 553 U.S. 723 (2008).

30. *See, e.g., Whitman v. American Trucking Associations*, 531 U.S. 457 (2001) ("[W]e have almost never felt qualified to second-guess Congress regarding the permissible degree of policy judgment that can be left to those executing or applying the law") (internal quotation omitted).

31. Kim Lane Schepple, *Small Emergencies*, 40 GA. L. REV. 835 (2006).

32. For useful introductions to and perspectives on Schmitt, *see* ELLEN KENNEDY, CONSTITUTIONAL FAILURE: CARL SCHMITT IN WEIMAR (2004); LAW AS POLITICS: CARL SCHMITT'S CRITIQUE OF LIBERALISM (David Dyzenhaus ed. 1998); WILLIAM E. SCHEUERMAN, CARL SCHMITT: THE END OF LAW (1999).

33. Schmitt lays out his theory in CARL SCHMITT, VERFASSUNGSLEHRE (1928), recently translated by Jeffery Seitzer, *see* CARL SCHMITT, CONSTITUTIONAL THEORY (Jeffrey Seitzer ed. & trans., 2007).

34. *See* CARL SCHMITT, THE CRISIS OF PARLIAMENTARY DEMOCRACY (Ellen Kennedy trans., 1985).

35. William E. Scheuerman, *The Economic State of Emergency*, 21 CARDOZO L. REV. 1869, 1887 (2000).

36. *Id.*

37. CARL SCHMITT, POLITICAL THEOLOGY: FOUR CHAPTERS ON THE CONCEPT OF SOVEREIGNTY 1 (George Schwab trans., 1985) (1922); *cf.* CARL SCHMITT, DIE DIKTATUR. VON DEN ANFÄNGEN DES MODERNEN SOUVERÄNITÄTSGEDANKENS BIS ZUM PROLETARISCHEN KLASSENKAMPF (1921). For an overview of these two works and their place in Schmitt's thought, see John P. McCormick, *The Dilemmas of Dictatorship: Carl Schmitt and Constitutional Emergency Powers, in* LAW AS POLITICS: CARL SCHMITT'S CRITIQUE OF LIBERALISM 217 (David Dyzenhaus ed., 1998).

38. SCHMITT, *supra* note 34; CARL SCHMITT, LEGALITY AND LEGITIMACY (Jeffrey Seitzer trans., 2004) (1932); WILLIAM E. SCHEUERMAN, BETWEEN THE NORM AND THE EXCEPTION: THE FRANKFURT SCHOOL AND THE RULE OF LAW (1994); Scheuerman, *supra* note 35.

39. Scheuerman, *supra* note 35, at 1887 (emphasis omitted). The description of the government's course of conduct, during the 2008 financial crisis as "regulation by deal," *see* Steven M. Davidoff & David Zaring, *Regulation by Deal: The*

Government's Response to the Financial Crisis, 61 ADMIN. L. REV. 463 (2009), fits our account perfectly.

40. WILLIAM E. SCHEUERMAN, LIBERAL DEMOCRACY AND THE SOCIAL ACCEL-ERATION OF TIME 124 (2004). In a later work, THE SITUATION OF EUROPEAN JURISPRUDENCE (1950), Schmitt seems to have worked around to the view that the customs and traditions of judge-centered legal professionalism could act as a check on the ever-increasing pace of modern lawmaking. *See* SCHEUERMAN, *supra*, at 127–43. This seems to us inconsistent with the larger arc of Schmitt's thought; here too, if the diagnosis is correct, the prescription seems hopeless. *Cf.* SCHEUERMAN, *supra*, at 140:

It is . . . unclear why we should expect recourse to either Savigny's cus-tomary law or Anglo-American common law to resolve the dilemmas at hand. To the extent that traditional forms of judge-centered legal practice are indeed cautious and time-consuming, they would seem ill-fitted to the imperatives of social acceleration. At the very least the misfit between the high-speed tempo of social and economic life and the slow-going pace of lawmaking would probably be even greater under the rule of common law courts than under elected legislatures.

41. Scheuerman, *supra* note 35, at 1888.
42. *See N. Jersey Media Group, Inc. v. Ashcroft*, 308 F.3d 198 (3d Cir. 2002), *cert. denied*, 538 U.S. 1056 (2003).
43. 542 U.S. 507 (2004).
44. 548 U.S. 557 (2006).
45. Aziz Huq, *What Good is Habeas?*, 26 CONST. COMM. 385 (2010); Benjamin Wittes & Zaahira Wyne, *The Current Detainee Population of Guantanamo: An Empirical Study* (2008), available at http://www.brookings.edu/reports/2008/1216_detainees_wittes.aspx.
46. Huq, *supra* note 45, at 421.
47. Huq, *supra* note 45, at 406.
48. Huq, *supra* note 45, at 429.
49. Huq, *supra* note 45, at 406.
50. For a good account, *see* DAVID WESSELL, IN FED WE TRUST: BEN BERNANKE'S WAR ON THE GREAT PANIC (2009).
51. Davidoff & Zaring, *supra* note 40.
52. John Cassidy, *Anatomy of a Meltdown*, THE NEW YORKER, Dec. 1, 1998, *avail-able at* http://www.newyorker.com/reporting/2008/12/01/081201fa_fact_cassidy.
53. For a clear statement of this view, *see* Jules Lobel, *Emergency Power and the Decline of Liberalism*, 98 YALE L.J. 1385, 1424–40 (1989). For more recent versions of this position, *see* David D. Cole, *Judging the Next Emergency: Judicial Review and Individual Rights in Times of Crisis*, 101 MICH. L. REV. 2565 (2003); Oren Gross, *Chaos and Rules: Should Responses to Violent Crises Always Be*

Constitutional? 112 YALE L.J. 1011 (2003). Some Madisonians put less emphasis on judicial review to ensure that the executive complies with constitutional
norms, but insist on congressional authorization. *See, e.g.,* Samuel Issacharoff
& Richard H. Pildes, *Between Civil Libertarianism and Executive Unilateralism:
An Institutional Process Approach to Rights During Wartime,* 5 THEORETICAL IN-
QUIRIES L. 1 (2004); Cass R. Sunstein, *Minimalism at War,* 2004 SUP. CT. REV.
47. We discuss their argument in chapter 3.

54. Robert F. Bruner & Sean D. Carr, *Lessons from the Financial Crisis of 1907,* 19 J.
APPLIED CORP. FIN. 115, 120 (2007).

55. Scheuerman, *supra* note 36, at 1887.

56. *See* Davidoff & Zaring, *supra* note 40.

57. *See* Note, *The International Emergency Economic Powers Act: A Congressional
Attempt to Control Presidential Emergency Power,* 96 HARV. L. REV. 1102 (1983).

58. The best treatments are Curtis A. Bradley & Jack L. Goldsmith, *Congressional
Authorization and the War on Terrorism,* 118 HARV. L. REV. 2047 (2005); David
Abramowitz, *The President, the Congress, and Use of Force: Legal and Political
Considerations in Authorizing Use of Force Against International Terrorism,* 43
HARV. INT'L L.J. 71 (2002).

59. Quoted in Abramowitz, *supra* note 59, at 73 (emphasis added).

60. *Id.*

61. Authorization for Use of Military Force, § 2(a), Pub. L. No. 107-40, 2001
U.S.C.C.A.N. (115 Stat.) 224.

62. Tom Daschle, *Power We Didn't Grant,* WASH. POST, Dec. 23, 2005, at A21.

63. Beryl A. Howell, *Seven Weeks: The Making of the USA PATRIOT Act,* 72 GEO.
WASH. L. REV. 1145 (2004); BERNARD D. REAMS, JR. & CHRISTOPHER T.
ANGLIM, USA PATRIOT ACT (2002).

64. Howell, *supra* note 64, at 1161–62.

65. *Id.* at 1178–79.

66. *See* Abramowitz, *supra* note 59, at 73.

67. *Id.* at 74–75.

68. *See* Howell, *supra* note 64.

69. Michael Kranish & Bryan Bender, *A Wait To See If Tax Breaks Will Swing Bailout
Vote,* BOSTON GLOBE, Oct. 3, 2008, at A1.

70. *See* Cole, *supra* note 54, at 2575–76; DAVID DYZENHAUS, THE CONSTITUTION
OF LAW: LEGALITY IN A TIME OF EMERGENCY (2006). *See also Korematsu v.
United States,* 323 U.S. 214, 242–48 (1944) (Jackson, J., concurring).

71. *See* SCHMITT, LEGALITY AND LEGITIMACY, *supra* note 39.

72. Emergency Economic Stabilization Act, Pub. L. No. 110-343, § 115(c), 2008
U.S.C.C.A.N. (112 Stat.) 3765, 3780 [hereinafter EESA].

73. *See* Deborah Solomon & Greg Hitt, *TARP Funds' Second Half Set for Release as
Senate Signs Off on Request,* WALL ST. J., Jan. 16, 2009, *available at* http://online.
wsj.com/article/SB123205759811587287.html.

74. EESA § 104.

75. *Free Enter. Fund v. Pub. Co. Accounting Oversight Bd.,* 537 F.3d 667, 679–80 &
n. 8 (D.C. Cir. 2008), affirmed in part and reversed in part on other grounds,
130 S. Ct. 3138 (2010).

76. EESA § 104.

77. Rick Pildes, *Update: Revising the Powers of the Secretary of the* Treasury, BALKINIZA-TION, Sept. 28, 2008, http://balkin.blogspot.com/2008/09/update-revising-powers-of-secretary-of.html.

78. Amit R. Paley, *Bailout Lacks Oversight Despite Billions Pledged*, WASH. POST, Nov. 13, 2008.

79. Neal Devins & David E. Lewis, *Not-So Independent Agencies: Party Polarization and the Limits of Institutional Design*, 88 B.U. L. REV. 459 (2008).

80. *Id.* at 491–98.

81. *See* Lisa Schultz Bressman & Robert B. Thompson, *The Future of Agency Independence* (Vanderbilt Law Sch. Pub. Law & Legal Theory, Working Paper No. 10-01, 2010), *available at* http://ssrn.com/abstract=1546103.

82. *Id.* at 2.

83. Donald F. Kettl, *The Savings-and-Loan Bailout: The Mismatch between the Headlines and the Issues*, 24 PS: POL. SCI. & POLITICS 441, 444 (1991).

84. *See Huntington Towers Ltd. v. Franklin Nat'l Bank*, 559 F.2d 863, 868 (2d Cir. 1977).

85. *Cf.* Sanford Levinson & Jack M. Balkin, *Constitutional Dictatorship: Its Dangers and Its Design*, 94 MINN. L. REV. 1789 (2010). The authors note accurately that discretionary power is lodged in multiple heads of the various executive agencies.

86. *See infra* ch. 3.

87. David Brooks, Op-Ed., *Revolt of the Nihilists*, N.Y. TIMES, Sept. 30, 2008, at A27.

88. Davidoff & Zaring, *supra* note 40.

89. *See* HOWELL & PEVEHOUSE, *supra* note 20; Kenneth R. Mayer, *Going Alone: The Presidential Power of Unilateral Action*, in THE OXFORD HANDBOOK OF THE AMERICAN PRESIDENCY, 427, 438–43 (2009).

90. For a catalogue of residual checks on presidential power, and executive power generally, *see* Alasdair Roberts, *Beyond the Imperial Presidency, available at* http://papers.ssrn.com/s013/papers.cfm?abstract_id=1106662. Although some of Roberts's checks are legal, most are political, and in any event they show only that presidential power is not as large as it could be. We do not read Roberts to deny the basic claim that government in the administrative state centers around the executive, with Congress and the courts relegated to secondary positions.

91. Jacob E. Gersen & Eric A. Posner, *Soft Law: Lessons from Congressional Practice*, 61 STAN. L. REV. 573 (2008).

CHAPTER 2

1. *See generally* William E. Scheuerman, LIBERAL DEMOCRACY AND THE SOCIAL ACCELERATION OF TIME (2004).

2. *See* ZACHARY ELKINS, TOM GINSBURG, & JAMES MELTON, THE ENDURANCE OF NATIONAL CONSTITUTIONS (2009).

3. *See* Donald Lutz, *Toward A Theory of Constitutional Amendment*, 88 Am. Pol. Sci. Rev. 355 (1994).

4. *See* Richard H. Fallon, The Dynamic Constitution (2004).

5. *See* Frederick A. Schauer, *Foreword: The Court's Agenda—And the Nation's*, 120 Harv. L. Rev. 4 (2006).

6. *See* Bruce Ackerman, We the People, Volume 1: Foundations (1993); Bruce Ackerman, We the People, Volume 2: Transformations (2000).

7. *See, e.g.*, Reynolds Holding, *The Executive Privilege Showdown*, Time, Mar. 21, 2007, *available at* http://www.time.com/time/nation/article/0,8599,1601450,00.html; Edward Epstein, *Dems Seek Showdown on War; House, Senate Leaders to Push Legislation That Would Force Bush to Withdraw Troops*, S.F. Chron., Mar. 9, 2007, at A1; Maura Reynolds, *Senate Vote Nears on Guantanamo Detainee Rights; Showdown Is Set Today on a Measure That Would Bar Prisoners' Access to Federal Court*, L.A. Times, Nov. 15, 2005, at A14.

8. *See* Sheryl Gay Stolberg, *Bush Moves Toward Showdown with Congress on Executive Privilege*, N.Y. Times, June 29, 2007, at A23.

9. *See* Adrian Vermeule, *Political Constraints on Supreme Court Reform*, 90 Minn. L. Rev. 1154, 1170 (2006).

10. The closest analogue in the literature is the useful idea of "constitutional hardball." *See* Mark Tushnet, *Constitutional Hardball*, 37 J. Marshall L. Rev. 523, 523 (2004).

11. *Myers v. United States*, 272 U.S. 52 (1926).

12. *Humphrey's Executor v. United States*, 295 U.S. 602 (1935).

13. *See* Akhil Reed Amar & Neal Kumar Katyal, *Executive Privileges and Immunities: The Nixon and Clinton Cases*, 108 Harv. L. Rev. 701 (1995).

14. John O. McGinnis, *Constitutional Review by the Executive in Foreign Affairs and War Powers: A Consequence of Rational Choice in the Separation of Powers*, 56 Law & Contemp. Probs. 293, 309–11 (1993).

15. *Ex parte Merryman*, 17 F. Cas. 144 (C.C.D. Md. 1861) (No. 9487).

16. In addition, Andrew Jackson refused to comply with the Supreme Court's decision in *Worcester v. Georgia*, 31 U.S. 515 (1832).

17. *Youngstown Sheet & Tube Co. v. Sawyer*, 343 U.S. 579 (1952).

18. *United States v. Nixon*, 418 U.S. 683 (1974).

19. Charles Gardner Geyh, When Courts & Congress Collide: The Struggle for Control of America's Judicial System (2006).

20. *Id.* at 66–67.

21. *Ex parte McCardle*, 74 U.S. (7 Wall.) 506 (1868).

22. Barry Friedman, *The History of the Countermajoritarian Difficulty, Part Two: Reconstruction's Political Court*, 91 Geo. L.J. 1 (2002).

23. *See* Peter J. Spiro, Book Review, *War Powers and the Sirens of Formalism*, 68 N.Y.U. L. Rev. 1338, 1356 (1993).

24. Daryl J. Levinson, *Empire-Building Government in Constitutional Law*, 118 Harv. L. Rev. 915 (2005).

25. *See* McGinnis, *supra* note 14.

26. Spiro, *supra* note 23, at 1356.

27. Jon Elster, Alchemies of the Mind 341–55 (1999).

28. *See* THOMAS C. SCHELLING, THE STRATEGY OF CONFLICT (1980).

29. On the role of focal points in the Battle of the Sexes game, *see* JAMES D. MORROW, GAME THEORY FOR POLITICAL SCIENTISTS 94–97 (1994).

30. *See* Jon Elster, *Unwritten Constitutional Norms* (unpublished manuscript, on file with the authors).

31. *See* STANLEY M. ELKINS & ERIC MCKITRICK, THE AGE OF FEDERALISM: THE EARLY AMERICAN REPUBLIC, 1788–1800 (1993).

32. HAROLD C. RELYEA & TODD B. TATELMAN, PRESIDENTIAL ADVISERS' TESTIMONY BEFORE CONGRESS: AN OVERVIEW (Cong. Research Serv., CRS Report for Congress Order Code RL31351, Apr. 10, 2007), *available at* http://www.fas.org/irp/crs/RL31351.pdf.

33. *See* Associated Press, *Texas Search For Democrats Is Ruled Illegal*, N.Y. TIMES, July 12, 2003, at A7.

34. *See, e.g.*, Michael J. Glennon, *The Use of Custom in Resolving Separation of Powers Disputes*, 64 B.U. L. REV. 109 (1984).

35. Spiro, *supra* note 23.

36. *See United States v. Midwest Oil Co.*, 236 U.S. 459 (1915). The example is discussed in Glennon, *supra* note 34, at 115–16.

37. *See* Spiro, *supra* note 23, at 1352–53, 1356.

38. For an argument that this is the appropriate interpretation of *opinio juris* in international law, *see* JACK L. GOLDSMITH & ERIC A. POSNER, THE LIMITS OF INTERNATIONAL LAW ch. 1 (2005).

39. We do not mean to imply that the expected policy choice will be the median's ideal policy choice; we assume that the optimal institutional allocation of authority minimizes the deviation from the median voter's preferences relative to other institutional arrangements.

40. In setting up the problem in this way, we exclude the possibility that one or both agents would prefer not to have authority over a particular issue because the issue is highly sensitive and politically dangerous. Such an assumption underlies some theories, for example, the theory of the "regulatory lottery," according to which Congress grants power to agencies in order to avoid having to make a politically sensitive decision. *See* Peter H. Aranson, Ernest Gellhorn, & Glen O. Robinson, *A Theory of Legislative Delegation*, 68 CORNELL L. REV. 1, 7 (1982). We have criticized this view in earlier work. *See* Eric A. Posner & Adrian Vermeule, *Interring the Nondelegation Doctrine*, 69 U. CHI. L. REV. 1721, 1746 (2002). Because there are few historical examples where two branches have tried to slough authority over an issue to each other, we think that this concern can be safely ignored. For the contrary view, *see* Levinson, *supra* note 24.

41. *See, e.g.*, ABHINAY MUTHOO, BARGAINING THEORY WITH APPLICATIONS (1999). We simplify considerably.

42. The institutions are aggregations, of course, which complicates the presentation of the argument but does not change our basic conclusions.

43. In imaginable cases, an agent will win lose the policy battle but win the authority battle. For example, a president might strike a deal with Congress that provides that the president will change policy and Congress will, by some explicit

act, recognize the president's authority. But this is not really a case of constitutional change through a showdown; it is a kind of incremental constitutional evolution that occurs through normal politics.

44. *See* David A. Strauss, *Common Law Constitutional Interpretation*, 63 U. CHI. L. REV. 877 (1996).

45. ACKERMAN, WE THE PEOPLE, VOL. 1, *supra* note 6; ACKERMAN, WE THE PEOPLE, VOL. 2, *supra* note 6.

46. LARRY D. KRAMER, THE PEOPLE THEMSELVES: POPULAR CONSTITUTIONALISM AND JUDICIAL REVIEW (2004).

47. Robert C. Post & Reva B. Siegel, *Protecting the Constitution from the People: Juricentric Restrictions on Section Five Power*, 78 IND. L.J. 1 (2003).

CHAPTER 3

1. The idea of "translation" derives from Lawrence Lessig, *Fidelity in Translation*, 71 TEX. L. REV. 1165 (1993).

2. *See* BRUCE ACKERMAN, BEFORE THE NEXT ATTACK (2006).

3. War Powers Resolution, Pub. L. No. 93-148, 87 Stat. 555 (1973).

4. National Emergencies Act, Pub. L. No. 94-412, 90 Stat. 1255 (1976).

5. International Economic Emergency Powers Act, Pub. L. No. 95-223, 91 Stat. 1626 (1977).

6. Ethics in Government Act, Pub. L. No. 95-521, 92 Stat. 1824 (1978).

7. Attorney General's Guidelines on Domestic Security Investigations (Apr. 5, 1976), reprinted in FBI STATUTORY CHARTER: HEARINGS ON S. 1612 BEFORE THE S. COMM. ON THE JUDICIARY, 95TH CONG. 18 (1978).

8. *See generally* Andrew Rudalevige, THE NEW IMPERIAL PRESIDENCY (2005).

9. Geoffrey S. Corn, *Clinton, Kosovo, and the Final Destruction of the War Powers Resolution*, 42 WM. & MARY L. REV. 1149 (2001).

10. PETER M. SHANE, MADISON'S NIGHTMARE: HOW EXECUTIVE POWER THREATENS AMERICAN DEMOCRACY 191 (2009).

11. Glenn E. Fuller, *The National Emergency Dilemma: Balancing the Executive's Crisis Powers with the Need for Accountability*, 52 S. CAL. L. REV. 1453, 1458 & n. 27 (1979).

12. *Dames & Moore v. Regan*, 453 U.S. 654 (1981).

13. *Beacon Products Corp. v. Reagan*, 633 F. Supp. 1191 (D. Mass. 1986), *aff'd*, 814 F.2d 1 (1st Cir. 1987).

14. Paul C. Light, MONITORING GOVERNMENT: INSPECTORS GENERAL AND THE SEARCH FOR ACCOUNTABILITY (1993).

15. William S. Fields, *The Enigma of Bureaucratic Accountability*, 43 CATH. U. L. REV. 505, 516–17 (1994) (reviewing Light, *supra* note 14).

16. *See* Authorization for Continuing Hostilities in Kosovo, 2000 OLC LEXIS 16 (Op. Off. Legal Counsel 2000).

17. Terry M. Moe & William G. Howell, *The Presidential Power of Unilateral Action*, 15 J. L. Econ. & Org. 132 (1999).

18. *See* Frederick Schauer, *When and How (If at All) Does Law Constrain Official Action?* (Va. Pub. Law & Legal Theory, Working Paper No. 2010-02, 2010), *available at* http://papers.ssrn.com/s013/papers.cfm?abstract_id=1494301.

19. Jide Nzelibe & Matthew Stephenson, *Complementary Constraints: Separation of Powers, Rational Voting, and Constitutional Design*, 123 HARV. L. REV. 617 (2010).

20. *See* Rudalevige, *supra* note 8.

21. Johan Steyn coined the term "legal black hole," *see* Johan Steyn, *Guantanamo Bay: The Legal Black Hole*, 53 INT'L & COMP. L.Q. 1 (2004), and David Dyzenhaus coined the term "legal grey hole," *see* DAVID DYZENHAUS, THE CONSTITUTION OF LAW: LEGALITY IN A TIME OF EMERGENCY 3 (2006).

22. DYZENHAUS, *supra* note 21, at 3.

23. *Id.* at 42.

24. *Id.*

25. *See* Richard Wolin, *Carl Schmitt, Political Existentialism, and the Total State*, 19 THEORY & SOC. 389, 396–401 (1990). *See generally* CARL SCHMITT, DIE DIKTATUR: VON DEN ANFÄNGEN DES MODERNEN SOUVERÄNITÄTSGEDANKENS BIS ZUM PROLETARISCHEN KLASSENKAMPF (1921).

26. John P. McCormick, *The Dilemmas of Dictatorship: Carl Schmitt and Constitutional Emergency Powers, in* LAW AS POLITICS: CARL SCHMITT'S CRITIQUE OF LIBERALISM 217 (David Dyzenhaus ed. 1998).

27. CARL SCHMITT, POLITICAL THEOLOGY: FOUR CHAPTERS ON THE CONCEPT OF SOVEREIGNTY 1 (George Schwab trans., 1985) (1922).

28. Schmitt focused on the substance rather than the procedure, but the latter is a short extension of his thought. *See* Mark Tushnet, *Emergencies and the Idea of Constitutionalism, in* THE CONSTITUTION IN WARTIME: BEYOND ALARMISM AND COMPLACENCY 39 (Mark Tushnet ed., 2005); *cf.* William E. Scheuerman, *Emergency Powers and the Rule of Law After 9/11*, 14 J. POL. PHIL. 61 (2006).

29. Tushnet, *supra* note 28, at 47 (quoting Louis Michael Seidman).

30. *See* SCHMITT, *supra* note 27, at 7.

31. *See, e.g.,* GIORGIO AGAMBEN, STATE OF EXCEPTION (Kevin Attell trans., 2005); William E. Scheuerman, *Carl Schmitt and the Road to Abu Ghraib*, 13 CONSTELLATIONS 108 (2006); Scheuerman, *supra* note 8.

32. *See, e.g.,* DYZENHAUS, *supra* note 21, at 18.

33. *See generally* LON L. FULLER, THE MORALITY OF LAW (rev. ed. 1969).

34. *See* David Dyzenhaus, *Schmitt v. Dicey: Are States of Emergency Inside or Outside the Legal Order?* 27 CARDOZO L. REV. 2005, 2026 (2006) ("[G]rey holes are more harmful to the rule of law than black holes").

35. *See generally id.*

36. *Id.* at 2029.

37. *See* Administrative Procedure Act, 5 U.S.C. § 702 (2000).

38. *Id.* § 551(1)(F), (G).

39. *Dalton v. Specter*, 511 U.S. 462, 470 (1994); *Franklin v. Massachusetts*, 505 U.S. 788, 796 (1992).

40. *See Franklin*, 505 U.S. at 800–801.

41. 493 F.3d 644 (6th Cir. 2007).

42. § 553(a)(1) (rulemaking); § 554(a)(4) (adjudications).

43. *See* S. Rep. No. 79-752, at 13 (1945); U.S. Dep't of Justice, Attorney General's Manual on the Administrative Procedure Act 26 (1947) (rulemaking) [hereinafter Attorney General's Manual]; *id.* at 45 (adjudication).

44. *Jean v. Nelson*, 711 F.2d 1455, 1477 (11th Cir. 1983).

45. *See Nademi v. INS*, 679 F.2d 811, 814 (10th Cir. 1982); *Malek-Marzban v. INS*, 653 F.2d 113, 115–16 (4th Cir. 1981); *Yassini v. Crosland*, 618 F.2d 1356, 1360 (9th Cir. 1980).

46. 321 F.3d 230 (1st Cir. 2003).

47. *Ventura-Melendez*, 321 F.3d at 233.

48. 359 F.3d 156 (2d. Cir. 2004).

49. 428 F.3d 916 (10th Cir. 2005).

50. Aviation and Transportation Security Act § 113(a), Pub. L. No. 107-71, 115 Stat. 597, 622 (2001).

51. *Merida Delgado*, 428 F.3d at 920.

52. *See* Dyzenhaus, *supra* note 34, at 2026.

53. *See, e.g.,* Jonathan Masur, *A Hard Look or a Blind Eye: Administrative Law and Military Deference*, 56 Hastings L.J. 441, 519–21 (2005); Peter Raven-Hansen, *Detaining Combatants by Law or by Order? The Rule of Lawmaking in the War on Terrorists*, 64 La. L. Rev. 831, 843–50 (2004).

54. 50 U.S.C. §§ 1701–7 (2000).

55. 333 F.3d 156 (D.C. Cir. 2003).

56. *Id.* at 162.

57. *Id.*

58. 477 F.3d 728 (D.C. Cir. 2007).

59. *Id.* at 734.

60. 5 U.S.C. § 553(b)(3)(B).

61. Attorney General's Manual, *supra* note 43, at 30.

62. S. Rep. No. 79-752, *supra* note 43, at 14.

63. Ellen R. Jordan, *The Administrative Procedure Act's "Good Cause" Exemption*, 36 Admin. L. Rev. 113, 121 (1974).

64. 370 F.3d 1174 (D.C. Cir. 2004).

65. *Jifry*, 370 F.3d at 1179 (quoting TSA determination).

66. *Id.* at 1180.

67. *See* Attorney General's Manual, *supra* note 43, at 30.

68. *See generally* Cass R. Sunstein, Laws of Fear: Beyond the Precautionary Principle (2005).

69. *Jifry*, 370 F.3d at 1179 (internal quotation marks removed).

70. *See* Cass R. Sunstein, *National Security, Liberty, and the D.C. Circuit*, 73 Geo. Wash. L. Rev. 693 (2005).

71. *See, e.g.,* 12 U.S.C. § 1821(j) (prohibiting certain forms of injunctive relief).

72. *See, e.g., Ward v. Resolution Trust Corp.*, 996 F.2d 99 (5th Cir. 1993).

73. *See* Stephen G. Breyer et al., Administrative Law and Regulatory Policy 222–28 (6th ed. 2006).

74. Dyzenhaus, *supra* note 21, at 47.

75. *See* Steyn, *supra* note 21.

76. *Rasul v. Bush*, 542 U.S. 466 (2004); *Boumediene v. Bush*, 553 U.S. 723 (2008).

77. Gerald L. Neuman, *Whose Constitution?* 100 YALE L.J. 909, 919–20 (1991).

78. *Rasul*, 542 U.S. at 498 (Scalia, J., dissenting).

79. *See id.* at 488 (Kennedy, J., concurring in the judgment) (advocating an approach that "would avoid creating automatic statutory authority to adjudicate claims of persons located outside the United States").

80. Keith Werhan, PRINCIPLES OF ADMINISTRATIVE LAW 310 (2007) (first alteration in original).

81. *Vermont Yankee Nuclear Power Corp. v. Nat'l Res. Def. Council*, 435 U.S. 519 (1978); *see generally* John F. Duffy, *Administrative Common Law in Judicial Review*, 77 TEX. L. REV. 113 (1998).

82. *See, e.g.*, DYZENHAUS, *supra* note 21, at 47–48.

83. Mark Tushnet, Book Review, *Dyzenhaus, The Constitution of Law*, 2007 PUB. L. 604, 605 (2007).

84. Evan J. Criddle, *Mending Holes in the Rule of (Administrative) Law*, 104 Nw. U. L. REV. COLLOQUY 309, 310 (2010).

85. *Youngstown Sheet & Tube Co. v. Sawyer*, 343 U.S. 579 (1952).

86. *See* Reuel E. Schiller, *Reining in the Administrative State: World War II and the Decline of Expert Administration*, *in* TOTAL WAR AND THE LAW 185 (Daniel R. Ernst & Victor Jew eds., 2002).

87. *Wong Yang Sun v. McGrath*, 339 U.S. 33, 40 (1950).

88. Criddle proposes to amend the APA to add a grab bag of procedural requirements to shore up the "good cause" escape hatch from notice-and-comment rulemaking, such as a requirement that agencies "give the public contemporaneous notice" of the need for the derogation. Criddle, *supra* note 84, at 109. Yet the APA already contains a similar requirement; *see* APA §553(b)(3)(B) (stating that when the agency invokes good cause, it must "incorporate[] the finding and a brief statement of reasons therefore in the rules issued"). It is not obvious why Criddle's proposal will, in operation, have any more bite than the extant requirement.

89. *See Youngstown Sheet & Tube Co. v. Sawyer*, 343 U.S. at 635–39 (1952) (Jackson, J., concurring).

90. Samuel Issacharoff & Richard H. Pildes, *Between Civil Libertarianism and Executive Unilateralism: An Institutional Process Approach to Rights During Wartime*, 5 THEORETICAL INQUIRIES L. 1 (2000). For a related view, *see* Cass R. Sunstein, *Minimalism at War*, 2004 SUP. CT. REV. 47 (2004).

91. *See* Moe & Howell, *supra* note 17.

92. Edward T. Swaine, *The Political Economy of* Youngstown, 83 S. Cal. L. Rev. 263 (2010).

CHAPTER 4

1. *See, e.g.*, Monty G. Marshall & Keith Jaggers, *Polity IV Project: Political Regime Characteristics and Transitions, 1800–2007*, at http:// www.systemicpeace.org/ polity/polity4.htm.

2. For a useful introduction, *see* Timothy Besley, Principled Agents? The Poltiical Economy of Good Government (2006).

3. The Constitution must also be self-enforcing as well; we will put aside this question. *See, e.g.*, Barry R. Weingast, *Self-Enforcing Constitutions* (Hoover Institution Working Paper, Nov. 2008), *available at* http://politicalscience. stanford.edu/faculty/documents/weingast-self-enforcing%20constitutions.pdf.

4. *See, e.g.*, John Ferejohn, *Incumbent Performance and Electoral Control*, 50 Pub. Choice 5 (1986); Morris Fiorina, Retrospective Voting in American National Elections (1981).

5. For the costs and benefits of periodic and continuous elections, see Adrian Vermeule, *Intermittent Institutions* (Harvard Law School Working Paper No. 10-13, 2010), *available at* http://papers.ssrn.com/s013/papers.cfm?abstract_id=1542104.

6. For a review of the research, see James M. Druckman & Lawrence R. Jacobs, *Presidential Responsiveness to Public Opinion, in* The Oxford Handbook of the American Presidency 160 (George C. Edwards III & William G. Howell eds., 2009).

7. We follow here the analysis in Torsten Persson, Gerard Roland, & Guido Tabellini, *Separation of Powers and Political Accountability*, 112 Q. J. Econ. 1163 (1997).

8. Geoffrey Brennan & Alan Hamlin, *A Revisionist View of the Separation of Powers*, 6 J. Theoretical Pol. 345 (1994).

9. Persson et al., *supra* note 7.

10. *Id.*; Matthew S. Shugart & John M. Carey, Presidents and Assemblies: Constitutional Design and Electoral Dynamics (1992).

11. *See, e.g.*, Ethan Bueno de Mesquita & Dimitra Landa, *An Equilibrium Theory of Clarity of Responsibility* (Jan. 22, 2008) (unpublished manuscript), *available at* http://home.uchicago.edu/~bdm/PDF/clarity.pdf; Jacob E. Gersen, *Unbundled Powers*, 96 Va. L. Rev. 301 (2010). Some empirical work suggests that the system of separation of powers could be superior to parliamentarianism because voters in the first system have greater ability to punish the executive. *See* Timothy Hellwig & David Samuels, *Electoral Accountability and the Variety of Democratic Regimes*, 38 B.J. Pol. S. 65 (2007). However, this work does not compare separation of powers with a single executive (for the good reason that the latter system does not formally exist). The logic of the argument—that voters do best when they can hold elected officials to account—favors the single executive over separation of powers, however.

12. Jide Nzelibe & Matthew Stephenson, *Complementary Constraints: Separation of Powers, Rational Voting, and Constitutional Design*, 123 Harv. L Rev. 617 (2010).

13. For one model of gridlock (involving inefficient equilibria), *see* Tim Groseclose & Nolan McCarty, *The Politics of Blame: Bargaining Before an Audience*, 45 J. Pol. Sci. 100 (2001).

14. For one more example, *see* Justin Fox & Stuart V. Jordan, *Delegation and Accountability* (Dec. 16, 2009), *available at* http://papers.ssrn.com/s013/papers. cfm?abstract_id=1524585 (evaluating trade-off between the risk of special-interest capture of the legislature and bureaucratic expertise).

15. B. DAN WOOD, THE MYTH OF PRESIDENTIAL REPRESENTATION (2009).

16. Jack Goldsmith, *The Cheney Fallacy*, THE NEW REPUBLIC, May 18, 2009, *available at* http://www.tnr.com/article/politics/the-cheney-fallacy?id=1e733cac-c273–48e5–9140–80443ed1f5e2.

17. We use "trust" and "credibility" as synonyms. In other words, we adopt a rational-ist account of trust rather than a nonrational or affective account, and thus follow the lead of Russell Hardin. RUSSELL HARDIN, TRUST AND TRUSTWORTHINESS 13–21 (2d ed. 2004). However, as will become apparent, we do not subscribe to Hardin's pessimism about the ability of institutions to successfully generate credibility in modern mass democracies. *See id.* at 151–72. For an overview of competing accounts of political trust, *see* Mark E. Warren, *Democratic Theory and Trust, in* DEMOCRACY AND TRUST, 310–45 (Mark E. Warren ed., 1999).

18. Here as elsewhere, we use the executive to include both the president and the agencies and cabinet departments. Although our examples will focus on the presidency, for concreteness and because the president is the most important case, the main point of our discussion apply equally to, say, a cabinet secretary or to the EPA, within their smaller spheres of authority.

19. Philippe Aghion et al., *Endogenous Political Institutions* 25 (Nat'l Bureau of Econ. Res., Working Paper No. 9006, 2003), *available at* http://www.nber.org/papers/w9006.

20. Daryl J. Levinson, *Empire-Building Government in Constitutional Law*, 118 HARV. L. REV. 915, 919–20 (2005).

21. In legal scholarship, the closest precedent for our work is Michael Fitts, *The Paradox of Power in the Modern State: Why a Unitary, Centralized Presidency May Not Exhibit Effective or Legitimate Leadership*, 144 U. PA. L REV 827, 878–91 (1996). However, Fitts does not use a rational choice approach, as we do, but focuses on matters of public psychology—for example, that the public wants powerful presidents to resolve disputes but then feels resentful when the dis-pute is not resolved in the desired manner. *Id.* at 839, 864–68; *see also* Cynthia Farina, *False Comfort and Impossible Promises: Uncertainty, Information Overload, and the Unitary Executive*, 12 U. PENN. J. CONSTITUTIONAL L. 357 (2010). We abstract from such issues. There is also a related literature in administrative law that implicitly argues that the president can be trusted but does not address the dilemma of executive credibility that is our focus. *See, e.g.,* Eric A. Posner & Adrian Vermeule, *Nondelegation: A Post-mortem*, 70 U. CHI. L. REV. 1331, 1344 (2003); Matthew C. Stephenson, *Public Regulation of Private Enforcement: The Case for Expanding the Role of Administrative Agencies*, 91 VA. L. REV. 93, 95–97 (2005). Matthew Stephenson also discusses problems of reliability of courts and members of Congress. *See* Matthew C. Stephenson, *Court of Public Opinion: Government Accountability and Judicial Independence*, 20 J.L. ECON. & ORG. 379, 380–81 (2004). Overall, the strand of political science literature that has had most influence on legal academia has focused on the problem of executive overreaching. *See, e.g.,* CLINTON ROSSITER, THE AMERICAN PRESIDENCY, 44–73 (1956); EDWARD CORWIN, THE PRESIDENT: OFFICE AND POWER, 1787–1984, 303–45 (4th ed. 1957). Other work in political science, especially

its rational choice analysis of institutions, is more directly relevant; we cite this work as appropriate in the body of the discussion.

22. A point that has been recognized by political scientists, *e.g.*, Rahul Sagar, *On Combating the Abuse of State Secrecy*, 15 J. Pol. Phil. 404 (2007).

23. *See, e.g.*, Richard E. Neustadt, Presidential Power and the Modern Presidents 187–91 (1990).

24. Wayne S. Cole, Roosevelt & the Isolationists 1932–45, 397 (1987).

25. Stephen Ambrose, Eisenhower, The President, Volume Two 513–15 (1984).

26. Walter LaFeber, *Johnson, Vietnam, and Tocqueville, in* Lyndon Johnson Confronts the World: American Foreign Policy 1963–1968, 49 (Warren I. Cohen & Nancy Bernkopf Tucker eds., 1994).

27. Stephen Ambrose, Nixon, Volume 3: Ruin and Recovery 1973–1990, 178, 182, 198 (1991).

28. Lawrence E. Walsh, Firewall: The Iran-Contra Conspiracy and Cover-up 231–32 (1997).

29. Haynes Johnson, The Best of Times 227 (2001).

30. Cole, *supra* note 24, at 239.

31. *Id.* at 367–69.

32. Stanley R. Sloan, *Negotiating Article 5*, NATO Rev. (Summer 2006), *available at* http://www.nato.int/docu/review/2006/issue2/english/art4.html.

33. *See* Truman Presidential Museum & Library, *Ideological Foundations of the Cold War*, http://www.trumanlibrary.org/whistlestop/study_collections/coldwar/; *see also* U.S. Department of State's Bureau of International Information Programs, chapter 12: Postwar America, *in* Outline of U.S. History, *available at* http://usinfo.state.gov/products/pubs/histryotln/postwar.htm.

34. *See* Richard E. Neustadt, Presidential Power and the Modern Presidents: The Politics of Leadership 40–49 (1990); Arthur M. Schlesinger Jr., The Imperial Presidency 128 (1973).

35. Schlesinger, *supra* note 34, at 129–30.

36. Stephen R. Graubard, Mr. Bush's War: Adventures in the Politics of Illusion 9, 122 (1992).

37. The vote on Authorization for Use of Military Force Against Iraq Resolution, Pub. L. 120-1, 105 Stat. 3 (1991), passed by less than 70 votes (250–183). The Senate vote was unanimous.

38. Graubard, *supra*, note 36, at 177–18.

39. *See* Alan Beattie, *US May Present New Resolution This Week; White House Determined to Disarm Saddam Even if Widespread International Support Withheld*, Fin. Times, Feb. 19, 2003, at 6.

40. Samuel L. Berger, *Testimony before the Eighth Public Hearing of the National Commission on Terrorist Attacks Upon the United States* 3–7 (Mar. 24, 2004), *available at* http://www.9–11commission.gov/hearings/hearing8/berger_statement.pdf.

41. James Patterson, Restless Giant, 380–83, 392–93 (2005); Haynes Johnson, *supra* note 29, at 406.

42. *Id.*

43. *See* Rob Willer, *The Effect of Government-Issued Terror Warnings on Presidential Approval Ratings*, 10 CURRENT RES. SOC. PO.'Y 1, 5, 10 (2004), *available at* http://www.uiowa.edu/~grpproc/crisp/crisp.10.1.html.

44. Richard Clarke, Clinton's counterterrorism chief, suggests that Clinton was not influenced by politics, at least for the initial decision to strike. *See* RICHARD A. CLARKE, AGAINST ALL ENEMIES: INSIDE AMERICA'S WAR ON TERROR 186 (2004). But then he says: "Our response to two deadly terrorist attacks was an attempt to wipe out al Qaeda leadership, yet it quickly became grist for the right-wing talk radio mill and part of the Get Clinton campaign. That reaction made it more difficult to get approval for follow-up attacks on al Qaeda, such as my later attempts to persuade the Principals to forget about finding bin Laden and just bomb training camps." *Id.* at 189.

45. Often, as in the case of surveillance of terrorist communications by the National Security Agency, the president cannot even announce the program, for to do so would reduce or eliminate its value, but must anticipate that the secret will eventually come out, in which case he will have to defend it.

46. Jonathan Mahler, *Terms of Imprisonment*, N.Y. TIMES, July 30, 2006, at 6.

47. For a textbook treatment *see* PATRICK BOLTON & MATHIAS DEWATRIPONT, CONTRACT THEORY 14–20, 129–70 (2005).

48. On some views, "what the voters would choose" is what the median voter would choose. *See* ANTHONY DOWNS, AN ECONOMIC THEORY OF DEMOCRACY 115–22 (1957). Our argument does not depend on this particular theory; it depends only on the assumption that there is some coherent criterion of public preference based on some aggregation of citizens' values and interests. We are agnostic about, and for present purposes need not take a stand on, the content of that criterion.

49. By statute, even classified presidential papers are unsealed after 12 years. Presidential Records Act of 1978, 44 U.S.C. § 2204 (2000). However, President George W. Bush's executive order may qualify this. *See* Exec. Order No. 13,333, 3 C.F.R. 815 (2001), *reprinted in* 44 U.S.C.A. §2204 (2001); Marcy Lynn Karin, *Note: Out of Sight, but Not Out of Mind: How Executive Order 13,233 Expands Executive Privilege While Simultaneously Preventing Access to Presidential Records*, 55 STAN. L. REV. 529, 548–52 (2002).

50. *See* Marc J. Hetherington, *The Political Relevance of Public Trust*, 92 AM. POL. SCI. REV. 791 (1998).

51. For a general comparison of these two methods, *see* James Fearon, *Electoral Accountability and the Control of Politicians: Selecting Good Types versus Sanctioning Poor Performance*, in DEMOCRACY, ACCOUNTABILITY AND REPRESENTATION 55, 70–84 (Adam Przeworski & Susan C. Stokes eds., 1999).

52. The enormous literature on this topic begins with A. Michael Spence, *Job-Market Signaling*, 87 Q. J. ECON. 355 (1973).

53. Geoffrey Brennan, *Selection and the Currency of Reward, in* THE THEORY OF INSTITUTIONAL DESIGN 257, 262–72 (Robert E. Goodin ed.,1996).

54. *See* BOLTON & DEWATRIPONT, *supra* note 47, at 169–70.

55. *Id.* This is a model that combines adverse selection and moral hazard.

56. Jon Elster, Ulysses and the Sirens 36–47, 99–103 (1979).
57. For criticisms, *see* Jon Elster, Ulysses Unbound 156–74 (2000); Jeremy Waldron, *Precommitment and Disagreement, in* Constitutionalism: Philosophical Foundations 271, 185–95 (Larry Alexander ed., 1998).
58. A somewhat analogous argument can be found in Daniel A. Farber, *Rights as Signals*, 31 J. Legal Stud. 83, 83–97 (2002). Farber argues that governments (not presidents) adopt judicially enforceable constitutional rights in order to signal that they value payoffs in the future, and thus will not drive off foreign investment in the long run by expropriating in the short run. *Id.* at 88–91.
59. Many of them might involve self-binding, depending on circumstances. For example, compare a president who appoints a commission, waits for its recommendation, and then acts, with a president who promises to appoint a commission, acts, and then receives its evaluation of his action. The first president does not engage in self-binding; he simply gains credibility prior to action (assuming that the commission supports him). The second president does engage in self-binding, and thus the mechanism works only if the president can be sanctioned if the commission criticizes his action. We will not belabor these details, except to note that the strict liability mechanism (*infra*) depends heavily on successful self-binding.
60. *United States v. Nixon*, 418 U.S. 683, 695–96 (1974), *Arizona Grocery v. Atchison*, 284 U.S. 370, 385–89 (1932). However, the Court has also said that for purposes of enforcing the constitutional "nondelegation doctrine," it is unimportant that an administrative agency has promulgated rules that channel its own discretion, even though such rules are binding on the agency unless and until changed. *Whitman v. American Trucking*, 531 U.S. 457, 472–76 (2001). For an overview of self-binding by agencies, *see* Elizabeth A. Magill, *Foreword: Agency Self-Regulation*, 77 Geo. Wash. L. Rev. 859 (2009).
61. In fact, the independent counsels who investigated Nixon were appointed under Department of Justice regulations that Nixon did not overturn; the regulations emerged from complicated background negotiations among Nixon, Attorney General Elliott Richardson, Chief of Staff Alexander Haig, and various senators. *See* K. A. McNeely-Johnson, United States v. Nixon, *Twenty Years After: The Good, The Bad and The Ugly–An Exploration of Executive Privilege*, 14 N. Ill. U. L. Rev. 251, 265–66 (1993). We offer a stylized version of the case to illustrate the point more cleanly.
62. *See* Neal Kumar Katyal, *Internal Separation of Powers: Checking Today's Most Dangerous Branch from Within*, 115 Yale L.J. 2314 (2006).
63. *Id.*
64. Bruce Ackerman, *How to Keep Future John Yoos Under Control*, Wash. Post, Feb. 23, 2010, at A19.
65. R. G. Lipsey & Kelvin Lancaster, *The General Theory of Second-Best*, 24 Rev. Econ. Stud. 11, 12 (1956).
66. For an introduction to this class of problems, *see* Adrian Vermeule, *Self-Defeating Proposals: Ackerman on Emergency Powers*, 75 Fordham L. Rev. 631 (2006).
67. *See* Katyal, *supra* note 62.
68. Other prominent commissions include the President's Commission on the Assassination of President Kennedy (the Warren Commission) and Pres-

ident Johnson's National Advisory Commission on Civil Disorders (the Kerner Commission), which reported on urban riots. For analysis of recent independent commissions, and for a sample of the diversity of issues covered by independent commissions, *see, e.g.,* Victoria S. Shabo, *"We Are Pleased to Report That the Commission Has Reached Agreement with the White House": The 9/11 Commission and Implications for Legislative-Executive Information Sharing,* 83 N. C. L. Rev., 1037, 1037–50 (2005); Ken Gish & Eric Laschever, *The President's Ocean Commission: Progress Toward a New Ocean Policy,* 19 Nat. Resources & Env't 17 (Summer 2004); Nkechi Taifa, *Codification or Castration? The Applicability of the International Convention to Eliminate All Forms of Racial Discrimination to the U.S. Criminal Justice System,* 40 Howard L.J. 641, 660–64 (1997) (criticizing the 1995 United States Sentencing Commission).

69. Commission on the Intelligence Capabilities of the United States Regarding Weapons of Mass Destruction, Report to the President, March 31, 2005 (2005), *available at* http://govinfo.library.unt.edu/wmd/report/wmd_report.pdf.

70. For models suggesting that a president can make credible commitments to the future direction of agency policy by appointing officials whose preferences are known to differ from the president's, *see* Daniel F. Spulber & David Besanko, *Delegation, Commitment and the Regulatory Mandate,* 8 J.L. Econ. & Org. 126, 127 (1992); Nolan McCarty, *The Appointments Dilemma,* 48 Am. J. Pol. Sci. 412, 421 (2004).

71. McCarty, *supra* note 70, at 422.

72. *Id.* at 423. The implication is that "the agencies that should be the most insulated from presidential control are those whose activities the president supports more than does Congress." *Id.* For an empirical overview of independent agencies, *see generally,* David E. Lewis, Presidents and the Politics of Agency Design (2003).

73. Cass Sunstein, Why Societies Need Dissent 54–73 (2003).

74. 28 U.S.C. § 591.

75. Julie O'Sullivan, *The Independent Counsel Statute: Bad Law, Bad Policy,* 33 Am. Crim. L. Rev. 463, 483–92 (1996).

76. *Cf.* Donald Wittman, *The Constitution as an Optimal Social Contract, in* The Federalist Papers and the New Institutionalism 73–84 (Bernard Grofman & Donald Wittman eds., 1989) (noting that where transaction costs are low, political actors can bargain around the separation of powers).

77. *See* Alex Cukierman & Mariano Tommasi, *When Does it Take a Nixon to Go to China?* 88 Am. Econ. Rev. 180, 190–92 (1998); Robert Goodin, *Voting Through the Looking Glass,* 77 Am. Pol. Sci. Rev. 420, 426–28 (1983).

78. For a rigorous analysis of this phenomenon in the context of cheap-talk games, see David Austen-Smith, Positive Political Theory I (1999).

79. However, there is a puzzling finding that the counterpartisanship effect is asymmetrical: in experiments, hawkish "voters" approved of dovish policies chosen by a hawkish "president," but dovish voters did not approve of hawkish policies chosen by a dovish president. *See* Lee Sigelman & Carol K. Sigelman,

Shattered Expectations: Public Responses to "Out-of-Character" Presidential Actions, 8 POL. BEHAVIOR 262, 274–76 (1986).

80. John Ferejohn suggests that agents might compete by offering their principals transparency, which lowers the costs to the principals of monitoring the agents, and thereby induces the principals to offer the agents greater discretion. *See* John Ferejohn, *Accountability and Authority: Toward a Theory of Political Accountability*, *in* DEMOCRACY, ACCOUNTABILITY, AND REPRESENTATION 131 (Adam Przeworski et al. eds., 1999). Empirically, the evidence offers only mixed support for this model. *See* James Alt et al., *The Causes of Fiscal Transparency: Evidence from the American States* 25–30 (EPRU Working Paper Series 2006-02, Feb. 2006), *available at* http://ideas.repec.org/p/kud/epruwp/06–02.html.

81. Murray Waas, *Libby Says Bush Authorized Leaks*, NAT'L J., Apr. 6, 2006, http://news.nationaljournal.com/articles/0406nj1.htm.

82. Simone Chambers, *Behind Closed Doors, Publicity, Secrecy, and the Quality of Deliberation*, 12 J. POL. PHIL. 389, 390–98 (2004); Jon Elster, *Arguing and Bargaining in Two Constituent Assemblies*, 2 U. PA. J. CONST. L. 345 (2000).

83. *Cf.* Woodward (blaming Tenet) and Risen (blaming Bush) for Iraq intelligence failure. Tenet was Risen's main source; Bush, among others, was Woodward's.

84. S.C. Res. 82, U.N. Doc. S/1501 (June 25, 1950); S. C. Res. 83, U.N. Doc. S/1511 (June 27, 1950).

85. Eugene Robinson, *An Easy Call: Lying*, N.Y. TIMES, May 12, 2006, at A21.

86. *Id.*

87. CNN, *Poll: 26% Suspect They've Been Wiretapped* (May 18, 2006), http://www.cnn.com/2006/POLITICS/05/18/nsa.poll/index.html.

88. The claim might not have to be based on their own calls. The damages would create a form of *qui tam* standing. There are complex questions about whether this would suffice as "injury in fact" for purposes of Article III. *See* Vt. *Agency of Nat. Resources v. United States ex rel. Stevens*, 529 U.S. 765, 771–78 (2000).

89. Even statutory authorization might not solve the problem, as courts are unwilling to force Congress to appropriate money for judgments. However, Congress seems to have been able to bind itself, as a practical matter. *See, e.g.*, Civil Liberties Act of 1988, 50 U.S.C.A. Appx. §§ 1989b *et seq.*, providing for individual payments of $20,000 for each survivor of Japanese internment camps and a $1.25 billion education fund. On October 9, 1990, the first nine payments were made. Children of the Camps, *WWII Internment Timeline*, available at http://www.children-of-the-camps.org/default.htm.

90. *See, e.g.*, Daryl Levinson, *Making Governments Pay Markets, Politics, and the Allocation of Constitutional Costs*, 67 U. CHI. L. REV. 345, 354–357 (2000); Daniel A. Farber, *Economic Analysis and Just Compensation*, 12 INT'L REV. L. & ECON. 129–32 (1992).

91. *See* COLE, *supra* note 24, at 478. Consider also Neustadt's discussion of Eisenhower's use of the news conference to enhance his reputation. Neustadt emphasizes rhetorical consistency and force, but this is another way of saying that people will not trust a president who takes questions but cannot answer them. NEUSTADT, *supra* note 34, at 68–72.

92. Lou Cannon, *Actor, Governor, President, Icon*, WASH. POST, June 6, 2004, at A01, *available at* http://www.washingtonpost.com/wp-dyn/articles/A18329–2004Jun5.html.

93. Coates Lear & James Bennet, *The Flack Pack: How Press Conferences Turn Serious Journalists into Shills*, WASH. MONTHLY, Nov. 1991, at 18.

94. Saul Levmore, *Precommitment Politics* 82 VA. L. REV. 567, 570 (1996). For related work, *see* SUSAN C. STOKES, MANDATES AND DEMOCRACY: NEOLIBERALISM BY SURPRISE IN LATIN AMERICA 6 (2001).

95. Levmore, *supra* note 94, at 575–84. The basic problem is that rules of contract law do not permit enforcement of such promises. Levmore offers ingenious suggestions for circumventing or finessing the problem, but to date those suggestions have not been adopted.

96. *The Real Agenda*, N.Y. TIMES, July 16, 2006, at 11.

97. On the point that the president might distort policies from the optimum so that the public can evaluate them, *see* Susanne Lohmann, *Electoral Incentives, Informational Asymmetries, and the Policy Bias Toward Special Interests*, 33 (U. S. Cal. L. Center, Working Paper No. 96-7 1995) and Ethan Bueno de Mesquita, *Politics and the Suboptimal Provision of Counterterror*, 61 INT'L ORG. 9 (2007).

98. LEWIS, *supra* note 72, at 71, 126, finds that (1) presidents generally oppose insulation of agencies from presidential control, *id.* at 71, and (2) agencies created by executive order are less likely to be insulated than agencies created by Congress, *id.* at 126.

CHAPTER 5

1. *See* Erik Voeten, *The Political Origins of the UN Security Council's Ability to Legitimize the Use of Force*, 49 INT'L ORG. 527 (2005).

2. *See* Simon Chesterman, *Unaccountable? The United Nations, Emergency Powers, and the Rule of Law*, 42 VAND. J. TRANSNAT'L L. 1509 (2009).

3. *See, e.g.*, PETER SINGER, ONE WORLD 147 (2004).

4. MICHAEL GLENNON, LIMITS OF LAW, PREROGATIVES OF POWER: INTERVENTIONISM AFTER KOSOVO (2001).

5. *See* INDEPENDENT INTERNATIONAL COMMISSION ON KOSOVO, THE KOSOVO REPORT 4 (2000).

6. *See* Eric Neumayer, *Do International Human Rights Treaties Improve Respect for Human Rights?*, 49 J. CONFLICT RESOL. 925, 950–51 (2005); Emilie M. Hafner-Burton & Kiyoteru Tsutsui, *Human Rights in a Globalizing World: The Paradox of Empty Promises*, 110 AM. J. SOC. 1373, 1395–1402 (2005); Oona A. Hathaway, *Do Human Rights Treaties Make a Difference?*, 111 YALE L.J. 1935, 1998 (2002); Linda Camp Keith, *The United Nations International Covenant on Civil and Political Rights: Does it Make a Difference in Human Rights Behavior?* 36 J. PEACE RES. 95 (1999); Todd Landman, PROTECTING HUMAN RIGHTS: A COMPARATIVE STUDY (2005); Emilie M. Hafner-Burton & James Ron, *Can the Human Rights Movement Achieve its Goals?* 12–17 (2008) (unpublished

manuscript), *available at* http://www.princeton.edu/~ehafner/pdfs/achieve_
goals.pdf; Emilie M. Hafner-Burton, *Right or Robust? The Sensitive Nature of
Repression to Globalization,* 42 J. PEACE RES. 679 (2005); Emilie M. Hafner-
Burton & Kiyoteru Tsutsui, *Justice Lost! The Failure of International Human
Rights Law To Matter Where Needed Most,* 44 J. PEACE RES. 407 (2007); BETH
A. SIMMONS, MOBILIZING FOR HUMAN RIGHTS (2009).

7. *But see* Curtis Bradley & Mitu Gulati, *Withdrawing from International Custom*
(2009) (unpublished manuscript).

8. For a collection of writings on this topic, *see* JEFFREY L. DUNOFF & JOEL P.
TRACHTMAN, RULING THE WORLD? CONSTITUTIONALISM, INTERNATIONAL
LAW, AND GLOBAL GOVERNANCE (2009).

9. For criticisms, *see* ERIC A. POSNER, THE PERILS OF GLOBAL LEGALISM 189–90
(2009).

10. Case T-315/01, *Kadi v. Council & Comm'n,* 2005 O.J. (C 281) 17.

11. *Military and Paramilitary Activities* (Nicar. v. U.S.), 1986 I.C.J. 14
(June 27).

12. *See* POSNER, *supra* note 9, at 173–74.

13. *See* Daniel Abebe & Eric A. Posner, *Foreign Affairs Legalism: A Critique* (Chicago
Pub. Law Working Paper No. 291, 2010), *available at* http://papers.ssrn.com/
s013/papers.cfm?abstract_id=1551300.

14. *See* Curtis A. Bradley, *The United States and Human Rights Treaties: Race
Relations, the Cold War, and Constitutionalism* (April 19, 2010) (unpublished
manuscript), *available at* http://papers.ssrn.com/s013/papers.cfm?abstract_
id=1593144.

15. 548 U.S. § 557 (2006).

16. *Filártiga v. Peña-Irala,* 630 F.2d 876 (1980).

17. *Roper v. Simmons,* 543 U.S. 551 (2005).

18. For the debate, *see* Eric A. Posner & Cass R. Sunstein, *The Law of Other States,*
59 STAN. L. REV. 131 (2006).

19. POSNER, *supra* note 9.

20. *See* JEREMY A. RABKIN, LAW WITHOUT NATIONS? WHY CONSTITUTIONAL
GOVERNMENT REQUIRES SOVEREIGN STATES (2005).

21. SAMUEL P. HUNTINGTON, THE THIRD WAVE: DEMOCRATIZATION IN THE
LATE TWENTIETH CENTURY (1991).

22. RAN HIRSCHL, TOWARDS JURISTOCRACY: THE ORIGINS AND CONSEQUENCES
OF THE NEW CONSTITUTIONALISM (2004).

23. Philipp Kiiver, *The National Parliaments in an Enlarged Europe and the
Constitutional Treaty* 85, 87–88, in THE CONSTITUTION FOR EUROPE AND AN
ENLARGED UNION: UNITY IN DIVERSITY? (Kirstyn Inglis & Andrea Ott eds.,
2005). This paragraph and the following paragraph are taken, with revisions,
from Tom Ginsburg & Eric A. Posner, *Subconstitutionalism,* 62 STANFORD L.
REV. 1583 (2010).

24. Kiiver, *supra* note 23 at 88–89.

25. See the Introduction by Paul Craig and Adam Tomkins, and the essays by
Lorne Sossin, Simon Evans, Denis Baranger, Giacinto della Cananea, Eberhard
Schmidt-Aβman and Christoph Möllers, in THE EXECUTIVE AND PUBLIC LAW:

Power and Accountability in Comparative Perspective (Paul Craig & Adam Tomkins eds., 2006).

26. *See* Eberhard Schmidt-Aβman and Christoph Möllers, *The Scope and Accountability of Executive Power in Germany*, in The Executive and Public Law, *supra* note 25 at 285–87.

27. *See* Adam Tomkins, *National Security, Counter-Terrorism and the Intensity of Review—A Changed Landscape?* 126 Law Q. Rev. (forthcoming 2010) (finding increasingly assertive review in the lower courts, although not necessarily in the House of Lords); Adam Tomkins, *Parliament, Human Rights, and Counter-Terrorism*, in Rescuing Human Rights (T. Campbell, K. Ewing, & A. Tomkins eds.) (forthcoming) (finding an increase in parliamentary oversight).

28. Tomkins, *National Security, Counter-Terrorism and the Intensity of Review—A Changed Landscape? supra* note 27, at 1 (quoting *Liversidge v. Anderson*, [1942] A.C. 206, 220 (per Viscount Maugham)).

29. *See* Paul Craig & Adam Tomkins, *Introduction* in The Executive and Public Law, *supra* note 25 at 1.

30. For a subtle account that describes both the constraints of the ECtHR on Russia and its limits, *see* Alexei Trochev, *All Appeals Lead to Strasbourg? Unpacking the Impact of the European Court of Human Rights on Russia*, 17 Demokratizatsiya 145 (2009).

31. *See* Eyal Benvenisti & George W. Downs, *The Empire's New Clothes: Political Economy and the Fragmentation of International Law*, 60 Stan. L. Rev. 595 (2007).

CHAPTER 6

1. *See, e.g.*, Stuart Taylor, Jr., *The Man Who Would Be King*, Atlantic Monthly, Apr. 2006, at 25–26, *quoted in* Sanford Levinson, Our Undemocratic Constitution: Where the Constitution Goes Wrong (And How We the People Can Correct It) 81 (2006). For another prominent example of tyrannophobia, *see* Arthur Schlesinger, Jr., The Imperial Presidency 377 (1st Mariner Books ed., 2004) (1973) (arguing that Jefferson's prophecy of "the tyranny of executive power" "appeared on the verge of fulfillment" (writing in 1973)); and see his apocalyptic introduction to the 2004 edition, *id.* at ix–xxiv. In a book published while our book was in press, Bruce Ackerman advocates significant reform of legal and political institutions to counter the risk of executive dictatorship. *See* Bruce Ackerman, The Decline and Fall of the American Republic (2010).

2. Ronald Wintrobe, The Political Economy of Dictatorship 43, 47 (1998).

3. Bruce Bueno de Mesquita et al., *Policy Failure and Political Survival: The Contribution of Political Institutions* 43 J. Conflict Resol. 147, 148 (1999).

4. Daron Acemoglu & James A. Robinson, Economic Origins of Dictatorship and Democracy 118 (2006); Carles Boix & Milan Svolik, *The Foundations of Limited Authoritarian Government: Institutions and Power-Sharing in Dictatorships* 1–4 (working paper, 2009), *available at* http://ssrn.com.ezp-prod1.hul.harvard.edu/abstract=1352065.

5. The median voter theorem is controversial, and authors make other assumptions as well.
6. This chapter can thus be thought of as a step in the direction of thinking about constitutional design from a behavioral law-and-economics perspective. That literature so far has largely focused on private law and some nonconstitutional public law issues. *See, e.g.,* BEHAVIORAL LAW AND ECONOMICS (Cass R. Sunstein ed., 2000).
7. Mark Tushnet helpfully noted to us that in principle one should distinguish the long-run costs and benefits of consolidated dictatorship from the short-run costs of a *transition* to dictatorship. If transition costs are very high, the switch to a dictatorship might be bad even if, in a steady state, dictatorship is no worse than democracy. (Of course, the same point might apply in reverse, to a switch from dictatorship to democracy.) However, we are unaware of large-number evidence on the transition question; the discussion in text refers to evidence on the long-run effect of dictatorship.
8. Casey B. Mulligan, Ricard Gil, & Xavier Sala-i-Martin, *Do Democracies Have Different Public Policies than Nondemocracies?* 18 J. ECON. PERSP. 51, 51–52 (2004).
9. DENNIS C. MUELLER, PUBLIC CHOICE III 423 (2003).
10. Edward L. Glaeser, Rafael LaPorta, Florencio Lopez-de-Silanes, & Andrei Shleifer, *Do Institutions Cause Growth?* 9 J. ECON. GROWTH 271, 282 (2004).
11. Robert T. Deacon, *Public Good Provision under Dictatorship and Democracy*, 139 PUB. CHOICE 241, 243 (2009).
12. Glaeser et al., *supra* note 10, at 285.
13. MUELLER, *supra* note 9, at 424 (citing Jody Overland, Kenneth L. Simons, & Michael Spagat, *Political Instability and Growth in Dictatorships* (2000) (unpublished working paper, later published in 125 PUB. CHOICE 445 (2005))).
14. Philippe Aghion, Alberto Alesina, & Francesco Trebbi, *Endogenous Political Institutions*, 119 Q.J. ECON. 565, 575 (2004), present a model in which a leader with relatively low insulation—meaning a leader who must gain the approval of (many) others before acting—is relatively more desirable as the risk aversion of the population increases.
15. Jon Elster, *Unwritten Constitutional Norms* (2009) (unpubublished manuscript).
16. *See* CLINTON ROSSITER, CONSTITUTIONAL DICTATORSHIP: CRISIS GOVERNMENT IN THE MODERN DEMOCRACIES 8 (Transaction Publishers 2002) (1948).
17. We thus by stipulation exclude certain types of "constitutional dictatorships" in the United States—the arguable cases being wartime presidential power. *See* ROSSITER, *supra* note 16. For a critical discussion of constitutional dictatorships, *see* Sanford Levinson & Jack M. Balkin, *Constitutional Dictatorship: Its Dangers and Design*, 94 MINN. L. REV. 1789 (2010). Levinson and Balkin believe that the U.S. executive currently has excessive power, which lends itself to abuse; and although they believe that to some extent constitutional dictatorship is unavoidable, they advocate increased checks on executive power in order to curb abuses and prevent unlimited dictatorship.
18. THE DECLARATION OF INDEPENDENCE para. 2 (U.S. 1776).

19. *Id.* at para. 30.

20. *Id.* at para. 31.

21. *See, e.g.,* Max M. Edling, A Revolution in Favor of Government: Origins of the U.S. Constitution and the Makings of the American State 66 (2003).

22. *Id.* at 67–68.

23. *See* Brendan McConville, The King's Three Faces: The Rise and Fall of Royal America, 1688–1776, 8–9, 311 (2006).

24. Gordon S. Wood, The Creation of the American Republic, 1776–1787, 135–36 (1969).

25. *Id.* at 404–12.

26. *Id.* at 466–67, 550–51.

27. Schlesinger, *supra* note 1, at 2.

28. *See, e.g.,* The Antifederalist No. 3, at 8, No. 25, at 66, No. 70, at 204 (Morton Borden ed., 1965). The papers are replete with references to "tyranny," "despotism," *etc.*

29. Edling, *supra* note 21, at 67.

30. Indeed, in Hamilton's comparison of the president to the British king and to American governors, he repeatedly emphasizes the more limited interpretations of the president's constitutional powers. *See* Federalist No. 69, at 396–402 (Alexander Hamilton) (Isaac Kramnick ed., 1987).

31. Of particular interest is the founders' disagreements about the executive prerogative to violate laws in order to protect the nation, and the intellectual history of this view. For reasons of space we cannot recount this story. For a brief, lucid account, *see* Levinson & Balkin, *supra* note 17; for a recent book-length treatment, *see* Benjamin Kleinerman, The Discretionary President: The Promise and Peril of Executive Power (2009).

32. For a standard account, *see* Schlesinger, *supra* note 1.

33. *Youngstown Sheet & Tube Co. v. Sawyer,* 343 U.S. 579 (1952).

34. *See, e.g,* Administrative Procedure Act, Pub. L. No. 79-404, 60 Stat. 237 (1946) (codified in various sections of 5 U.S.C.); U.S. Const. amend. XXII (setting term limits after FDR); War Powers Resolution, Pub. L. No. 93-148, 87 Stat. 555 (1973) (codified at 50 U.S.C. §§ 1541–48 (2000)); National Emergencies Act, Pub. L. No. 94-412, 90 Stat. 1255 (1976) (codified as amended at 50 U.S.C. §§ 1601–51 (2000 & Supp. III 2003)); International Emergency Economic Powers Act, Pub. L. No. 95-223, 91 Stat. 1626 (1977) (codified as amended at 50 U.S.C. §§ 1701–6 (2000 & Supp. III 2003)); Ethics in Government Act, Pub. L. No. 95-521, 92 Stat. 1824 (1978) (codified as amended at 28 U.S.C. §§ 591–98 (2000)); and Foreign Intelligence Surveillance Act, Pub. L. No. 95-511, 92 Stat. 1783 (1978) (codified as amended at 50 U.S.C. §§ 1801–63 (2000 & Supp. III 2003)) (various framework statutes after Nixon).

35. *See, e.g.,* Schlesinger, *supra* note 1, at 122–23, 409.

36. *Id.* at 127–28, 163–70.

37. *Id.* at 210–12.

38. As noted above, we exclude from our definition of dictator the time-limited

dictator; arguably, certain wartime presidents such as Lincoln and FDR had time-limited dictatorial powers.

39. George Washington, FAREWELL ADDRESS (Sept. 17, 1796).

40. *See* John C. Yoo, *Andrew Jackson and Presidential Power*, 2 Charleston L. Rev. 521 (2008).

41. WILLIAM MANCHESTER, AMERICAN CAESAR: DOUGLAS MACARTHUR, 1880–1964, 679–83 (1978).

42. A few other distinguished military leaders became minor presidents, including William Henry Harrison, Zachary Taylor, and Ulysses Grant. Theodore Roosevelt, a great president, could not be considered a great military leader on the basis of his minor exploits in the Spanish-American War.

43. BENJAMIN L. ALPERS, DICTATORS, DEMOCRACY, AND AMERICAN PUBLIC CULTURE: ENVISIONING THE TOTALITARIAN ENEMY, 1920s–1950s 15 (2003). The name would be dropped in 1937.

44. Raymond Gram Swing, *Forerunner of American Fascism, in* HUEY LONG 90, 90–103 (Hugh Davis Graham ed., 1970).

45. Alpers, *supra* note 43, at 105–7, 205–6.

46. Pub. L. No. 79-404, 60 Stat. 237 (1946) (codified in various sections of 5 U.S.C.).

47. Alpers, for example, argues that what we call tyrannophobia—an excessive fear of tyranny—led to persecution of dissenters and others who opposed American foreign policy during World War II and the cold war, which was presented by the government as a conflict with dictatorship. Alpers, *supra* note 43, at 301–2.

48. WORLD VALUES SURVEY, http://www.worldvaluessurvey.org (last visited July 15, 2009). The surveys we use were conducted over a 10-year period from 1999 to 2008; different countries were surveyed in different years.

49. *Id.,* question E114.

50. *Id.,* question E121.

51. AREND LIJPHART, PATTERNS OF DEMOCRACY: GOVERNMENT FORMS AND PERFORMANCE IN THIRTY-SIX COUNTRIES 132–33 (1999).

52. The two survey variables are highly correlated. Our data set consists of 191 countries, but we have survey results for only 84 countries (in the case of Strong Leader) and 65 countries (in the case of Democracies Squabble). For Strong Leader, the mean was 35 percent, ranging from 3 to 78 percent. For Democracies Squabble, the mean was 49 percent, ranging from 13 to 80 percent.

53. *See* Adam Przeworski et al., *What Makes Democracies Endure?* 7 J. DEMOCRACY 39, 41 (1996); ANGUS MADDISON, THE WORLD ECONOMY: HISTORICAL STATISTICS 58–69, 87–89, 100–101, 105, 110, 142–48, 180–87, 218–24 (2003).

54. MADDISON, *supra* note 53, at 62.

55. Per Capita Personal Income by State, http://bber.unm.edu/econ/us-pci.htm (last visited Jul. 24, 2009).

56. Przeworski et al., *supra* note 53 at 41 (citing SEYMOUR MARTIN LIPSET, POLITICAL MAN: THE SOCIAL BASES OF POLITICS 51 (1981)).

57. Acemoglu & Robinson, *supra* note 4, at 173–220; *see also* CARLES BOIX, DEMOCRACY AND REDISTRIBUTION 21–23, 37–38 (2003).

58. A problem with this model is that it is unclear why the promise of the franchise

is any more credible than would be a promise of direct redistribution; if the revolutionary masses cannot reassemble, elites can revoke the franchise they previously promised or else engage in vote-rigging, as in Iran in 2009. The model must add an epicycle, to the effect that revoking elections is a more clear betrayal of the promise to redistribute and will thus create a focal point that allows the masses to coordinate on an uprising. *Cf.* Barry R. Weingast, *The Political Foundations of Democracy and the Rule of Law*, 91 Am. Pol. Sci. Rev. 245, 246 (1997). If this is common knowledge among elites and masses, then the initial promise of the franchise will be credible.

59. Jess Benhabib & Adam Przeworski, *The Political Economy of Redistribution Under Democracy*, 29 Econ. Theory 271, 274–75 (2006).

60. There is a vigorous debate in comparative politics about whether the facts show that homogeneity—of ethnicity, language, religion, or wealth—is conducive to or even necessary for democracy. Yet the weight of the findings holds that homogeneity on these dimensions is at least appreciably correlated with democracy. (For a recent overview of the literature and an argument against the conventional view, *see* M. Steven Fish & Robin Brooks, *Does Diversity Hurt Democracy?* 15 J. Democracy 154 (2004).)

61. Benhabib & Przeworski, *supra* note 59, at 274.

62. *See* List of Countries by Income Equality, http://en.wikipedia.org/wiki/List_of_countries_by_income_equality (last visited Apr. 24, 2010).

63. Przeworski et al., *supra* note 53, at 44–47.

64. *Id.* at 47; *see* Juan J. Linz, *Presidential or Parliamentary Democracy: Does It Make a Difference? in* The Failure of Presidential Democracy 3, 6–8 (Juan J. Linz & Arturo Valenzuela eds., 1994).

65. Wintrobe, *supra* note 2, at 259–62; Scott Mainwaring, *Presidentialism in Latin America*, 25 Latin American Research Review 157 (1990)

66. Bruce Ackerman, The Failure of the Founding Fathers: Jefferson, Marshall, and the Rise of Presidential Democracy 27–35 (2005).

67. José Antonio Cheibub, Presidentialism, Parliamentarism, and Democracy (2007).

68. Scott Plous, The Psychology of Judgment and Decision Making 107–88 (1993).

69. See our earlier discussion of the evidence regarding the greater likelihood that tyranny takes place in poorer societies (as the United States was before modern times) than in richer societies.

70. *See generally* Alexis de Tocqueville, Democracy in America (Harvey C. Mansfield & Delba Winthrop trans., 2000) (1835), especially Part II, ch. 9 and Part IV, chs. 1 & 6. Tocqueville believed that American mores, ideological commitments, and institutions posed a number of dangers, but despotism in the usual sense was not one of them.

71. See Richard Hofstadter, *The Paranoid Style in American Politics, in* The Paranoid Style in American Politics and Other Essays 3, 29–40 (1965); Richard Hofstadter, *The Pseudo-Conservative Revolt—1954, in* The Paranoid Style in American Politics and Other Essays, *supra*, at 41, 46.

72. Tocqueville, *supra* note 70, at 257–58.
73. This implication is, however, in tension with the data suggesting that in richer (and presumably technologically more advanced) societies, people are more likely to disapprove of a strong executive.
74. *See e.g.,* Jonathan Hartlyn, *Presidentialism and Colombian Politics, in* THE FAILURE OF PRESIDENTIAL DEMOCRACY, *supra* note 64, at 294, 295–96.
75. *Id.*; Linz, *supra* note 64; Przeworski et al., *supra* note 53, at 44–46.
76. RAOUL BERGER, GOVERNMENT BY JUDICIARY: THE TRANSFORMATION OF THE FOURTEENTH AMENDMENT (1977).
77. As another possible example of self-defeating precautions against tyranny, term limits on the executive might induce coups or other constitutional crises. Anticipating that they will be barred from standing for reelection, powerful executives might decide to subvert the constitutional order altogether. *See* FEDERALIST No. 72, at 414 (Alexander Hamilton) (Isaac Kramnick ed., 1987) (an executive facing term limits "would be much more violently tempted to embrace a favorable conjuncture for attempting the prolongation of his power, at every personal hazard"). However, a forthcoming study of the effect of term limits across constitutional democracies finds little evidence of such an effect. *See* Melkinsburg, *On the Evasion of Executive Term Limits* (unpublished manuscript, 2009).
78. CASS R. SUNSTEIN, LAWS OF FEAR: BEYOND THE PRECAUTIONARY PRINCIPLE 27–32 (2005).
79. THE FEDERALIST No. 47, at 303 (James Madison) (Isaac Kramnick ed., 1987).
80. Amanda L. Tyler, *Suspension as an Emergency Power,* 118 YALE L.J. 600, 627–30 (2009); *Boumediene v. Bush,* 128 S. Ct. 2229, 2247 (2008).
81. *See* WILLIAM E. LEUCHTENBURG, THE SUPREME COURT REBORN: THE CONSTITUTIONAL REVOLUTION IN THE AGE OF ROOSEVELT 137, 146 (1995).
82. Pub. L. No. 93-148, 87 Stat. 555 (1973) (codified at 50 U.S.C. §§ 1541–48 (2000)).
83. Pub. L. No. 94-412, 90 Stat. 1255 (1976) (codified as amended at 50 U.S.C. §§ 1601–51 (2000 & Supp. III 2003)).
84. Daryl J. Levinson & Richard H. Pildes, *Separation of Parties, Not Powers,* 119 HARV. L. REV. 2311, 2316–30 (2006).
85. FORREST MCDONALD, NOVUS ORDO SECLORUM: THE INTELLECTUAL ORIGINS OF THE CONSTITUTION 250 (1985).
86. Bruce Ackerman, *The New Separation of Powers,* 113 HARV. L. REV. 633, 643–46 (2000).
87. Duverger's law. MAURICE DUVERGER, POLITICAL PARTIES: THEIR ORGANIZATION AND ACTIVITY IN THE MODERN STATE 217 (Barbara North & Robert North trans., Wiley 2d Eng. ed. rev. 1963).
88. There are significant scholarly controversies here. For a finding that fragmented parties do not create risks to democracy, and indeed that fragmentation and proportional representation (usually thought to produce fragmentation) are *negatively* correlated with democratic collapse, *see* Abraham Diskin et al., *Why Democracies Collapse: The Reasons for Democratic Failure and Success,* 26 INT'L. POL. SCI. REV. 291, 299–300 (2005).

89. Entering the terms "Bush" and "Hitler" into Google yields 6,820,000 hits; "Obama" and "Hitler" yield twice that.

90. Terry M. Moe & William G. Howell, *The Presidential Power of Unilateral Action*, 15 J. Law Econ. & Org. 132 (1999).

91. Schlesinger, *supra* note 1, at 377.

92. *See, e.g.,* Hossein Jalilian, Colin Kirkpatrick, & David Parker, *The Impact of Regulation on Economic Growth in Developing Countries: A Cross-Country Analysis*, 35 World Dev. 87, 87–88 (2007).

93. For examples of "tangible security harms" resulting from civil-libertarian rules that constrain executive power, *see* Eric A. Posner & Adrian Vermeule, Terror in the Balance: Security, Liberty, and the Courts 24–26 (2007); Adrian Vermeule, *Libertarian Panics*, 36 Rutgers L.J. 871 (2005).

94. Nixon and many of his predecessors engaged in such behavior.

95. Schlesinger, *supra* note 1, at 210. *See also* Cynthia R. Farina, *False Comfort and Impossible Promises: Uncertainty, Information Overload, and the Unitary Executive*, 12 U. Penn. J. Const. L. 357 (2010).

96. We do not claim, however, that we live in the best of all possible worlds. When the executive engages in abuses, legal or constitutional reform may be justified. *See, e.g.,* Levinson & Balkin, *supra* note 17, who propose a number of creative reforms. However, we believe they go astray by starting with the premise that the United States already has a kind of constitutional dictatorship or nearly so, and then arguing that (therefore?) additional checks are justified. Indeed, this last argument is in tension with their recognition that some type of discretionary executive action is necessary in cases of emergency. *Id.* at 5. Their paper is motivated by the historical fear that republican governments are in danger of collapsing into dictatorships. *Id.* at 4–5. Our argument is that this historical fear is (by now) exaggerated.

CONCLUSION

1. *See* Alasdair Roberts, *Beyond the Imperial Presidency, in* Alasdair Roberts, The Collapse of Fortress Bush: The Crisis of Authority in American Government 164 (2008).

2. For a lucid discussion of how Delaware courts avoided ruling on the Bear, Stearns–J.P. Morgan Chase merger, *see* Marcel Kahan & Edward Rock, *How to Prevent Hard Cases From Making Bad Law: Bear Stearns, Delaware, and The Strategic Use of Comity*, 58 Emory L.J. 713 (2009).

3. Brian Loveman, The Constitution of Tyranny: Regimes of Exception in Spanish America (1993).

INDEX

solutions, 133–37
theory of, 129–33
Truman, Harry and, 125–26
Criddle, Evan, 107, 109
crisis, 13, 19, 31–32, 33, 41–42, 48–49,
    50–59, 77, 81, 86, 95, 156, 180
    (*see also* emergency)
    during the, 43–48
    economic, 16, 33, 40, 59, 86, 101–3, 192,
        197, 201, 208
    financial, 128, 142, 208
    self-fulfilling, of authority, 59–60
Cromwell, 176, 183, 185, 187

decentralization, 22, 24, 30, 181
deception strategy and credibility, 124
Declaration of Independence, 181–82, 187
delegation, 3, 7, 8, 9, 11, 19, 27, 31–32, 34,
    44, 45, 47, 51, 110, 130, 143, 153, 206
democracies, 4, 12, 14, 16, 20, 32, 33, 39, 42,
    59, 64, 65, 90–91, 113, 115, 126, 152,
    180, 186, 189–92, 198, 201–2, 208
    dictatorship and, 177, 180–81
    foreign, 170–74
Democratic Republic of Congo, 162
Democratic Party, 39–40, 47, 48, 144
Department of Justice, 47, 86
Detainee Treatment Act (2005), 34
Dicey, Albert Venn, 4
dictatorship, fear of. *See* tyrannophobia
Dyzenhaus, David, 4, 9, 90, 92, 96–97, 103,
    107

Economic Stabilization Act (1970), 99
Eisenhower, Dwight, 7, 74, 124, 185, 186
elections and electoral process, 115–17
emergency, 3, 7–8, 9, 31, 41, 45, 47, 50–54,
    85–87, 90–94, 102–10, 113, 122, 145,
    158, 165, 181, 191, 199, 200, 207–8
Emergency Economic Stabilization Act
    (EESA), 13, 39, 40, 47–48, 49, 51, 55,
    58, 59, 101, 102–3
Emergency Petroleum Allocation Act
    (1973), 99 (*see also* crisis)
Epstein, Richard, 4
Ethics in Government Act, 85
European Commission, 173
European Court of Human Rights (ECtHR),
    174
European Court of Justice (ECJ), 160, 173

European integration, 172
European Union (EU), 172
Exchange Stabilization Fund, 38
executive, 9, 14, 25, 26–27, 33–34, 106
    abuse, 184
    agencies, 5–7, 12, 56–57, 208
    bounded rationality and, 194
    constitutional showdown and, 75
    constraints on, 4–5, 113–35
    crisis and, 43, 44, 48, 60
    and globalization, 174–75
    government, 11–15
    ill-motivated, 26, 29, 122, 132, 135, 136,
        137, 139, 140, 142, 146, 148, 149–53
    liberal legalism and, 43
    power, 172–73, 187
    powerful, 184–85
    prerogative, 9
    problems for judicial oversight of, 29
    self-binding, 123, 137
    signaling, 123, 137–50
    well-motivated, 26, 29, 123, 130–31, 132,
        135, 136, 137–38, 141–142, 145, 145,
        147–53
Executive Office of the President, 6, 7

Faubus, Orval, 73
Federal Aviation Administration (FAA), 100
Federal Deposit Insurance Corporation
    (FDIC), 40, 41
Federal Housing Finance Agency, 56
Federal Reserve Board, 7, 38, 44, 49, 50, 57,
    58–59, 128, 142
Financial Stability Oversight Board, 55
FISA Amendments Act (2008), 34
Ford, Gerald, 185
France, 124, 155, 173, 189
Fuller, Lon, 92

Garzón, Baltasar, 164
Gates, Robert, 143
Geithner, Timothy, 40, 121
General Assembly, 155–56, 161
Geneva Conventions, 166
Genocide Convention, 157
George III, 176, 182, 183
Germany, 124–25, 173, 185, 189
Gingrich, Newt, 120, 144
globalization and executive, and global
    liberal legalism, 174–75

global liberal legalism, 154
  domestic courts and foreign relations law and, 165–69
  foreign courts and universal jurisdiction and, 163–65
  foreign democracies and, 170–74
  globalization and executive and, 174–75
  human rights regime and, 157–32
  international courts and, 160–163
  international law and, 155–57
  jus cogens norms and, 159
  normative basis of, 169–70
Grant, Ulysses S., 70
Great Depression, 124
Greece, 126
Greenspan, Alan, 6
Grenada, 74
grey holes, 10, 85, 89, 92, 96–97, 103, 104, 106, 108, 109, 112
  good cause exception, 99–101
  soft look review and, 97–99

Hamdan v. Rumsfeld (2006), 36, 166
Hamdi v. Rumsfeld (2004), 35, 207
Hamlin, Alan, 118
Hirschl, Ran, 172
Hitler, Adolf, 176, 195
Holy Land Foundation for Relief and Development v. Ashcroft (2003), 98
Home Affordable Modification Program, 40–41
House Judiciary Committee, 47
House of Representatives, 69
Housing and Urban Development, 56
Howell, William, 28
human rights regime and global legal liberalism, 157–59
Hume, David, 24
Hussein, Saddam, 127

impeachment and constitutional change, 68–69
imperial presidency, 12, 14, 199
independent commissions, 141–42
Independent Counsel Statute, 143
India, 171
Indonesia, 167, 171, 189
information asymmetries, 26, 29, 79–80, 106
Inspector General Act (1978), 9, 85, 86–87

Inspector General for Civil Liberties and Civil Rights, 47
institutional process view, 109, 110
intelligible principle, 8
International Court of Justice (ICJ), 156, 160–62, 163
International Covenant on Civil and Political Rights (ICCPR), 157, 166
International Covenant on Economic, Social and Cultural Rights (ICESCR), 157
International Criminal Court (ICC), 162, 170
International Emergency Economic Powers Act (1977), 44, 86, 98
international law and global legal liberalism, 155–57
Internet Age, 208
Interstate Commerce Commission (1887), 8
invisible hand mechanisms, 22–23
Iran, 147
Iraq, 126–27, 129, 141, 147
Islamic American Relief Agency (IARA) v. Gonzalez (2007), 98
Italy, 126, 173

Jackson, Andrew, 184, 186
Jackson, Robert, 109
James II, 176
Japan, 125, 171
Jifry v. FAA (2004), 100
Joe McCarthy, Joe, 197
Johnson, Andrew, 24, 68, 70
Johnson, Lyndon B., 124, 185
Judgment Fund, 149
judiciary, 10, 14, 18, 29, 30, 57, 70, 77, 116, 120, 165, 170, 174
jus cogens norms and global legal liberalism, 159
Justice Department
  Office of Legal Counsel, 87, 140

Kadi v. Council & Comm'n (2005), 160
Katyal, Neal, 139, 140
Kennedy, Anthony, 104
Kenya, 127
Kiiver, Philipp, 172, 174
Knox, Frank, 125, 144
Kosovo conflict, 86, 87
Kuwait, 126, 127

LaHood, Ray, 143
Latin America, 171, 208
leader and public, difference between, 114–115
Leahy, Patrick, 47
legal checks, 178, 195, 201, 206
legality, 85, 89, 90, 104, 108, 112 (*see also*
    individual entries)
    and legitimacy, 5, 33, 52, 54, 57
legislatures, 4, 7–8, 14, 19, 26, 33–34, 43, 44,
    60, 107, 119, 172, 174, 183
    precrisis state and, 42–43
    representative, 3, 14, 64
legitimacy, 59, 64, 82, 100, 110, 129, 157
    deficit, 30–31
    and legality, 5, 33, 52, 54, 57
    political, 64
    of power, 12
    Security Council and, 155
Lehman Brothers, 38
Levi Guidelines (1976), 85
Levinson, Daryl, 20
liberal legalism, 3–4, 14–15, 62, 64 (*see also*
    constitutional change; global legal
    liberalism; statutory framework)
    Congress and, 41
    executive and, 43
    fallacy of, 5
    problems of, 7–10
liberty, 18, 20, 116, 120, 121
    civil, 35, 37, 45, 47, 113, 116, 121, 130,
    132, 136, 145, 153, 178, 201, 202
Lincoln, Abraham, 11, 12, 69, 145, 153, 184,
    185, 186, 200
Liversidge v. Anderson (1942), 173
Locke, John, 9
"logic of escalation," 183
Long, Huey, 186

MacArthur, Douglas, 186
Madison, James, 4, 18, 23, 27, 153
Mao Tse Tung, 176, 195
Marshall Plan, 125
McCardle, Ex Parte (1868), 70
Merida Delgado v. Gonzales (2005), 96
Merryman, Ex parte (1861), 69
Military Commissions Act (2006), 29, 36
monitoring, 19, 27–31, 49, 54, 145, 148, 161,
    172, 201, 208–9
    compliance, 87
    Madisonian, 25

Moussaoui, Zacarias, 96
multilateralism, 146–48, 151, 155
Mussolini, Bennito, 186, 195

Napoleon I, 185–86
National Emergencies Act, 9, 55, 85, 86, 87,
    199
National Industrial Recovery Act, 8
National Intelligence Act, 9
national security, 10, 25, 26, 28, 30, 47, 49,
    50, 85, 88, 96, 101, 104, 110, 129, 130,
    132, 135, 136, 173
National Security Agency, 26, 94, 148
New Deal, 8, 65–66, 82, 121, 202
news conference, 149
Nicaragua, 86, 161
1984, 176
Nixon, Richard, 37, 69–70, 121, 124, 138,
    143, 144, 184, 199, 200, 201, 209
    impeachment of, 69
Nixon, United States v. (1974), 69
nondelegation doctrine, 8
North Atlantic Treaty Organization, 125
notice-and-comment rulemaking, 97, 99,
    101
Nuclear Regulatory Commission, 96

Obama, Barack, 6, 37, 49, 121–22, 143, 144,
    176
    administration, 40–41, 49, 128, 142,
    207
Office of Information and Regulatory Affairs
    (OIRA), 6
oversight, legal and political functions of, 25

partisanship, 13, 27–28, 42, 122, 142–44,
    143, 147
Patriot Act (2001), 13, 34, 46–47, 50, 60,
    103
Paul, Ron, 49
Paulson, Henry, 39, 49, 56, 59, 121, 128
Pentagon Papers, 30
Persson, Torsten, 118
Pevehouse, Jon, 28
Philippines, 171
Pinochet, Augusto, 164
plebiscitary presidency, 16, 204–5, 206
Poland, 126
political checks, 177, 178, 195–96, 202, 204,
    208

DATE DUE

MAR - - 2011